VALUES AND PLANNING

Values and Planning

edited by

Huw Thomas
Department of City and Regional Planning
University of Wales College of Cardiff

Avebury

Aldershot • Brookfield USA • Hong Kong • Singapore • Sydney

Published by
Avebury
Ashgate Publishing Limited
Gower House
Croft Road
Aldershot
Hants GU11 3HR
England

Ashgate Publishing Company
Old Post Road
Brookfield
Vermont 05036
USA

British Library Cataloguing in Publication Data

Values and Planning
  I. Thomas, Huw
  307.1

Library of Congress Cataloging-in-Publication Data

Values and Planning/edited by Huw Thomas.
  p.   cm.
  ISBN 1 85628 306 2: £35.00
  1. Policy sciences.   2. Planning.   3. Values.
  I. Thomas, Huw, 1954–.
  H97.V338   1994
  320'.6–dc20

Typeset in 11pt Times by Manton Typesetters, 5–7 Eastfield Road, Louth, Lincolnshire, England.

Printed and bound in Great Britain by Hartnolls Limited, Bodmin, Cornwall

Contents

Contents

Acknowledgements

This project took some time to complete, as authors juggled commitments; I am grateful to them for their forbearance, and also to Suzanne Evins, of Ashgate, for her patience in awaiting a manuscript. Maureen Pether produced a manuscript with her customary skill and goodwill.

List of contributors

Timothy Beatley   Department of Urban and Environmental Planning, School of Architecture, University of Virginia, USA.

Jerome E. Bickenbach   Department of Philosophy, Queen's University, Kingston, Ontario, Canada.

John Forester   Department of City and Regional Planning, Cornell University, USA.

Sue Hendler   School of Urban and Regional Planning, Queen's University, Kingston, Ontario, Canada.

Charles Hoch   School of Urban Planning and Policy, University of Illinois at Chicago, USA.

Nicholas Low   School of Environmental Planning, University of Melbourne, Australia.

Beth Moore Milroy   School of Urban and Regional Planning, University of Waterloo, Ontario, Canada.

John Punter   Centre for Planning, University of Strathclyde, Scotland, UK.

Nigel Taylor   School of Town and Country Planning, Faculty of the Built Environment, University of the West of England, UK.

Huw Thomas   Department of City and Regional Planning, University of Wales College of Cardiff, UK.

Michael J. Thomas   School of Planning, Oxford Brookes University, UK.

Chapter 1

Introduction

Huw Thomas

Evaluation permeates the practice and rhetoric of planning, yet professional and academic discussions of values and value judgements in planning remain underdeveloped. Although there are some excellent discussions of particular aspects of evaluation it could hardly be claimed that discussions of values, and their role in planning, have traditionally been a significant item on professional or scholarly agendas. The explosion of interest during the 1970s in substantive questions in moral philosophy has caused some ripples among planning theorists (e.g. Faludi 1989; Harper & Stein 1992), yet it is astonishing that Nicholas Low's contribution to this volume (Chapter 6), for example, is one of so very few which have explicitly considered the relevance of the vast literature on competing theories of justice to planning. However, times are changing, and the significance of evaluation to planning is receiving increasing attention. One important aim of this book is to review significant theoretical discussions outside planning which can assist with developing a discussion of the role of values and evaluation within it.

The historical indifference to value theory is the result of the ways in which both the profession of planning and the academic study of it have developed. The exclusionary strategy of professionalisation of an occupation involves the creation of barriers to entry and the colonisation of a particular sphere of activity. The winning of acceptance that the profession has some kind of specialised technical expertise is a fundamental component of controlling entry to it. The planning profession worldwide has sought to do just this. Inevitably, in so doing, it has shifted the focus of professional attention – in discussions and literature – towards topics which lend themselves to being presented as 'purely technical' matters.

In the UK, in particular, this tendency has been reinforced by the bureaucratisation of the profession through employment in local (and to a lesser extent, central) government. The tradition that technical officers should serve the government of the day 'impartially', whatever its party, has strengthened the incentive to try to divorce 'planning' from 'politics', though as Eric Reade (1987) has pointed out, this has not prevented planners from smuggling in evaluation under the cover of 'technical' discussions.

Charles Hoch's argument in Chapter 10 of this book suggests that, in academic life, too, there have been material interests which have been served by denying recognition to the significance of values to planning. The quest for academic credibility – and with it academic survival – has pushed planners in academe into viewing themselves as social scientists, and accepting a considerable amount of ideological baggage as a result, including, at certain times, a concern for 'value-free' analysis. Hoch writes of the US experience, but it has clear resonances in UK planning education over the last thirty years.[1] Until the 1960s British planning education was heavily influenced by the ideologies of professional practice, not least because there was a well-established tradition of part-time teaching by (often distinguished) practitioners. Only in the late 1960s did career academics begin to work in British planning education in any numbers, a consequence of an expansion of education which also saw an increase in undergraduate education. Many of the courses were established in the new polytechnics, which had to seek external validation of them. It was the search for a respectable underpinning for new courses which seems to have been especially influential in pushing much of British planning education towards social science and general theories of planning imported from public administration. The effect was the same as in the USA, however – a concern for analysis, technique and procedure, but little room for discussion of value judgements.

Of course, the ideological impulse to avow a divorce of the technical from the evaluative did not mean that the practice of planning was somehow purged of values. On the contrary, in the early 1970s Jon Gower Davies (1972) produced an incisive, and justly celebrated, critique of the submerged value systems of planning.[2] A central feature of the ideology he unearthed was the value ascribed to 'progress'. This was rarely rigorously defined, but implicitly endorsed the continued exploitation of scientifically-based technologies and accepted a crude (but potent) distinction between 'traditional' and 'modern' ways of life, with the latter seen as desirable, and exemplified by a range of dichotomies – notably: Western capitalist societies, as opposed to 'tribal', 'backward', 'developing' countries; and, within Western societies, progressive metropolitan social formations and ways of life as opposed to a variety of socially, economically and geographically peripheral ways of life (Hall 1992).

However, the acceptance of progress fell far short of an acceptance of the avant-garde. Jonathan Raban's (1974, p.160) analysis of contemporary urban life concluded that: 'The idea that the city is in essence a rational structure, and that evidence of irrationality is a sign of decadent deviation from its intrinsic cityness ... accounts for the curious sense of unreality that pervades so much of the literature of town planning.' Such critiques reminded observers that far from being value-free, the intellectual underpinnings of analyses and prescriptions in planning adopted (generally unwittingly) the values of the post-Enlightenment modernist outlook with its focus on human control of nature and society (McLennan 1992), such control being executed through projects rationally conceived and executed. The attitude towards nature and society which has dominated the theory and practice of modern town planning is one which locates the planner, as analyst/intervener, outside the phenomena she or he seeks to understand and influence. From this vantage point the planner first understands the object of attention (society, nature), and then controls, orders, shapes – in general, changes it – as appropriate.

This approach contains epistemological principles which have distinctive implications for discussions of values. It involves a model of how knowledge is obtained which stresses the importance of very specific modes of acquiring and validating evidence, of a separation between knower and known, and of the irrelevance of all but a few of the personal characteristics of the knower – the relevant few including, for example, certain intellectual capacities.[3] From this picture of understanding as, in essence, impersonal in its operation, and of the knower as inhabiting a position outside the phenomena being understood, certain characteristics of knowledge and its acquisition follow. Importantly, there can be no differences which are irreconcilable *in principle*, because the relevant point of observation can be taken up by anyone (since it is an intellectual position not dependent on any personal characteristics) and methods of acquiring evidence can be replicated; secondly, the model introduces a distinction between gaining knowledge or understanding and undertaking some form of engagement with a phenomenon. Moreover, this model carries with it an emphasis on the alleged essential similarity of all human beings, by virtue of their having the capacity for knowledge acquisition (their rationality), as opposed to an emphasis on their differences (such as culture or gender); this is one major support for the view that moral and political judgements and standards must be universalisable (i.e. must be, in some sense, applicable to all people and all societies). All these characteristics, in their own ways, have served to discourage the discussion of the role of values in planning.

In the UK, for example, the empiricist interpretation of the Enlightenment view of knowledge has held that evaluative judgements cannot constitute *knowledge*. At most they might have a factual component (see e.g. Hare 1952), but their distinctiveness, as evaluations, is their non-factual, emotive, or subjective element (the term used varies from one writer to another). As Mackie (1977, p.38) puts it, speaking of the possibility of 'objective values': 'if we were aware of them, it would have to be by some special faculty ... utterly different from our ordinary ways of knowing everything else'. He concludes that there is no evidence of any such faculty, nor of 'objective values'. For professionals or academics influenced by such views, and keen to emphasise their technical expertise and proficiency, there was little to gain in concerning themselves with the bases of value judgements. And even those adhering to a different intellectual tradition, in which it was claimed that value judgements could be rationally grounded, still faced the awkward fact that, apparently, the resolution of disputes over questions of value did not lend themselves to widely supported procedures, in the way that disputes in science did. For those establishing professional or intellectual credentials, therefore, dabbling in value questions held little attraction because, however sophisticated the discussion, there seemed no way of *forcing* people to acknowledge the technical or intellectual superiority of the planner in that sphere. So planners eschewed any significant discussion of questions about values while generally accepting without question key modernist tenets regarding the essential perfectability (through the application of reason, science and technology) of society, and (in practice) the universal applicability of the mores and technical principles they were imbibing and developing in the West.

This rather comfortable position has been undermined as intellectual critiques, embedded in real changes in social life and popular perceptions (Giddens 1990), have accumulated. As Squires (1993, p.2) has put it, the 'post-modern condition' has involved: 'The rejection of all essentialist

4

and transcendental conceptions of human nature; the rejection of unity, homogeneity, totality, closure and identity; the rejection of the pursuit of the real and the true ... the celebration of fragmentation, particularity and difference; the acceptance of the contingent and apparent.' One result of this intellectual ferment has been to raise politically and morally significant questions about hitherto generally accepted key dimensions of the practice of planning. The relationship of humanity to the physical environment, what constitutes the public interest, and the nature of rationality are three important examples of aspects of planning which are considered in this volume (by Beatley, Taylor and Milroy, in Chapters 2, 5 and 7 respectively), where debates have been sharpened by critiques of modernism.

Another consequence have been attempts to establish principled evaluative positions in aesthetics, ethics and politics – to establish that not 'anything goes'. Punter, Low and Forester (in Chapters 3, 6 and 9 respectively) are especially concerned about this question. Whatever the merits of individual attempts to address the problem, it is quite clear that questions about the nature of values, and how we conceptualise and find out about them, have become more than footnotes to an epistemology whose central concern is with intellectually underpinning Western science.

These debates are continuing in a wide range of academic disciplines worldwide, and are informed by the insights, arguments and experiences of those who have experienced the oppression legitimised by the products of the 'Enlightenment Project', and are clearly beginning to impinge on planning theory. Beauregard (1992, p.9) sums up the position: 'As planning theorists we seem suspended between outmoded and bankrupt positions [of] functional rationality, critical distance, universalising stances, totalising perspectives of apolitical practices and a variety of challenges emanating from postmodern, poststructuralist, hermeneutic, deconstructionist, post colonial and feminist perspectives.' However, as the contributions to this book show, the intellectual terrain remains contested, and its implications for discussions about value and planning ambiguous.

Chapter 7 by Milroy and Chapter 9 by Forester exhibit in a particularly direct fashion the ways in which the debates and perspectives to which Beauregard refers are influencing discussions in planning theory. Milroy, drawing on an evolving corpus of feminist critiques of post-Enlightenment epistemology, focuses on the implications for planning, and evaluation within it, of the demise of the disembodied rational subject (which, she argues, is an image which coincides with the conventions of masculinity).[4] She concludes with a range of prescriptions for professionals and academics which include constructing a 'feminine genealogy associated with design', and refusing 'complicity in exploiting the motherhood function of women in all designs for structures and processes'. She also concludes that planners must find 'a new place from which to speak', one which does not assume an intellectual or practical supremacy, in so doing echoing a theme in the critique of the forms and intellectual underpinning of modernity which theorists such as Giddens (1990) have highlighted – the exposure of the experts' feet of clay.

Forester, influenced by the same general intellectual thrust, argues, in Chapter 9, for a 'discursive ethics' which recognises, in civic and political association and activity, the actual material perspectives, values and judgements of a diverse populace. What is striking about Forester's essay is the very deliberate weight attached to the public character of the planning process, of its being – in reality – a process of state involvement in the development and use of land with a variety of consequences for different publics.

It is this public character which has made the public interest such a potent notion in planning, yet, interestingly, Taylor's argument for a defensible and usable conception of the public interest, in Chapter 5, portrays it as, in some way, a common denominator among individual interests, with the latter abstracted, to some extent, from their particular circumstances. In that sense, the public interest, as Taylor portrays it, is something which might well be calculable without recourse to the discursive techniques advocated by Forester. And Low, in discussing justice and planning, makes no critique of the use of 'disembodied individuals' – of the kind frowned upon by Milroy and Forester – by theorists such as Rawls.

It should be clear, therefore, that this book is a product of a period of intellectual and professional ferment in planning, and presents no unified intellectual programme or prescription for action. The brief for contributors was that their discussions of aspects of the interpenetration of planning and evaluation should connect with relevant debates and schools of thought outside planning itself. Each chapter, therefore, presents a distinctive perspective in a continuing debate, as well as allowing interested readers a guide to further explanation of the issues, often with the benefit of a summary of key texts or ideas.

As the preceding discussion has hinted, the richness of the individual chapters has meant that they relate in a number of ways, allowing a correspondingly large number of ways of grouping them. A simple, if crude, approach divides the book into three. Chapters 2 to 4 consider some ways in which values enter three particular spheres of planning activity – environmental management, design/aesthetic control, and heritage/conservation. Each of these areas has received increased political and professional prominence as critiques of modernism have accumulated. It is an interesting question whether widespread recognition of the global environmental change has itself eroded modernist optimism about technology, or whether such recognition was, in fact, dependent upon prior (and increasing) disquiet about the modernist faith in virtually inexorable progress for a rationally organised, scientifically-based society. As faith in progress and an assured future has dimmed, so some have sought refuge in the (retrospective) certainties of the past. However, increasingly, such succour seems inadequate, and there is now widespread interest in exploring principles which can guide design and conservation practice.

The possibility of global environmental or ecological disaster raises issues of political control and the relationship of the individual to the 'juggernaut' of modern society (Giddens 1990), and also acute questions of the ethical basis on which environmental policy should be founded. Yet 'environmentalism' is a notoriously ambiguous term, and Beatley's survey of theories of environmental ethics (see Chapter 2) shows clearly how some still incorporate the modernist ethos of nature as an object to be controlled and manipulated. As Beatley notes, one critique of such positions identifies the search for mastery with the dominance of patriarchal structures, which suggests that a well-founded environmental ethic must be built on a radical epistemological reappraisal and reconstruction. Milroy's contribution (Chapter 7) provides more than an indication of what that might involve. Beatley's own concerns are perhaps more political than epistemological, as he constructs a 'middle-range' position which can garner a broad base of political support. Such a project is undoubtedly important as a way of making some immediate progress in improving our relationship with the natural environment, but it might be thought to beg questions about how (if at all) constructive debate aimed at *changing views* is to take place between advocates of different ethical theories. It is this kind of issue which exercises Forester in Chapter 9.

One of Punter's major concerns (see Chapter 3) is that aesthetic judgement be freed from the grip of a small band of 'experts'. Indirectly, the empiricist/scientist epistemology of, say, John Mackie lends support to the notion that aesthetic sensibility is the preserve of an elite. The empiricist picture may not allow that aesthetics is a form of knowledge, but its emphasis on the separation of object and perceiver encourages the idea that aesthetics involves a particular (heightened) form of sensibility cultivated by only a select few, as Cooke (1990) points out. Punter, following a wide-ranging review of the literature, is adamant that in the sphere of design, at least, engagement with artifacts is a legitimate component of aesthetic appreciation. The question he must then face is whether such engagement alone is sufficient for aesthetic appreciation, a position which is in danger of leading to a populist relativism (and, with it, a further – if different – challenge to the status of aesthetic judgement). His discussion of this, and other important issues, is fascinating and illuminating.

Keith and Cross (1993, p.4) aver that 'central to postmodernist social forms is the continual reflection on the nature of time'. Michael Thomas, in Chapter 4, relates these intellectual reflections to popular and professional attitudes towards, and emotional investment in, conservation of the 'historic' built environment. A particularly valuable aspect of his discussion is his placing it within the context of aesthetic sensibilities more generally.

Chapters 5 to 8 analyse concepts and approaches which are central to planning and are, themselves, evaluative (or highly valued by planners). The public interest is one, and Taylor, in Chapter 5, argues for the rehabilitation of a concept which has been criticised by some as ideology masquerading as objectivity. He counters the claim that the idea of 'interests' is inherently evaluative, gaining content only within a particular moral perspective, and suggests that a coherent notion of the public interest is available which can serve as a justification of planning activity. However, it is a moot point whether the conception *he* outlines and defends is one which professional planners would feel themselves to be invoking in their more expansive justifications of their activity. This does not invalidate Taylor's project, but rather illustrates the tension between planners' occasional ideological aspirations to be serving the public interest by helping to bring about a society which will be better for all (see e.g. Donnison & Soto 1980), and the realities of radical individualism and social divides in contemporary Western societies – as a result of which the notion of the public interest, when typically used in the sphere of planning, typically collapses into denoting the interests of the state, or its administrators (McAuslan 1980).

The two chapters which follow provide a vivid illustration of the intellectual ferment which surrounds discussions of values in planning.

Low's review of the more influential conceptions of social justice (Chapter 6) and Milroy's exploration of the implications for planning of feminist epistemological critiques (Chapter 7) differ in their intellectual referents, approach and presentation. Low undertakes the task of relating the work of Rawls, Nozick and others to planning. Although he discusses theorists such as Walzer, who Harvey (1993), for example, has described as seeking to accommodate post-modernist concerns, his general approach is to argue within the same epistemological framework as Rawls and Nozick – a framework which makes no such concessions, and which Milroy questions. Nevertheless, there are intimations of an overlap or convergence of interests, as Low concludes by highlighting the importance of confronting power relations in seeking justice, a problem which Forester (Chapter 9) also flags (and has addressed elsewhere), and which underlies Milroy's concerns.

The final three chapters of the book are, in their different ways, reflective overviews of the implications of the evaluative dimension in planning.

Chapter 8, by Bickenbach and Hendler, and Chapter 9, by Forester, are responses to the fluid intellectual and political circumstances described in this introduction and illustrated by the essays in this book. If it is an illusion to envisage planning as part of a grand project creating an ordered, rational and aesthetically pleasing world through the activities of trained technicians in a basically benign state, then, in Bickenbach and Hendler's words, what 'moral mandate' has it? And if planners acknowledge the messiness, the moral ambiguity, the moral conflict of the world in which they work (as Hoch, in Chapter 10, advocates), then how do they act, what do they do? Forester provides some general principles and guidelines for action. A fundamental question which his account of evaluative judgement raises is whether discursive agreement is a solid enough basis for the development of 'principled positions' (Squires 1993), a potential difficulty of which he is clearly aware (see note 1, Chapter 9).

In Chapter 10, the final chapter of the book, Hoch considers how the role of values in planning has been incorporated into the education of planners. Although he confines his discussion to the USA, his tale of a general disavowal of the significance of questions of value is one which will be just as familiar to an audience outside that country. Hoch criticises the social science-influenced 'rational method' approach to curriculum design as having ignored the messiness of the real world of planning, which is inextricably bound up with moral, political and aesthetic judgements, and hence produces graduates who are ineffective in the 'real world' – they are analysts, not 'doers'. Again, for the British planner and academic, this has a familiar ring. However, in considering education it might be useful to distinguish between two issues:

(i)   the issue of training planners who can 'do', who are implementers;
(ii)   the issue of turning out planners who can think systematically and clearly about the moral/political significance and value of their work.

These two issues are different. In a highly politicised atmosphere it can sometimes be useful to be able to understand moral and political categories, if only to understand the views of others. But this falls short of actually reflecting upon your own values and the choices facing you. One comes across a number of planners who are *effective*, in the sense of understanding real estate, *Realpolitik*, the development process, the way residents' groups work etc., but they *never* question the value of what they do. They are effective doers, but *amoral* doers. Such people lead one to question Hoch's apparent concern for effectiveness as a valued goal in itself.

These sketchy remarks can do no more than gesture towards the wealth of argument and insight contained in the book's essays: virtues which surely betoken the development of a wide-ranging debate about values and planning within the profession and in academe.

NOTES

1   The rest of this paragraph draws on, and compresses, analysis first presented in Thomas (1980, 1981).
2   In my view, a defect of an otherwise marvellous piece of work is that, while Davies suggests it is planners, collectively, who are the authors of various misconceptions about the role of values in guiding practice, he fails to explain why this might be so by placing them in any kind of social context.
3   Although, as Milroy reminds us in Chapter 7 of this book, it has been argued that the knowing subject in this model is, crucially, gendered (and male).
4   It is important to point out that her contribution to this volume develops a particular line of argument on these issues, and she has written elsewhere (e.g. Milroy 1992) about the variety of feminist perspectives which can be found in the literature.

REFERENCES

Beauregard, R., 1992, 'Introduction to Planning Theories, Feminist Theories: A Symposium', *Planning Theory*, Vols 7–8, pp. 9–12.

Cooke, P., 1990, *Back to the Future*, London: Unwin Hyman.

Davies, J. G., 1972, *The Evangelistic Bureaucrat*, London: Tavistock.

Donnison, D. and Soto, P., 1980, *The Good City*, London: Heinemann Educational.

Faludi, A., 1989, 'Procedural Rationality and Ethical Theory', *Planning Outlook*, Vol. 32(1), pp. 55–65.

Giddens, A., 1990, *The Consequences of Modernity*, Cambridge: Polity Press.

Hall, S., 1992, 'The West and the Rest: Discourse and Power', in Hall, S. and Mgieben, B. (eds), *Formations of Modernity*, Cambridge: Polity Press, pp. 275–320.

Hare, R., 1952, *The Language of Morals*, Oxford: Oxford University Press.

Harper, T. L. and Stein, S. M., 1992, 'The Centrality of Normative Ethical Theory to Contemporary Planning Theory', *Journal of Planning Education and Research*, Vol. 11(2), pp. 105–16.

Harvey, D., 1993, 'Class Relations, Social Justice and the Politics of Difference', in Squires, J. (ed.), *Principled Positions*, London: Lawrence and Wishart, pp. 85–120.

Keith, M. and Cross, M., 1993, 'Racism and the Postmodern City', in Cross, M. and Keith, M. (eds), *Racism, the City and the State*, London: Routledge, pp. 1–30.

Mackie, J., 1977, *Ethics*, Harmondsworth: Penguin.

McAuslan, J. P., 1980, *The Ideologies of Planning Law*, Oxford; Pergamon.

McLennan, G., 1992, 'The Enlightenment Project Revisited', in Hall, S., Held, D. and McGrew, T. (eds), *Modernity and its Futures*, Cambridge: Polity Press, pp. 327–55.

Milroy, B. M., 1992, 'Some Thoughts About Difference and Pluralism', in *Planning Theory*, Vols 7–8, pp. 33–8.

Raban, J., 1974, *Soft City*, London: Hamish Hamilton.

Reade, E., 1987, *British Town and Country Planning*, Milton Keynes: Open University Press.

Squires, J., 1993, 'Introduction', in Squires, J. (ed.), *Principled Positions*, London: Lawrence and Wishart, pp. 1–13.

Thomas, H., 1980, 'The Education of British Town Planners, 1965–75', *Planning and Administration*, Vol. 7(2), pp. 67–78.

Thomas, H., 1981, 'Developments within the Education of British Town Planners', in Thomas, H. and Thomas, W. K., *Planning Education in the 1970s*, Working Paper No. 55, Oxford: Oxford Polytechnic, pp. 1–20.

Chapter 2

Environmental ethics and the field of planning: Alternative theories and middle-range principles

Timothy Beatley

THE ETHICAL NATURE OF ENVIRONMENTAL PLANNING AND POLICY

There is little disagreement that the condition of the natural environment continues to deteriorate and that the global environmental predicament worsens each year. The scale and magnitude of these environmental problems continues to expand, with problems of acid deposition, defor-estation, massive species extinction, dramatic global population increases and global warming, among others, elevating the environmental crisis to new levels. The worsening environmental situation raises serious ques-tions about the ethical standards employed in contemporary planning and policy-making (or the lack thereof). Many believe that environmental problems can only be effectively addressed through a new awareness of environmental ethics, and through an acknowledgement of certain funda-mental moral obligations to, and relative to, the natural world. This essay explores the subject of environmental ethics, and the implications that this body of writing and thinking has for environmental planning and policy. I will argue that this subject has considerable implications for planning practice and for guiding land use and environmental policy.

More specifically, I have several objectives in this essay. I would first like to introduce the subject of environmental ethics, and briefly survey the theoretical landscape, giving the reader a sense of the diversity and richness of the thinking in this area. Second, once the landscape has been surveyed, I would like to offer some thoughts about what these different ethical positions and theories suggest about planning and public policy. I will argue in the latter portions of the essay that, despite the significant differences in the foundational principles and underlying concepts of a number of the major competing theories of environmental ethics, there is considerable overlap and likely agreement about planning and policy implications. I will suggest that there are certain 'middle-range' environmental principles or obligations that would be embraced by those subscribing to quite different ethical theories.

The topic of environmental ethics, as a subject of academic and scholarly focus, as well as a subject of popular attention, is a relatively recent one. In the US context, many of the early beginnings can certainly be traced to such conservation luminaries as John Muir and Gifford Pinchot, and the literary works of Emerson, Thoreau and others. The emergence of contemporary ethics as a subject of serious attention is perhaps best marked by the groundbreaking work of Aldo Leopold, most notably through Leopold's *A Sand County Almanac* (1949). In Leopold's essay 'The Land Ethic' he put forth a new philosophical and policy agenda that set the tone for much of the discourse and writing to follow in environmental ethics. Among other things, Leopold was sharply critical of what he saw as the prevailing economic view of the environment: a short-sighted view, and one in which human beings were seen as being apart from – and indeed morally above – other forms of life and the environment as a whole. Leopold argued for a new and different posture towards the natural environment, one which viewed the human species, instead of conqueror of nature, as 'member and plain citizen' of it, and a citizen of this larger biotic community. The concept of community, then, was essential to Leopold. Just as we are part of human communities and thus have obligations to them, so also do we have obligations to the larger biotic community. In Leopold's words (1949, p.85):

The land ethic simply enlarges the boundaries of the community to include soils, water, plants and animals, or collectively: the land ... a land ethic changes the role of Homo Sapiens from conqueror of the land community to plain member and citizen of it. It implies respect for his fellow members, and also respect for the community as such.

While Leopold's views remain controversial and far from being realised, they have in many ways served to set in motion a very active and vibrant debate about what our ethical posture towards the natural environment ought to be, and the extent and nature of our ethical obligations to, or relative to, the natural environment. In academic circles discussions about environmental ethics have surfaced in many places. For example, there is now a growing sub-field of environmental ethics within moral philosophy, a *Journal of Environmental Ethics*, and a great many books, articles and symposia addressing the subject (e.g. see Attfield 1983; Callicott 1989; Hargrove 1989; Nash 1989; Regan 1984; Rolston 1988; Van De Veer & Pierce 1986).

The field of planning has not been quick to incorporate environmental ethics into its theory and practice. Unfortunately, literature within planning which explicitly addresses the subject of environmental ethics is virtually non-existent (for exceptions, see Beatley 1989; Jacobs, forthcoming). Moreover, planning curricula, at least at US universities, pay scant attention to theories and concepts of environmental ethics. A recent survey of US planning schools, for instance, found only three programmes which offered a fully-fledged course on the subject (out of 81 schools responding; see Martin & Beatley, forthcoming).[1] Consideration of environmental ethics in graduate planning theory classes would also seem logical and appropriate, but a recent US survey of planning theory courses found virtually no consideration of this subject (Klosterman 1992).[2]

Despite the lack of specific attention paid to the area of environmental ethics, there is a trend towards greater attention to the ethical dimensions of planning practice, as evidenced by the adoption of the American Planning Association Set of Ethical Principles and recent action by the Planning Accreditation Board (PAB) requiring planning programs to address values in their curricula. This shift towards greater attention to ethical issues may also herald greater emphasis on environmental ethics.

THE SCOPE OF ENVIRONMENTAL ETHICS

As a body of scholarship and thought, what does environmental ethics encompass and what is its theoretical and practical scope? At the most general level, environmental ethics might be defined as that area of thought and moral discourse dealing with our ethical duties to, and relative to, the natural environment. As Taylor (1986, p.3) notes, it is: 'concerned with the moral relations that hold between humans and the natural world. The ethical principles governing those relations determine our duties, obligations, and responsibilities with regard to the Earth's natural environment and all the animals and plants that inhabit it.' Environmental ethics, then, is clearly about choices and decisions, and it concerns questions of right and wrong, good and bad. It is important to recognise that the consideration of environmental ethics is not an optional question. Rather, the failure to consider environmental ethics directly is itself a form of ethical choice, albeit of a *de facto* sort. Even those who have little or no regard for environmental impacts on the natural environment *have* a set of environmental ethics – they simply treat the environment or environmental considerations as having little or no value. Before examining in detail any particular ethical positions or theories, it will be instructive to attempt to develop a broad framework for organising or categorising many of these different approaches.

An initial important question in defining the scope of environmental ethics and in categorising different theories of environmental ethics is how we conceive of the relevant moral community involved – that is, *to whom* or *to what* do we have ethical duties or obligations? There are several different dimensions to this question, including a biological dimension, a temporal dimension and a spatial/geographical dimension.

The first dimension, which I refer to as *biological*, involves the fundamental issue of whether moral obligations extend beyond the human species, and whether other forms of life, or the larger ecosystem itself, have *intrinsic* value. Within the environmental ethics literature there is a distinction frequently made between *anthropocentric* views and those which might be said to be *non-anthropocentric*. Historically, our ethical posture has been heavily anthropocentric – that is, placing the human species at the centre of the moral universe. Anthropocentric theories see the environment primarily as a human 'resource', to satisfy human needs and wants. Nature and the natural environment have no intrinsic value or inherent worth, but are only valuable to the extent that they serve the *instrumental* needs of *Homo sapiens*. William Baxter, in his memorable book, *People or Penguins* (1974, p.5), sums up the anthropocentric view well:

My criteria are oriented to people, not penguins. Damage to penguins, or sugar pines, or geological marvels is, without more, simply irrelevant. One must go further, by my criteria, and say: Penguins are important because people enjoy seeing them walk about rocks... In

15

short, my observations about environmental problems will be people-oriented, as are my criteria. I have no interest in preserving penguins for their own sake.

Non-anthropocentric views, on the other hand, disagree sharply with Baxter and others, and hold, for various different reasons, that nature, or elements of nature, have inherent worth and intrinsic value, irrespective of the value they may hold instrumentally to human beings. Several of the more important of these positions are described in detail below.

Other dimensions can also be important in defining the relevant moral community. The *temporal* dimension involves fundamental questions about the moral timeframe of planning and policy decisions. Is it the case that moral obligations are owed primarily to the present generation, or are obligations owed to the future and to future generations? This perspective is considered in more detail in a later section. The *geographical* dimension involves questions about the extent of *duties beyond borders*, and whether or not we are obligated to consider environmental impacts and degradation which occur to other communities, states, and nations (many of our contemporary environmental problems, from groundwater contamination to global warming, involve difficult moral trade-offs between those who are, in some sense, geographically close and those who are not).

Once the moral community is defined in some sense, there are difficult questions about the extent and nature of our obligations. A common distinction made in ethics and moral philosophy is between *deontological* (or duty-based) ethical theories, and those which are *teleological* (or utilitarian). *Teleological* theories – utilitarianism being the most dominant form – hold that:

the basic or ultimate criterion or standard of what is morally right, wrong, obligatory, etc., is the nonmoral value that is brought into being. The first appeal, directly or indirectly, must be to the comparative amount of good produced, or rather to the comparative balance of good over evil. (Frankena 1973, p.14)

Deontological, or duty-based theories, on the other hand, hold that:

there are other considerations that may make an action or rule right or obligatory besides the goodness or badness of its consequences –

certain features of the act itself other than the *value* it brings into existence, for example the fact that it keeps a promise, is just, or is commanded by God or by the state. (Frankena 1973, p.15)

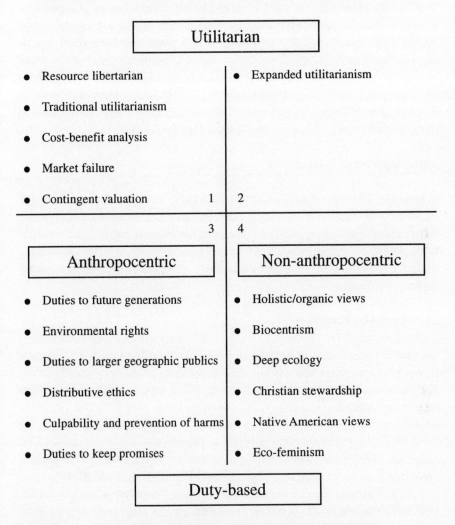

Figure 2.1   Categorising theories of environmental ethics

Note: the concepts and theories contained in each quadrant are meant to be illustrative, not exhaustive. Moreover, no attempt is made within each quadrant to array the theories along the two axes.

Source: Beatley (forthcoming).

These initial questions allow us to construct at least a crude theoretical framework for organising and classifying concepts and theories of environmental ethics. While there are undoubtedly many other variables or dimensions upon which positions could be classified, Figure 2.1 captures two of the most important: the extent to which a position is *utilitarian* versus *duty-based*, and the extent to which positions have been developed in each of these quadrants; Figure 2.1 presents several of the more important of these. A full exploration of these different moral perspectives is found in Beatley (forthcoming). While I lack the space here to discuss each of these perspectives fully, what follows is a more detailed examination of several of the more prominent positions.

Anthropocentric theories

Within the anthropocentric camp, several prominent ethical positions can be identified, and are discussed below, including: the resource libertarian view; the utilitarian/economic view; environmental rights, and obligations to future generations. The major non-anthropocentric viewpoints briefly described below include: biocentrism, ecocentrism, deep ecology and eco-feminism.

The resource libertarian

To many, the natural environment is merely a collection of proprietary resources to be used and exploited as individual property-owners see fit. Forests are to be harvested, coastlines are to be developed, and water is to be appropriated and consumed. The environment generally has no value beyond how the individual landholder or proprietor believes it can be used profitably, and short-term profit is usually the key motivation. The *resource libertarian* is generally suspicious of government or collective constraints on individual use of the environment, or on individual behaviour which affects the environment. Such restrictions are often characterised as curtailments on personal freedom, and as such are seen as antithetical to democracy and a free market economy. If a private landholder wishes to destroy endangered species, habitats or to fill wetlands located on his or her property, they should be left to do so – believing that ultimately it ought to be up to individuals to determine how and when to use land and the natural environment. It is through such numerous and unencumbered individual decisions, so the theory holds, that the broader

18

public interest will be served. (In its focus on the sanctity of private ownership and use of the natural environment, this position could also easily be classified as *deontological*.)

The resource libertarian view also finds expression in public lands policy. At least in the US, many publicly-owned lands have essentially been expropriated by individuals and commercial interests (ranchers, miners, timber companies) who express the desire to use and exploit these lands without (or with minimal) government control. In recent years, as public pressures to further curtail the use of existing public lands such as national forests and grazing areas (e.g. Bureau of Land Management land) continue to rise, private land rights groups have formed around the USA. Under the banner of the 'wise use' movement, groups such as The Center for the Defense of Free Enterprise and the Wilderness Impact Research Foundation have been active in opposing expanded public ownership and control, and are quick to charge that such actions undermine the system of personal freedoms (e.g. see O'Callaghan 1992).

For those concerned with establishing ethical public policy relative to the natural environment, the resource libertarian position is hard to defend. It fails to acknowledge the inherently public or collective nature of the natural environment, or the myriad external effects of individual actions and resource decisions. To most environmentalists the idea of absolute or nearly-absolute ownership of such things as coastal marshes or Sequoia redwood forests is difficult to accept.

The utilitarian/economic view

Arguably, the dominant ethical view in US policy circles – the *utilitarian* model – sees as ethically correct those decisions about the natural environment which serve to *maximise* human benefits, ideally through the rubric of the market system. Where the market system in some sense works imperfectly or *fails*, for example in the case of environmental pollution or *negative externalities*, government intervention is justified to correct such allocative inefficiencies. The use of benefit-cost techniques and thinking have become widespread and pervasive approaches to making environmental decisions, applied to everything from decisions about whether to construct a flood control project to whether to adopt a proposed emission standard to whether or not an area should be designated as a wilderness (e.g. see Kelman 1985). One of the first actions taken by President Reagan was the issuing of Executive Order #12291 (still in force), which requires agencies such as the Environmental Protection Agency (EPA) to conduct benefit-cost analyses for any proposed environmental regulation and prevents any action where the calculated benefits do not exceed the costs. Interestingly, a bill has been introduced in the US Congress in 1991 and again in May 1993, entitled the 'Human Protection Act', which would apply similar benefit-cost standards to the listing process under the federal Endangered Species Act, long viewed as a law that did not have to depend on such economic justifications.

The utilitarian/economic view generally assumes that all environmental goods and services can be *priced* and monetary values placed on them; that values are determined through personal preferences and the casting of dollar 'votes', and that environmental and non-environmental goods can be compared through the common dollar metric. Through the practice of *discounting* (putting all benefits and costs in terms of present value), the utilitarian paradigm tends to devalue the future. Considerable effort has been expended in recent years to place monetary values on many elements of the natural environment, from visibility in national parks to endangered species to wilderness areas. The primary tool has been the so-called technique of 'contingent valuation'. (For recent examples, see Schulze et al. 1983; Lancaster 1991.)

Critics of the economic view see it as, at best, difficult to place quantitative prices on all elements of the environment and, at worst, immoral to try. The very act of placing a price on something (from a species of animal to a national park) serves to cheapen it, and ignores broader moral issues and obligations (e.g. the prospect of these things having intrinsic value, that they should be preserved out of obligations to future generations).

Environmental rights

There are also other non-utilitarian variants of anthropocentric ethics. One such variant can be seen in the concept of *environmental rights*, or the fundamental notion that all human beings have certain environmental entitlements guaranteed by virtue of their humanity. These are rights that must be respected even where they are not socially efficient or optimal under a utilitarian model. Evidence of this type of rights-based thinking can, I believe, be seen in contemporary environmental policy, in the USA and elsewhere. Environmental rights may involve rights *to* things, such as rights of access to mountains and rivers and beaches, or rights to be *free from* excessive levels of pollution. There is much of this thinking in the establishment of national pollution standards, for instance the National Ambient Air Quality Standards under the Clean Air Act. A potentially very powerful concept (again in the US context) is the so-called *public-trust doctrine*, a common law doctrine which protects public access to navigable waters, shorelines and beaches (at least the wet-beach in most US states, e.g. see Sax 1971). Along the same lines, efforts have been made to gain passage of a federal constitutional right to environmental protection, and a number of state constitutions in fact include provisions establishing the right to a liveable environment.[3] The 'Earth Charter', drafted for the Rio Earth Summit (though never adopted), contains similar wording, stating that 'all individuals have the fundamental rights to freedom, equality, and an environment adequate for their health and well-being' (*Earth Ethics*, p.11).

There are, of course, certain difficulties in an environmental rights position. These include difficulties (theoretical and practical) in determining what the extent of these rights are, and whether they can legitimately vary from one country, region or culture to the next.

Future generations

Arguments about the need to protect the environment have also frequently been made based on our ethical obligations to posterity and to future generations (e.g. see generally Sikora & Berry 1978; Partridge 1981). The federal National Environmental Policy Act (NEPA), for instance, calls on us to 'fulfil the responsibilities of each generation as trustee of the environment for succeeding generations'.

This paradigm argues that, while it may be difficult to know precisely what preferences future generations will have, we can be reasonably assured that they will want and need clean air, clean water, open space, toxic-free communities, etc. Moreover, this perspective argues that we should *keep options open* for future generations, and avoid making irreversible decisions (such as causing the extinction of species or the destruction of old-growth forests). Others have argued that not only do we have a moral responsibility not to pass along an environmentally compromised planet, but that obligations in fact exist to clean up and restore degradations and to pass along a healthier and more liveable planet.

Obligations to future generations have been derived and defended in many ways. Rawls (1971) argues for something he calls the 'just savings principle', believing that rational individuals deciding on the principles of social justice (and under a 'veil of ignorance') would acknowledge certain obligations to their immediate descendants. Still others have argued for such obligations based on more radical social contract theory (e.g. that all generations ought to be represented, at least theoretically, when determining the conditions and principles of the social contract). Still others argue for obligations to future generations based on utilitarianism (e.g. see Attfield 1983).

Sceptics towards such obligations point to our difficulty in determining even what the *current* generation needs and wants, never mind what future generations will desire (can we really be certain that future generations will value, say, an endangered cave invertebrate, if the present generation does not appear to?) and, to many, arguments about keeping options open appear circular. If we argue, for example, that a pristine river should not be damaged so that future generations can decide whether it should be preserved, won't future generations be similarly constrained by such a 'keeping the options open' standard?

Biocentric and other non-anthropocentric views

In more recent years, and building on the intuitions of Leopold, a number of non-anthropocentric ethical perspectives on the environment have been discussed and advocated. These include: animal rights/welfare; duties to species and duties to protect endangered species and biodiversity; biocentrism; ecocentrism; deep ecology, and eco-feminism, among others. There are a number of different ways of slicing this theoretical pie, and a greater or lesser number of camps depending on who is doing the classifying. Because of limited space, only several of the more prominent of these positions are profiled here.

Ecocentric and biocentric ethical views change the moral locus dramatically. No longer are benefits or impacts to the human species the moral *sine qua non*. Rather, the natural environment, or particular elements of the natural environment, have moral value and worth, irrespective of the value placed on them by human beings. There are a number of theoretical variants, and biocentric and ecocentric views are briefly described here.

Biocentrism and ecocentrism

Biocentrism, as the name implies, seeks to rearrange the ethical universe, placing life (Greek *bios*), or the biotic community, at the centre, rather than *Homo sapiens* (following Leopold in many ways, I might add). In environmental philosophy, one of the most detailed and comprehensive biocentric works is Paul Taylor's *Respect for Nature* (1986). Taylor argues for a biocentric world-view, which comprises four core beliefs:

(a) The belief that humans are members of the Earth's community of Life in the same sense and on the same terms in which other living things are members of that community.
(b) The belief that the human species, along with all other species, are integral elements in a system of interdependence such that the survival of each living thing, as well as its chances of faring well or poorly, is determined not only by the physical conditions of its environment but also by its relations to other living things.
(c) The belief that all organisms are teleological centres of life in the sense that each is a unique individual pursuing its own good in its own way.
(d) The belief that humans are not inherently superior to other living things. (Taylor 1986, pp. 99–100)

Assuming such a biocentric outlook, *respect for nature* (Taylor argues) is the only reasonable moral posture. Obviously the potential policy ramifications of such an outlook are substantial, and Taylor lays out a set of basic rules of conduct and priority principles for resolving conflicts between *Homo sapiens* and other forms of life. Central to these principles is the notion that the human species must not violate the basic interests (survival) of other forms of life merely to satisfy non-basic human desires. In Taylor's words:

> The central idea ... is that, in a conflict between human values and the good of ... wild animals and plants, greater weight is to be given to basic than to nonbasic interests, no matter what the species, human or other, the competing claims arise from [this] ... prohibits us from allowing nonbasic interests to override basic ones. (Taylor 1986, p.278)[4]

Such philosophical biocentricism, then, constructs a moral foundation based on the inherent value of all life – the assumption that all living organisms have a good of their own. It expands the moral community, in a fashion reminiscent of Albert Schweitzer, to give moral weight and consideration to other lifeforms, and the larger ecosystems that harbour and sustain them.

Such a system in effect assigns moral rights to other non-human entities which create ethical constraints on human policy and behaviour.

For those holding an ecocentric ethic, it is not individual life which has inherent worth, but rather the larger ecosystem. The ecosystem has such inherent worth because of its complexity, interconnectedness and persistence (e.g. see Rolston 1988).[5] Despite the theoretical differences between these biocentric and ecocentric moral perspectives, their practical implications are quite similar. Biocentrics like Taylor, for instance, advocate protecting and preserving larger ecosystems because this will tend to ensure protection for the greatest number of individual lifeforms.

Many policy-makers and citizens alike remain unconvinced about the intrinsic value and inherent worth of nature. It is frequently argued that an anthropocentric moral outlook is unavoidable given the fact that it is *Homo sapiens* doing the valuing. The biocentric assumptions of Taylor are, to many, difficult to accept (are humans really not inherently superior to other living creatures?), and ecocentric theory has been criticised as generating an 'ought' from an 'is' (i.e. moral value derived merely from factual or empirical conditions; e.g. the complexity and interconnectedness of the ecosystem; see Callicott 1989; Taylor 1986).

Deep ecology

Deep ecology represents a different approach to thinking about our environmental obligations. Coined by Norwegian philosopher Arne Naess, the term deep ecology refers to the idea of achieving a deeper ecological consciousness and a more fundamental alteration of the human–nature relationship (e.g. Naess 1973). Much contemporary US environmental policy, from the Clean Water Act to the National Environmental Policy Act, is characterised as *shallow* ecology, in that it represents only minor tinkering or changes at the margin. Central to deep ecology is a fundamental *identification* with nature, and the struggle to achieve a larger *ecological self*:

If we experience the world as an extension of ourselves, if we have a broader and deep identification, then we feel hurt when other beings, including nonhuman beings are hurt. (Devall 1980)

In the concept of the Ecological Self, human interests and natural interests become fused and there is no need to appeal to the traditional discourse of rights and values. The integrity of the biosphere is seen as the integrity of our own persons; the rights of the natural world are implied in our right to be human and humane. (Manes 1990)

Deep ecology, then, is critical of biocentric theories, such as Taylor's, which seek to set up philosophical systems for adjudicating between the rights and interests of nature and its various constituent parts. Rather, deep ecology seeks to promote in humans an ethic which sees harm to nature as harm to ourselves.

Considerable scepticism has been expressed about the feasibility and practicality of the deep ecology outlook, at least in the short term. It is too much to expect, many believe, that more individuals will be able to achieve the deeper ecological unity desired. While this may be something for our society to strive for, such a moral posture represents a radical reorientation, not likely to be achievable in the foreseeable future. Moreover, while deep ecology espouses a particular relationship to the natural environment, it can be criticised for not encouraging or putting forth a defensible moral theory to support it (and the movement has in fact drawn from and incorporated various aspects of the other theories discussed here, e.g. see Devall & Sessions 1985).

Eco-feminism

Eco-feminism shares many of the underlying beliefs and perspectives of deep ecology. It contends that much of the destructive and exploitative relationship we have had towards the natural world is the result of *androcentric* (man-centred) values. It draws parallels between the dominance and exploitation of men over women, and the dominance of the human species over the natural world. To eco-feminists, a solution to the environmental crisis is not possible without also overcoming male domination in society.

Eco-feminism stresses the feminine element of the natural world – the notion of Mother Earth as a 'nurturing home for all life', which should be respected and revered as it was in certain pre-modern societies (Oelschlaeger 1991). Eco-feminists believe that the environmental crises can be addressed in part through the adoption of a feminine perspective – a perspective which emphasises the need for a nurturing and respectful stance towards nature, rather than an exploitative and manipulative stance.

In most other theoretical respects eco-feminism and deep ecology are quite similar. Some eco-feminists, however, are suspicious about the deep ecologists' desire to promote an *ecological self*, or a merging of human and natural interests. To some, this represents a return to a male-dominated world, and negates much of the feminists' progress in asserting individual rights and identity. In most respects, however, deep ecology and eco-feminism share common basic underlying tenets, with similar planning and policy implications.

EXPLORING THE COMMON MORAL GROUND: IDENTIFYING SOME MIDDLE-RANGE ETHICAL PRINCIPLES

Where, then, does this quick review of alternative ethical positions leave the planning field? At a philosophical level it is clear that there is considerable disagreement among these views about the appropriate ethical posture of *Homo sapiens*, and the extent to which the natural environment and its various elements have intrinsic value. I personally find considerable ethical appeal, at least at an intuitive level, in a hierarchical ecocentric approach – one which attaches inherent worth at both organism and ecosystem levels, but which assigns moral priority to protecting ecosystem integrity (and priority to larger, broader ecosystemic levels).[6] It is based both on a belief that individual organisms can be shown to have a good of their own, and that the complexity, persistence and integrative nature of ecosystems argues for their intrinsic value. Ecosystems, then, and the living creatures and natural processes that comprise them, *do* have moral worth, in my view, and as such must be respected in our planning decisions about the use of land and the environment.

Despite these theoretical differences, however, I would suggest that there are considerable and fundamental areas of agreement. While ecocentric and biocentric views attach intrinsic value to different aspects of the environment (one to the ecosystem as a whole, the other to the many lifeforms that flourish in the ecosystem), both agree that protecting and sustaining the ecosystem is morally requisite. While proponents of anthropocentric duties to future generations may be sceptical of the notion of the intrinsic value of other lifeforms or the natural system, for example, they will tend to have in common with ecocentrists and deep ecologists the perceived need to protect endangered species, wilderness and open land. It is my view that there are a number of what might be called *middle-range ethical principles* that can provide guidance for human action, and on which considerable agreement might be reached between these different ethical camps (and these intermediate principles give more practical expression to my own moral outlook). These middle-range principles will not be universally embraced. Those subscribing to the resource libertarian view are not likely to find any of them supportable or acceptable, nor will many utilitarians (though this is likely to depend on individual opinions about the actual extent of benefits and costs). And, moreover, the middle-range principles discussed below do assume a common sense of the value and importance of the natural environment and the care with which it ought to be used or impacted.

I have no definitive list of middle-range principles, but these diverse ethical positions do seem to suggest certain ethical concepts and imperatives. I offer the following as some crude starting points that might be helpful in promoting discussion and dialogue.

Reducing the human footprint

Most of the ethical positions discussed here would agree that the human species has a moral obligation to substantially reduce its *footprint* on the world (or what we might refer to as the 'principle of the minimal footprint'). In a practical sense, such an ethical goal implies numerous things, including perhaps: serious efforts to promote population control globally (the prospects of global population levels reaching 12 billion or more are incredibly daunting); efforts to reduce air and water pollutants substantially, and efforts to protect and preserve remaining areas of wilderness and open space.

From a planning point of view, such a principle of the minimal footprint suggests serious re-evaluation of our prevailing patterns of growth and development, and the ways our cities and population centres have been organised. In the USA, with a few state and local exceptions, we currently tolerate an extremely inefficient and damaging pattern of low-density urban sprawl, which in large part accounts for many of our more serious environmental problems, from degradation of the Chesapeake Bay in my home state to air quality problems in Southern California to threats to endangered species in Texas to loss of beaches, dunes, and coastal environments in Florida and elsewhere, among many other environmental problems.

Promoting sustainability

There is also considerable agreement that current patterns of development and resource use are not sustainable in the long run. The last decade has seen the tremendous popularising of the concept of 'sustainable development' – a concept strongly advocated by the World Commission on Environment and Development (WCED – the Brundtland Commission). In the commission's influential report, *Our Common Future*, sustainability is defined as 'meeting the needs of the present without compromising the ability of future generations to meet their own needs' (WCED 1987, p.43). What are increasingly called for are economic and development models which are respectful of the carrying capacities of the biosphere, and which require 'society to live on the "interest" of our ecological endowment' (Rees 1990, p.18), while maintaining and protecting the ecological 'capital'. Obligations to promote sustainability imply numerous potential planning and policy changes, including: substantially reducing the level of timber harvesting (and the use of clear-cutting and other non-sustainable harvest practices); reducing production demands on soils and agricultural lands; reducing the extraction and wasteful use of groundwater and surface waters, and so on. Promoting sustainability provides further support for population control policies, development and use of renewable forms of energy (e.g. greater use of solar power), and reducing the overall human footprint.

Recently, there have been efforts to explore the meaning of sustainability at local and community level. The notion of 'sustainable communities' (other terms are frequently used, such as sustainable cities, eco-cities, green cities, and so on) suggests that our cities and communities can and ought to be organised in ways which minimise resource consumption (e.g. energy, water), the generation of wastes (air pollution, solid waste), and promote greater liveability and social equity (e.g. Van der Ryn & Calthorpe 1991). Such new approaches to human settlement patterns should include: substantially higher densities and more compact and contiguous growth patterns; greater reliance on mass transit and alternative modes of transportation to the automobile; more energy-efficient development; development patterns which avoid sensitive lands, including areas of high biodiversity, among other components (e.g. see Walter et al. 1992). There are some signs of progress in the USA. At the federal level, for example, the new transportation bill (the Intermodel Surface Transportation Efficiency Act of 1991) is a landmark piece of legislation offering the prospect of much greater support for mass transit and alternative forms of transportation.[7] At more local levels, for instance, there are increasingly impressive models of developments and towns and cities organised around more ecologically sensible and sustainable principles (e.g. see Beatley et al. 1988).

Satisfying basic needs and exhausting viable alternatives

There is much agreement in principle among many of the positions surveyed that environmental destruction or degradation should only be tolerated to satisfy *important* or *essential* or *basic* human needs. Moreover, an obligation exists at every level of decision-making to consider viable and feasible *alternatives* which are less destructive.

Unfortunately, perhaps, such standards are very subjective and very much 'eye of the beholder' concepts. What one person may view as a basic or essential human need, another may view as superfluous. Are sporting and recreational facilities, such as golf courses or baseball fields, essential human needs, and thus defensible even when they are extremely environmentally destructive? What about the traditional US household lawn, very water-consumptive and environmentally wasteful? Also, what is a feasible alternative to one person is impractical or not feasible to another. The important element of such a principle, however, is the good-faith effort to explore alternatives, and to question the importance of uses and activities that result in unnecessary environmental destruction.

There are some signs of movement in this direction. A recent example is the US Environmental Protection Agency's (EPA) veto of the so-called Two Forks dam in Colorado. The project was intended to serve as a drinking-water supply for the Denver area, and the EPA concluded that there were indeed practicable alternatives to constructing the dam (and the resulting loss of wetlands), including water conservation. While the EPA has historically been timid in exercising its veto authority in such cases, the action does serve to illustrate the importance of such a *practicable alternatives* standard.

There are few who would advocate an environmental ethic that prohibits all human impacts on, or alteration of, the natural environment. Rather, what is demanded is a more critical view of alternatives, and allowance of degradation/alteration only for extremely important or essential human goals, and only when other less damaging options have been exhausted.

Expanding the moral timeframe

Most of the ethical positions surveyed above would concur that the human species has a clear obligation to expand the moral timeframe. Much of the prevailing decision-making ethic has taken an inappropriately narrow view of the temporal moral community. Clearly our environmental decisions, individually and· cumulatively, have tremendous potential impact on future environmental conditions and the quality of the future existence of all life. The typical approach is either to completely disregard the future, or to seriously devalue it (e.g. through the technique of discounting). Even those of us in the field of planning typically take very narrow views. Local comprehensive or land-use plans typically assume a twenty-year or thirty-year time horizon, for understandable reasons. It seems that public officials and citizens alike have difficulty conceptualising about their communities very far into the future. Tonn (1986) argued for a need for 500-year plans, and it does seem that we must, as a society, become better at thinking longer-term. Planners are perhaps in the best position to advocate such longer timeframes.

Preventing irreversible actions

Consistent with expanding the moral timeframe, there is some consensus among these different theories that the human species has a special moral duty to prevent irreversible actions and, to the extent possible, not unnecessarily foreclose the options available to future generations.

There are many examples of planning conflicts which involve irreversible actions. In the USA, recent protracted debates have centred around the extinction of species (and the stringency of the federal Endangered Species Act), and the destruction of irreplaceable landforms and habitats (e.g. old-growth forests in the Northwest, destruction of wilderness such as the Arctic National Wildlife Refuge in Alaska, etc.). It is also clear that planning frequently involves land-use and resource decisions which can set in place patterns and trends that are later difficult to constrain or stop. A standard of preventing irreversible actions may, for instance, suggest the need to prevent the construction of a road or highway which may forever change a pristine natural area because of the secondary causal pressures resulting from it.

Quality over quantity

The human species has a moral duty to begin to emphasise quality over quantity, and community over individualism. Movement towards a more sustainable relationship with planet Earth will likely have to involve some willingness on the part of individuals, families, communities and society to rethink the notion of 'progress'. Progress at each level has tended to emphasise material goods, and the quantity of such goods. Leopold is among many who have questioned the current definition of 'progress', suggesting in contrast that we may be in a period of 'regress':

> Our grandfathers were less well-housed, well-fed, well-clothed than we are. The strivings by which they bettered their lot are also those which deprived us of [passenger] pigeons. Perhaps we now grieve because we are not sure, in our hearts, that we have gained by the exchange. The gadgets of industry bring no more comforts than the pigeons did, but did they add as much to the glory of the spring? (Leopold 1949, p.109)

Consistent with the importance of stressing basic or essential human needs, the implications for planning here are numerous, further supporting the need for neighbourhoods and land-use patterns which promote development of community, and rich interpersonal relations. Planners are in a position to create and promote those modes of social organisation that may be able to overcome contemporary consumption-oriented lifestyles (e.g. by promoting integration of home and work, creating integrative public spaces, and reducing auto-dominated transportation systems, promoting greater aesthetic appreciation). The recent movement in design and planning circles in the US towards *neo-traditional* communities is a positive sign of some of these changes (albeit on small scales).

Ecological economics

There is a moral duty to adjust the existing economic system to better reflect the true costs of environmental degradation and destruction, and to promote more ecologically sustainable economies. Most agree that our current free market systems clearly do not take adequate account of environmental damage and destruction and must be altered in one way or another. For utilitarians or market proponents this often means govern-

31

ment interventions to correct for *market failures*. For others, the problems are more fundamental and go to the centre of the growth-orientation and bias found in traditional capitalism (e.g. see Daly 1977). Despite the range of views about the virtues and desirability of market economies, there is, I believe, considerable support from most or all factions for initiatives which promote a greater *ecological economics*. These initiatives, while not necessarily sufficient, will tend to promote a more environmentally responsive economic system. The specific policy and planning initiatives range from developing green Gross National Products to carbon taxes to marketable pollution permits.

New concepts of land ownership

Most contemporary theories of environmental ethics would also agree that there is need to formulate and defend new concepts of land ownership which overcome traditional property-rights views of land. Many of our recent efforts to protect the environment – protections given to wetlands, river corridors, endangered species – impinge on the desires of private landowners to use their land freely. There is an increasing charge that such restrictions amount to government *takings* of land, prohibited by the US Constitution without just compensation. A recent decision by the US Supreme Court in *Lucas* v. *South Carolina Coastal Council*,[8] reiterates just how far such movement needs to occur. This case involved two extremely vulnerable beachfront lots on a dynamic South Carolina barrier island on which the owner was prevented from building houses. The lower court found in favour of the landowner's holding that the shoreline regulation was indeed an unconstitutional taking. The South Carolina Supreme Court reversed, holding that all that the state was doing was preventing the creation of a public harm. The US Supreme Court reversed and remanded, holding that the South Carolina Supreme Court had erred in its reasoning. It further reinforced the legal holding that, where land regulations leave no reasonable economic use for its owners (and the regulations are not simply attempting to enforce pre-existing common law nuisance restrictions), it is likely to be found to be a taking, requiring public compensation. To many it seems odd that society must compensate landowners when they are prevented from building in fragile and dangerous places, and in ways which jeopardise both ecological integrity and personal safety.

The current US Supreme Court notwithstanding, what we must ultimately evolve towards at a societal level is an understanding of land ownership which sees as many ethical *duties* as rights – duties to respect, nurture, and care for the land. Moreover, there is no absolute right, I would contend, to use or develop land or to reap high profits from its use where significant environmental destruction is the outcome. Where such activities fundamentally change the natural character of the land, the presumption must be against allowing extensive development.[9] Certainly, hand in hand with such changes we must continue to explore ways to mitigate the financial impacts of new land and environmental regulations where possible. These techniques might include the use of transferable development rights, compensatory forms of regulation, and probably more extensive public land acquisition programmes.

Promoting connectivity with the environment

Deep ecology is perhaps the ethical approach most committed to promoting greater connectivity with the environment. The concept of *identification* is, as we have seen, central to this approach – essential to reaching a point where we experience damage to the natural environment as damage to ourselves. Subscribers to many different ethical theories are likely to concur with the need to promote such connectivity. Promoting such connection clearly involves many factors beyond the realm of planning, including greater attention to environmental education in our school systems, and a much greater appreciation for the myriad ways in which we are interconnected with the natural environment. From a planning perspective, however, such a goal further reinforces the need to incorporate the natural environment into land-use and development designs where possible, and to maximise opportunities for human exposure to the natural environment (e.g. getting people out of their cars, providing direct pedestrian access to parks and open spaces, etc.). Such exposure and appreciation will clearly help to reinforce the other environmental ethical standards mentioned above.

Important here, as well, is the nurturing of a proprietary view of the natural environment – one where collective indignation is expressed at the filling of a local wetland or the destruction of a local forest. Leopold (1949, p.225) expressed similar sentiments in seeking a community where farmers and landowners would be given 'social approbation for right actions: social disapproval for wrong actions'.

Bioregionalism has often been advocated – frequently by deep ecologists – as the necessary cure for the lack of personal connection and responsibility for these types of actions. Bioregionalism suggests the importance of focusing on certain biologically distinct areas for planning and political reasons. Bioregionalism implies a sense of personal (and political) connection to a bio-region, and the responsibility to be involved in decisions about its planning and management. One of the most important actions individuals can undertake, according to advocates of bioregionalism, is simply to stay put – observing that (at least in the US context) part of the problem in developing connectivity is the often transitory nature of individuals and families.

CONCLUSIONS

This essay has briefly surveyed the theoretical landscape of environmental ethics, describing the major strands of philosophy and thought in this area. While little attention has been paid to the subject of environmental ethics in the planning field, the moral questions and issues raised are indeed central to the profession. Moreover, there is a burgeoning body of writing and thought that can be helpful to planners in clarifying their own values, and in guiding a variety of public and private decisions about the environment. While much is often made about the many differences between various theories and concepts of environmental ethics (anthropocentric v. non-anthropocentric, biocentric v. ecocentric), it is argued here that there is much more common ground than sometimes thought. While different world-views may disagree about the underlying justification and defence of our environmental obligations, they often seem to agree on what have been called middle-range principles. Focusing attention on these – both in planning education and professional practice – may often be more productive than emphasising the gulf that exists between different world-views.

NOTES

1   While few programmes offer an entire course in environmental ethics, some 64 per cent of the responding programmes did indicate that one or more planning faculty members taught environmental ethics as an explicit component of another course. It is hard to tell, however, how much coverage the subject actually gets in other courses and a review of syllabi uncovers little specific reference either to ethics in general, or environmental ethics in particular.

2 While planning theory courses do appear to increasingly incorporate consideration of planning ethics, this has largely to do with more narrow questions of professional ethics, with little consideration of the substantive questions about our ethical relationship to land and the environment. It is surprising to this author, for instance, that planning theory students are not given some exposure to Leopold's 'Land Ethic', and similar discussions which would seem to be at the heart of what planning is or should be. (See Klosterman 1992.)

3 For example, the Pennsylvania Constitution states that 'The people have a *right to* clear air, pure water, and to the preservation of the natural, scenic, historic and aesthetic values of the environment.' For a review of these provisions and their practical and legal weight, see Banner (1976).

4 In Taylor's framework he does allow for certain exceptions to this rule – allowing certain human non-basic interests to overrule the basic interests of other life (under the principle of minimum wrong). These exceptions involve interests that play an important role in the 'overall view of civilised life that rational and informed people tend to adopt autonomously as part of their total world outlook', and occupy a central place in 'peoples' rational conception of their own true good' (Taylor 1986, p.281). Thus, while an art museum might not constitute a basic interest in a physiological sense, filling a wetland to build one may be justified because of its centrality to civilised life. Taylor does stipulate that when such harms are created, alternatives must be chosen which minimise the harms done.

5 These types of holistic or organic views suffer from certain practical uncertainties: namely, at what ecosystem level does inherent value adhere? Is it the larger global or planetary ecosystem to which obligations are owed? What about, at the other end of the continuum, the five-acre coastal marsh; do holistic environmental ethics obligate us to protect and preserve this as well? One response is to hold that each ecosystem level has inherent value, but that moral priority adheres in the larger ecosystem level.

6 My own particular ethical framework is considerably more inclusive than this, incorporating anthropocentric and deontological obligations as well. My framework includes, for instance, duties to future generations, distributive obligations, and extra-jurisdictional duties, among others. A full presentation of this framework can be found in Beatley (forthcoming).

7 Among other things, this bill gives state and local governments greater flexibility in using federal transportation monies, allowing monies to be spent on public transit, car pooling, cycleways and other uses besides constructing highways. Moreover, each state will have to spend a minimum of 10 per cent of its yearly allocation on so-called 'transportation enhancement activities', which include (among a list) provision of facilities for pedestrians and bicycles. The Act also substantially strengthens state and local transportation planning.

8 *Lucas* v. *South Carolina Coastal Council*, 112 S. Ct. 2886 (1992).

9 This principle has been perhaps most eloquently articulated by the Wisconsin Supreme Court in its landmark decision *Just* v. *Marinette*. The court upheld a local shoreline zoning ordinance which prevented a landowner from filling and building on a wetland site. The court stated that: 'An owner of land has no absolute and unlimited right to change the essential natural character of the land so as to use it for a purpose for which it was unsuited in its natural state and which impairs the rights of others. The exercise of the police power in zoning must be reasonable and we think it was not an unreasonable exercise of that power to prevent harm to public rights by limiting the use of private property to its natural use' (56 Wis 2nd at 11, 201 N.W.2d).

REFERENCES

Attfield, R., 1983, *The Ethics of Environmental Concern*, New York, NY: Columbia University Press.

Banner, J. W., 1976, 'A Constitutional Right to a Liveable Environment in Oregon', *Oregon Law Review*, Vol. 55, pp. 239–51.

Baxter, W. F., 1974, *People or Penguins: The Case for Optimal Pollution*, New York, NY: Columbia University Press.

Beatley, T., 1989, 'Environmental Ethics and Planning Theory', *Journal of Planning Literature*, Vol. 4, pp. 1–32.

Beatley, T., forthcoming, *Ethical Land Use: Principles for Policy and Planning*, Baltimore, MD: Johns Hopkins University Press.

Beatley, T., Brower, D. and Brower, L. A., 1988, *Managing Urban Growth: Small Towns and Rural Areas*, Chapel Hill, NC: University of North Carolina Centre for Urban and Regional Studies.

Callicott, J. B., 1989, *In Defense of the Land Ethic: Essays in Environmental Philosophy*, Albany, NY: State University of New York Press.

Daly, H., 1977, *Steady-State Economics*, San Francisco, CA: W.H. Freeman.

Devall, B., 1980, 'The Deep Ecology Movement', *Natural Resources Journal*, Vol. 20, pp. 299–322.

Devall, B. and Sessions, G., 1985, *Deep Ecology: Living as if Nature Mattered*, Salt Lake City, UT: Gibbs M. Smith.

Earth Ethics, 1991, 'The Earth Charter', Vol. 3(1), pp. 11–12.

Frankena, W., 1973, *Ethics*, Englewood Cliffs, NJ: Prentice-Hall.

Hargrove, E. C., 1989, *Fundamentals of Environmental Ethics*, Englewood Cliffs, NJ: Prentice-Hall.

Jacobs, H., forthcoming, 'Contemporary Environmental Philosophy and its Challenge to Planning Theory', in Hendler, S. (ed.), *Planning Ethics: A Reader in Planning Philosophy, Practice and Education*, New Brunswick, NJ: Centre for Urban Policy Research, Rutgers University.

Kelman, S., 1985, 'Cost-benefit Analysis and Environmental Safety and Health Regulation: Ethical and Philosophical Considerations', in Wachs, M. (ed.), *Ethics in Planning*, New Brunswick, NJ: Centre for Urban Policy Research, Rutgers University.

Klosterman, R. E., 1992, 'Planning Theory Education in the 1980's: Results of a Second Course Survey', *Journal of Planning Education and Research*, Vol. 11, pp. 130–40.

Lancaster, J., 1991, 'Value of Intangible Losses from Exxon Valley Spill Put at $3 Billion', *The Washington Post*, 20 March.

Leopold, A., 1949, *A Sand County Almanac*, Oxford: Oxford University Press.

Manes, C., 1990, *Green Rage: Radical Environmentalism and the Unmaking of Civilization*, Boston: Little, Brown.

Martin, E. and Beatley, T., forthcoming, 'Our Relationship with the Earth: Environmental Ethics in Planning Education', submitted to the *Journal of Planning Education and Research*.

Naess, A., 1973, 'The Shallow and the Deep, Long Range Ecology Movement, Summary', *Inquiry*, Vol. 15, pp. 95–100.

Nash, R., 1989, *The Rights of Nature: A History of Environmental Ethics*, Madison, WI: University of Wisconsin Press.

O'Callaghan, K., 1992, 'Whose Agenda for America', *Audubon*, September/ October.

Oelschlaeger, M., 1991, *The Idea of Wilderness*, New Haven, CT: Yale University Press.

Partridge, E. (ed.), 1981, *Responsibilities to Future Generations: Environmental Ethics*, Buffalo, NY: Prometheus.

Rawls, J., 1971, *A Theory of Justice*, Cambridge, MA: Harvard University Press.

Rees, W. E., 1990, 'Sustainable Development and the Biosphere: Concepts and Principles', *Teilhard Studies*, No. 23, Spring/Summer.

Regan, T. (ed.), 1984, *Earthbound: New Introductory Essays in Environmental Ethics*, Philadelphia, PA: Temple University Press.

Rolston III, H., 1988, *Environmental Ethics: Duties to and Values in the Natural World*, Philadelphia, PA: Temple University Press.

Sax, J. L., 1971, *Defending the Environment: A Strategy for Citizen Action*, New York, NY: Alfred A. Knopf.

Schulze, W. D. et al., 1983, 'The Economic Benefits of Preserving Visibility in the National Parklands of the Southwest', *Natural Resources Journal*, Vol. 23, pp. 149–74.

Sikora, R. I., and Berry, B. (eds), 1978, *Obligations to Future Generations*, Philadelphia, PA: Temple University Press.

Taylor, P. W., 1986, *Respect for Nature: A Theory of Environmental Ethics*, Princeton, NJ: Princeton University Press.

Tonn, B. E., 1986, '500-Year Planning: A Speculative Provocation', *Journal of the American Planning Association*, Vol. 52, pp. 185–93.

Van De Veer, D. and Pierce, C. (eds), 1986, *People, Penguins and Plastic Trees: Basic Issues in Environmental Ethics*, Belmont, CA: Wadsworth.

Van der Ryn, S. and Calthorpe, P., 1991, *Sustainable Communities*, San Francisco, CA: Sierra Club Books.

Walter, B., Arkin, L. and Crenshaw, R., 1992, *Sustainable Cities: Concepts and Strategies for Eco-City Development*, Los Angeles, CA: Eco Home Media.

WCED (World Commission on Environment and Development), 1987, *Our Common Future*, Oxford: Oxford University Press (The Brundtland Report).

Chapter 3

Aesthetics in planning

John Punter

To know what something is like in advance of the experience of it, is to have an imaginative apprehension of that experience. The ability to participate imaginatively in future experiences is one of the aims of aesthetic education, and it is only by the cultivation of present discrimination, and the present sense of what is appropriate, that it can be properly achieved. It is this aesthetic education which has enabled men to build structures and streets that have remained agreeable beyond the expiry of their ephemeral purposes. (Scruton 1979, pp. 243–4)

INTRODUCTION

Questions of aesthetics are fundamental to town and country planning in the sense that judgements about the physical quality of proposed development, or the environment at large, are central to most planning systems and their control and enhancement functions. And yet the assumptions upon which such judgements are based, let alone the theoretical bases of such assumptions and their relationship to aesthetic theory, are rarely discussed. Every opportunity is taken to circumvent the difficult questions about aesthetic judgement, either by dismissing them, or by applying so-called 'common sense' principles or simplified ideas about environmental quality.

In the UK, aesthetic issues in planning have traditionally been subsumed in the concept of 'amenity', which, while not being legally defined (a dictionary definition suggests 'the quality of being pleasant'), is sufficiently vague to allow a huge range of interpretations as to what is 'injurious to amenity' and therefore should not be given planning permission (Cullingworth 1976, pp. 156–7). In the United States the landmark 1950 Supreme Court decision (*Berman* v. *Parker*) upheld 'spiritual as well as physical, aesthetic as well as monetary' values in community regulation of public welfare, but aesthetic practice has been oriented, at least until recently, essentially towards preservation of historic areas, views (especially from highways) and trees (Duerksen 1986, pp. 1–4). In France the National Rules of Urban Planning, enshrined in the Code de L'Urbanisme, are explicit about control of aesthetics and allow refusal of a permit for a proposed development if the situation, architecture, dimensions or natural appearance would damage the character or interests of surrounding areas, natural or urban landscapes (DoE 1989, p.195).

There is a recognition underlying every campaign for and every system of aesthetic regulation, that planning should attempt to satisfy higher-order needs in the form of an attractive urban and rural environment. Yet there is also concern about the regulation of taste, and restriction on the freedom of the individual. In the UK in particular there has been a long-standing central government view that aesthetics is subjective, and that design regulation should only be encouraged in high-quality environments where the context can strongly influence design solutions (Punter 1986–7). This highlights the essential pragmatism, if not anti-intellectualism, of those charged with overall regulation of the planning system, but it also clearly illustrates the lack of a solid theoretical base for aesthetic judgement. Of course, such a position is defensible in the absence of clear consensus about the nature and bases of both townscape/ landscape beauty or environmental preferences. For, while the social and environmental sciences have contributed a great deal to our understanding of the problems, they have not as yet been able to develop a clear perspective that could inform judgement (Jarvis 1991).

This essay will attempt to review aesthetic theory briefly, and to establish its relevance to urban and rural landscapes and planning regulation. It will explore the particular nature and dimensions of urban and rural environmental experience, the bases of aesthetic value judgements, and the question of beauty. It will conclude by examining some of the practical implications for planning and design control.

THE HISTORY OF AESTHETIC THEORY

Two of the reasons why planning has failed to develop a clear concept of aesthetics lie beyond any intrinsic professional inadequacy. In the first place, the philosophy of aesthetics, like many areas of philosophical enquiry, is still marked by competing traditions and differential lines of enquiry (Beardsley 1966) and is frequently described as an intellectual disaster area (Scruton 1979; Forrest 1988). In the second place, the relationship between the traditional objects of aesthetic enquiry – the arts – and planners' interest in the environment has never been successfully resolved, although a number of aestheticians have explored architecture and landscape as objects of aesthetic interest.

There is not space here to provide a history of aesthetic thought, and useful overviews are available elsewhere (Beardsley 1966; Holgate 1992, pp. 16–42). However, it is necessary to be aware of how different ideas about aesthetics have shaped landscapes and townscapes through time, enriching our cultural and visual environment and providing objective records of intellectual ideals that, in many instances, are now treasured artifacts protected through conservation legislation and planning controls. The most concise account of these ideas is Gibson's (1989) identification of five aesthetic traditions that have influenced both the creation and re-shaping of landscapes and townscapes and ways of seeing and enjoying them. These include the rationalist perspectives developed in the Renaissance and clearly expressed by the eighteenth-century landscape gardeners; the picturesque tradition which supplanted it later in the eighteenth century; the sublime of the nineteenth-century romanticists; the realism of the turn of the century, celebrating the everyday landscape; the revival of a form of rationalism in twentieth-century modernism, and its post-modern replacement by Surrealism. However, a variety of textbooks on landscape architecture, architecture, urban design and planning provide insights into the prevalence of particular aesthetic ideas through history (Turner 1986; Mordaunt-Crook 1989; Morris 1979), while some, most notably Geoffrey Scott's *Architecture of Humanism* (1914), are able to demonstrate and critique the persistence of certain key ideas. The planner needs to understand such material in order to comprehend the cultural inheritance that she or he is charged with preserving or enhancing, and to understand that, although aesthetic theories and tastes change through time, many persist and constitute part of the dialectic of personal or group values.

40

THE PHILOSOPHICAL DEBATES

Because the very scope and content of aesthetics often seems elusive, the historical debate and its philosophical underpinnings remain critical to an understanding of competing traditions. Much of the controversy revolves around efforts of different philosophers to equate the concept of beauty with that of aesthetics, while simultaneously narrowing and mystifying the former, excluding such aspects as utility, morality, associations, symbolism, artistic intention or skill, or even non-visual sensations (Holgate 1992, pp. 18–19). As beauty was defined in a progressively more rarefied manner, so genuine aesthetic experience was characterised as being 'disinterested' or detached from practical concerns or desires, and focused on the material properties of the object to the exclusion of any 'extraneous' factors (Holgate 1992, pp. 17–20, 32–5; Bourassa 1991, pp. 28–36).

A second major controversy revolves around the problem of whether beauty or aesthetics resides in the object or the subject, and this has led to the development of two bodies of work, on formal and experiential aesthetics respectively, that are often difficult to integrate. Formal aesthetics deals with the physical qualities of the object – architecture, buildings, streets, spaces and landscape – using concepts such as scale, proportion, enclosure, composition and flow of space. Experiential aesthetics concentrates upon the interaction of subject and object and the experience of the observer, which is mediated by personal and cultural values and the meanings that are attributed to artifacts.

Then there is the prevalent tendency to deny the accessibility of art, beauty and aesthetics to those untrained in art criticism or aesthetic philosophy. This is consistent with the idea of beauty as a rarefied quality, and the aesthetic moment as a high-order intellectual experience. Such ideas are frequently linked with arguments about good taste, which themselves have a history in aesthetics, being variously defined as a special faculty, an aesthetic attitude, or a capacity to divine what is right or 'appropriate'. Most arguments about good taste are circular, but, of course, 'good taste' tends to be defined by the most powerful or articulate groups in the community. Holgate (1992, p.39) suggests that most philosophers agree that taste is innate, but that it can be refined by education and experience.

All these arguments raise the issue of elitism in aesthetic judgements. However, it is important to recognise that better informed or more fully refined aesthetic judgements are possible, and that the question of whose

41

judgements should prevail (in architecture, urban design, planning or public art) is a political and not necessarily an aesthetic choice. A complete rejection of notions of aesthetic training, design awareness or visual literacy leads to a descent into relativism and the loss of any basis for qualitative judgement.

Finally, it must be recognised, when dealing with environmental aesthetics, that architecture occupies a privileged place in the debate because it has been regarded as a fine art and treated in a similar way to sculpture and painting, with its formal qualities exhaustively analysed, particularly through the concept of style. Landscapes, or particular locations, have been treated in a similar way through their associations with painting, or by regarding them as views or prospects, objects of self-conscious contemplation. However, such perspectives ignore the fact that landscape is simultaneously art, artifact and nature, just as architecture is 'commodity, firmness and delight', and the relationships between each of these three not mutually exclusive categories are very complex.

CONCEPTUALISING THE AESTHETIC AS PART OF THE EVERYDAY

Finding a way through this philosophical minefield has defied many an able scholar. However, one of the most helpful perspectives on environmental aesthetics comes from Raymond Williams's linguistically-based analysis, which reveals that the word 'aesthetic' only appeared in English in the nineteenth century, and was first borrowed from German in a Latin form (*aesthetica*). This usage embraced the study of beauty as phenomenal perfection apprehended through the senses. By contrast, the Greek root of 'aesthetics' contains a broader conception, and is not concerned with beauty *per se* but with the conditions of sensuous perception. It is this latter meaning which has been largely lost as subjective 'sense activity' has become emphasised as the basis of art and beauty (Williams 1979, pp. 31–2; see also Holgate 1992, pp. 17–24). In the process, philosophical treatises on 'the beautiful' and 'principles of good taste' have tended to obscure social or cultural interpretations of aesthetic judgement.

The difference between these two competing definitions of aesthetics becomes clearer in the respective antonyms. The antonym of the Latin root is 'unaesthetic', or 'ugly', while that of the Greek root is 'anaesthe-

sia', or 'experiencing nothing' (Williams 1979, pp. 31–2). In attempting
to grapple with environmental aesthetics, where all aspects of the experience are important, it is more productive to abandon a preoccupation
with phenomenal perfection and 'the beautiful', and to return to the
Greek and broader Kantian conception of aesthetics as 'the conditions of
sensuous perception'. By rejecting a preoccupation with visual appearance, beauty and subjective sense activity, we can recover the explana-
tory power of social or cultural interpretations (widely-shared views
acquired through common experience, education and culture) as the bases
of aesthetic judgement, and reduce the damaging isolation and
marginalisation of 'aesthetic considerations' as opposed to practical or
utilitarian concerns. For, as Scruton (1979, p.240) argues, aesthetic judgement is closely related to practical matters in all aspects of building (and
landscaping) as well as in furnishings, clothing and manners.

More than any other philosopher of aesthetics, it was John Dewey who
decried the practice of separating art from life and asserted the importance of keeping the aesthetic as part of everyday life, maintaining that
aesthetic experience was a particularly engaged, intense or heightened
form of normal experience. He also emphasised the way in which aesthetic appreciation developed new meanings which in themselves af-
forded new interpretations and modes of enjoyment of the objects
(Beardsley 1966, pp. 332–42), and this idea is particularly relevant to
townscape and landscape experience.

Of course, townscapes and landscapes have frequently been discussed
as if they were works of art and objects of phenomenal perception. The
very origins of the term 'landscape' in Dutch painting – its limitation to
natural scenery, the focus upon 'pleasing prospects' as objects of contemplation, the exclusion of figures (people) from the view – are all significant conventions imposing a limited perspective, and one can explore the
same kind of preoccupations in the concept of 'townscape' (Punter 1981;
Williams 1973).

Clearly, when dealing with the environment as opposed to the arts, it is
counter-productive to sever aesthetic qualities from other aspects of an
object, since the aesthetic appreciation of townscapes and landscapes is
closely related to their practical utility and to their meanings to groups
and individuals. As John Costonis, a US lawyer with long-standing involvement in aesthetic regulation, has succinctly expressed it, the aesthetics of the art gallery have no place in the (planning) courtroom
(Costonis 1989).

By placing aesthetic experience alongside everyday experience it is possible to treat it in conjunction with the more practical and more common urban experiences of way-finding and navigation, seeking out services and facilities, exercise and relaxation, people-watching or socialising, or even environmental 'work' like gardening, farming or construction. As Charles Jencks (1988, p.50) has noted, 'architecture is generally perceived inattentively or with the greatest prejudice of mood and will' as we go about our daily business in the city, although there may be occasions when it becomes the principal focus of our attention because of our purposive action (tourism, study, searching) or because of objective conditions (lighting, position in the visual field, etc.), or indeed because of the sheer beauty of a building or a piece of countryside. Similarly, the nature of urban experience is often dictated by the throng of people, the pattern of activities and land uses, the need to negotiate crowds, street furniture and traffic, or to read the physical information on signs and find desired facilities, rather than by any attempt to appreciate the quality of built form *per se*. For example, research has shown that the visual field rarely extends above shop fascia level for the majority, and is dominated by the floorscape, its furniture and its occupants (Prak 1977).

To explore the continuity of aesthetic and practical experiences, Donald Appleyard defined three modes of response to the environment – the responsive, the operational and the inferential (Appleyard 1979, pp. 205–7; see also Brower 1988). These categories are useful to describe both typical behaviours and academic approaches to townscape and landscape.

The responsive mode embraces the aesthetic dimension and is concerned with emotional response to the environment, using it as a stimulus for feelings and associations. It tends to be the mode of the outsider, especially the tourist or designer, and it employs much specific art, aesthetic and design language to evoke its response. A key example would be Gordon Cullen's book *Townscape* (1961), which celebrated the sensual and emotional possibilities of visual exploration of the city.

The second mode, the operational, describes the everyday experience, the search for task-directed information about how to find and use facilities and amenities in the environment, how to preserve life and limb, and how to be comfortable and relaxed in the process. The search is for useful information rather than architectural experience or sensory delight, although the latter may intrude from time to time. A key example would be Kevin Lynch's exploration of *The Image of the City* (1961), which tried to isolate the 'imageabilty' of built form and its influence on people's mental maps.

The third mode of response, the inferential, deals with questions of the meaning of environmental information, a major omission from both *The Image of the City* and *Townscape*. It looks at the different inferences drawn from the same environmental information by people with different social status, lifestyles, ethnicity and personal history. It deals with the symbolic content of the environment and the meaning it carries for people – personal associations, group identities, community history, and even aesthetic ideology (often differentially interpreted) in the form of architectural statements. It explores how people generalise their experience to develop environmental cognition. Much has been written, but there has yet to be a truly classic example of such an inferential approach. Charles Jencks's *The Language of Post-Modern Architecture* (1989) does explore the question of architectural meaning, though the book rarely escapes from differential professional and critics' perspectives on buildings.

Of course, individuals are continually shifting between operational, responsive and inferential modes, and there is a constant tension and dialectic at work. As people go about their daily lives, fulfilling their everyday needs, so their modes of perception and the qualities they wish to extract from townscapes and landscapes change. By using Maslow's (1954) definition of a six-stage hierarchy of human needs we can suggest how physiological requirements relate to higher-order cognitive and aesthetic requirements, and how different modes of perception might be broadly related to such needs. From a planner's perspective there is a need to cater for safety, comfort, shelter and ease of movement (operational needs), ensuring ease of way-finding, accessibility and a sense of place (inferential needs), and developing a stimulating, attractive and creative environment (responsive needs – see Figure 3.1). Placing aesthetic needs alongside the need for shelter, security, identity, status and self-expression, and thinking about differential modes of environmental experience, helps to clarify the tasks of urban designers, development controllers and local planners in re-shaping the environment.

Appleyard's modes of perception	Maslow's hierarchy of human needs	Some design considerations
Operational	*Physiological* food, shelter, health	• adequate accommodation, utilities and services • comfort • ecologically sound and stable
	Safety and security protection from danger, pollution; privacy	• road safety • surveillance • privacy • accessibility/permeability
Inferential	*Affiliation* belonging, community	• community facilities • a sense of identity/place • legibility
	Esteem status and recognition	• ownership • individuality
	Self-actualisation creativity	• opportunities for personalisation and participation in design • variety, visual appropriateness
Responsive	*Cognitive/aesthetic* intellectual and sensual stimulation	• cultural/recreational opportunities • quality townscape and landscape richness

Figure 3.1 Reconciling modes of perception and human needs in the environment (after Faulkner 1978; reproduced in Walmsley 1988, pp. 60–1)

BASES OF AESTHETIC VALUES – AN EXPERIENTIAL PERSPECTIVE

Much debate has centred on the bases of aesthetic value systems and how these affect aesthetic experience and environmental preferences. Bourassa's exploration of *The Aesthetics of Landscape* (1991) groups these theories into three general categories – the biological, the cultural and the personal – noting the long-standing tension between biologically-based theories of aesthetics and those that view aesthetics as a strictly cultural phenomenon. Dewey (1929) saw all three factors as necessary components of aesthetics. Bourassa reinforces this view by drawing on a wide variety of work in psychoanalysis, psychology and neurophysiology that suggests their relevance to the development of the human intellect. While recognising the difficulties in distinguishing between the biological, the cultural and the personal, Bourassa goes on to review a wide range of landscape aesthetics literature. We can now draw out and amplify those ideas of most relevance to planning and urban design.

Biological theories/laws

Biological theories of aesthetics are those that are based upon human genetic characteristics and seek to explain aesthetic preferences in terms of physiological characteristics, or as adjuncts to the satisfaction of fundamental human biological needs in manipulating the environment. Neurophysiological theories have tried to relate the tripartite structure of the brain (a primitive reptilian brain; a palaeo-mammalian brain or limbic system, similar to that in many animals, and a neo-mammalian brain or neo-cortex – a highly sophisticated brain found mainly in humans) to different types of discrimination and aesthetic preference. Research has shown how the limbic system is geared towards self-preservation and the perpetuation of the species, and operates on the basis of feelings and emotions. Peter Smith has explored the possibility that there are 'deep structures' in the limbic system that control environmental symbolism and determine certain archetypal preferences, including the effects of gigantism, bright colour, enclosure, water, exposure, protection, or even of primitive ideas of 'prospect and refuge' in rural and urban landscapes (Smith 1977: Appleton 1975). Smith, Kaplan and others also explore the human brain's more sophisticated preferences for complexity, ambiguity and mystery, but recognise the parallel need for coherence, legibility and

47

orientation that are all related to the information-processing capabilities of the brain. Much of this writing is suggestive and highly tentative (Kaplan & Kaplan 1989). Some of it, notably perhaps prospect-refuge theory, is reductionist in the extreme (Appleton 1975; Tuan 1976). Yet, as Bourassa reminds us, most biological theories are habitat-based in their emphasis upon human evolution. Ethnological studies in particular have provided a rich vein of ideas about urban environmental preferences and aesthetics that include concepts of territoriality, defensible space, proxemics (personal space preferences and behaviours) and privacy that are particularly relevant to issues of safety and status in housing and urban design (Newman 1973; Hall 1966), though deciding where bio-logical factors become cultural, and avoiding the trap of environmental determinism, is always problematic (Coleman 1985).

Cultural theories

Cultural theorists argue that 'aesthetic behaviour is transmitted socially through the use of language and other tools', and that this is what distin-guishes cultural from biological preferences. They see the means of communicating culture as being primarily symbolic in character, and acknowledge that landscapes and townscapes are important to both the expression and preservation of cultural identity. Bourassa catalogues a wide variety of studies that demonstrate cultural differences in aesthetic values consistent with age, sex, ethnicity, income, occupation and life-style differentials. But he pays particular attention to two sets of variables – environmental expertise (professionals and non-professionals), and familiarity (insiders and outsiders) – which emerge as of key impor-tance particularly in the literature on urban perception and planning (Figure 3.2). These two dimensions subsume many educational, profes-sional orientation and social class factors (expertise), as well as nation-ality, ethnicity, social grouping and even age-sex factors (familiarity). They are particularly important in any discussion of aesthetic values in planning, urban design and landscape architecture since they help to explain the often quite different perspectives of lay and professional observers, and the frequently yawning gap between the users of envi-ronments and those who design them. Craik, Gans, Appleyard, the Kaplans and Relph, and many other self-critical professionals and envi-ronmental commentators, have noted that professional education and experience, combined with a self-conscious existential 'outsider's' per-

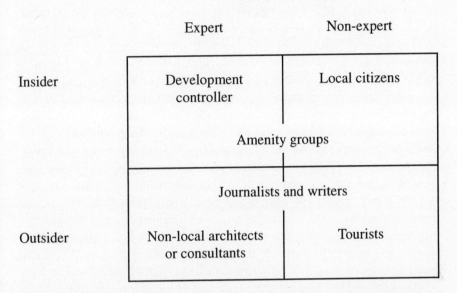

Professional Status

Figure 3.2   A typal framework for analysing the aesthetic attitudes of cultural groups (adapted from Bourassa 1991, p.109)

spective, create quite different perspectives on environmental aesthetics (see the synthesis in Bourassa 1991, pp. 90–109). Bourassa's typology is helpful in providing a warning to planners – and other designers who need to consider the aesthetic preferences of lay people – of the dangers of professional expertise and lack of familiarity with the local scene when it comes to urban design or design control. But the framework is also useful in defining particular modes of environmental behaviour, such as the outsider-non-expert attitudes of tourists, or the expert-outsider writings of the architectural critic.

Other cultural theorists concentrate upon the meanings derived from townscape and landscape. They regard the environment as a 'vast mnemonic system for the retention of group history and ideals' (Lynch 1961, p.126). John Costonis has developed a cultural stability/identity approach to preservation issues, arguing that questions of beauty are not the main force behind aesthetic regulation, and that it is 'our individual and social needs for stability and reassurance in the face of environmental changes' which are fundamental. Costonis argues against traditional conflations of aesthetics with beauty. In legal aesthetics, people come first; their emotional investment in environmental features, second; and the formal qualities of the objects, last (Costonis 1989, p.45).

Costonis's substitution of experiential for formal aesthetics – his focus upon the public's desire for stability and identity in the environment rather than upon the sensory or formal attributes of beauty – emphasises the sentiments, associations, and meanings that individuals and groups attach to the urban and rural landscape. In the British context these have been explored by a variety of cultural critics, following principally in the steps of Raymond Williams, whose literary-based analysis of *The Country and the City* (1973) uncovers a particular consciousness linking high culture with historical and contemporary landscape and townscape values. Williams charts the emergence of the complex of values that are encapsulated by rural fundamentalism, anti-urbanism, and enlightened stewardship of the land, and which are central to British planning ideology (e.g. green belts, village envelopes, conserved countryside, listed buildings, etc.). Meanwhile, Wiener, Newby, Wright and Hewison have in turn explored the anti-industrialism, anti-modernism, selective re-creation of 'tradition', the manufacturing of heritage and the all-pervasive conservation ethic, and the general gentrification of taste that together constitute the prevailing aesthetic (Wiener 1981; Newby 1979; Wright 1985; Hewison 1988). Williams explains how we project on to landscapes and nature some of our deepest aspirations and fears – sometimes culturally and sometimes socially derived – and how such landscapes then come to symbolise and epitomise those values of a more meaningful, more sharply observed, wholesome and 'good' life usually associated with the past or with childhood (Williams 1973; see e.g. Shoard 1979). In the contemporary period, Forty and Moss (1980) have argued that a similar complex of aesthetic and social values are associated with the neo-vernacular architecture of national housebuilders, introduced to the idea by architect-planners looking to preserve some regional landscape identity through design guidance. NIMBYism (the 'Not In My Back Yard' syndrome), a fundamental aspect of much local planning, needs to be subjected to the same kind of profound cultural analysis (BDOR 1992).

Bourdieu reaffirms the social class basis of aesthetics when he argues that 'no judgement of taste is innocent – we are all snobs'. He considers that the aesthetic choices people make are all distinctions: choices made in opposition to those made by other classes that constitute the basis for social judgement (Bourdieu 1984, pp. 9–61). He illustrates how dominant theories of art (particularly the Kantian disinterested aesthetic) reinforce the social dimensions in society by becoming part of the cultural or symbolic capital deployed essentially by intellectuals of the dominant class to maintain the distance between itself and the lower classes. Such symbolic capital will include house styles, restored buildings, landscaping, architecture, designer labels (name architects), historic buildings or even positional goods like prestige addresses, protected villages or countryside (Jager 1986; Dovey 1993). These ideas have particular relevance in the contemporary period in the context of the 'aestheticisation of everyday life', where advertising (the art of capitalism?) and its promotion of fashion, style and myth produces a proliferation of signs, images, dreams and meanings (Featherstone 1991, pp. 65–82). Such meanings are largely divorced from context and reality, and directed towards conspicuous and continuous consumption and the seemingly endless proliferation of differential products, lifestyles and taste cultures, developing 'the city as an emporium of styles' (Raban 1974).

Such concepts lie at the heart of post-modernism: a convenient catch-all phrase for contemporary culture, but also a concept developed particularly from analysis of contemporary architecture and urban landscape. Analysis of the social production of the built environment, and of the reciprocal and recursive relationship between the built environment, society and individuals, has begun to explore the whole question of the symbolic content of the built environment, how it is produced and what its effects are on human perception and behaviour (see Figure 3.3; Knox 1984). Researchers have begun to ask questions about the aesthetic values of designers and controllers, and to question their influence in mediating economic processes. Critics of post-modernism, like David Harvey, have interpreted post-modernism as a fetishism – a concern with surface appearances that successfully conceals underlying meanings, particularly the real bases of economic processes (exploitation, expropriation, profiteering) conflating populism and market orientation in order to facilitate the 'creative destruction' (concentrated investment and widespread disinvestment) of capitalism (Harvey 1989). Others have applied similar perspectives to gentrification, redevelopment, retailing, conservation, waterfront reclamation, festivals and spectacles, and vernacular architecture (Jager 1986; Shields 1989; Dovey 1993; Forty & Moss 1980) to reveal the social and economic processes being expressed in the townscape.

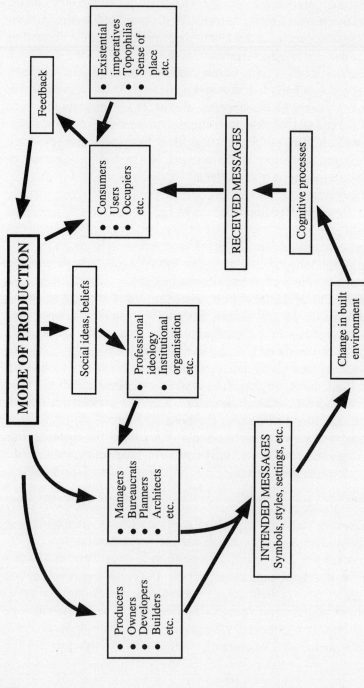

Figure 3.3 The study of meanings in landscape and townscape: signs, symbolism and settings; a framework for analysis (after Knox 1984, p.119)

Such critiques are of considerable relevance to planning since they directly challenge some of its best-publicised, most sought-after 'achievements'. However, work on the symbolism of landscapes remains fragmented and focused upon the spectacular rather than the everyday, and it has not yet come to grips with ordinary landscapes. Nor has it adequately grappled with the role of the individual in the interaction between society and the environment. Environmental/cultural theorists can tend to posit the idea of people as cultural dupes, ignoring their individuality and their ability to exploit the environment for their own purposes (Whitehand 1992, p.623), and it is important to recognise the variety of conscious and unconscious responses to different phenomena.

Personal strategy theories

Concern with the individual is at the heart of Bourassa's third set of categories of aesthetic experience, that of personal strategy theories. Exponents of personal strategy theory are not easy to identify. Most researchers in this area have merely sought to relate personality directly to preferences, without considering biological or cultural factors. This is clearly the least well-developed of Bourassa's three categories, but it is based upon the proposition that 'through intellectual activity ... the individual can transcend biological constraints on his or her behaviour' (Bourassa 1991, p.110). Identifying such transcendent behaviour is, of course, problematic, and the whole category might be viewed merely as a form of extreme subjective individualism, but theories of creativity do provide some support for such behaviour. Bourassa notes that most changes in cultural rules start out as innovative personal strategies, either perceptual strategies on the one hand (e.g. Gordon Cullen or Raymond Williams), or design strategies on the other (e.g. Le Corbusier, Richard Rogers). A key point in landscape preferences is that personal experience and creativity will modify cultural and biological rules and produce a measure of individuality and idiosyncrasy that needs to be acknowledged.

The importance of personal experience and creativity should be obvious to design professionals, most of whom have deliberately sought both a wide range of environmental experience and different forms of design education, and who have attempted, in various formal and informal ways, to develop creative syntheses of these (e.g. in journalism or academic writing, brief writing, environmental designation and enhancement, or actual design). Lay people attempt different, perhaps less ambitious, creative syntheses through story-telling, gardening, personalisation, DIY, etc. Each conveys subtly different conceptions of place, taste and environmental self-expression. As noted earlier, the meanings and associations attached by people to places have been frequently neglected in favour of the more pragmatic 'operational' perspective on human behaviour, or the more esoteric, contemplative outsider's perspective of the designer/aesthetician.

Personal strategies also embrace many forms of architectural and landscape criticism, and while most of these reveal the biases of professional expert-outsiders, they are important in shaping tastes and providing insights into various forms of theory. Attoe (1979) has developed an exhaustive categorisation of architectural criticism grouped into three broad types – normative, interpretive and descriptive – and this is particularly useful in revealing the individual perspective of each critic, whether it be a renowned architectural writer or a resident opposing a planning application (Figure 3.4). Critics play a major role in defining the meanings of buildings and shaping public opinion. Prince Charles, for example, has used the crudest form of visual analogy ('the lowest form of architectural criticism – not to be taken seriously', suggests Abercrombie, 1984, p.126) to damn contemporary development proposals in London like the National Gallery, 'a carbuncle on the face of a much-loved friend', or No. 1 Poultry, 'resembling nothing so much as a 1930s wireless' (Jencks 1988, pp. 43–50). Recent compilations of professional criticism reveal the diversity of perspectives, the all-important conflicts between different architectural doctrines (which are frequently incomprehensible to the public, and only serve to emphasise the gap between lay and professional tastes), and the general lack of systematic criticism and *post hoc* evaluation (Buchanan 1988; *Weekend Guardian* 1989).

One important body of work which might be fitted into the concept of personal strategy, particularly because of its attempt to grapple with the imaginative and creative dimensions of the aesthetic, is Scruton's writings on architecture and art (Scruton 1979). One of the very few recent thoroughgoing treatments of the aesthetics of architecture, Scruton's approach of downplaying the concept of art in aesthetics, and attempting to restore aesthetics to a central place in everyday experience, is consistent with approaches advocated earlier in this chapter. He describes aesthetic judgement as a common practical wisdom, an application of that sense of what 'fits' which governs every aspect of daily existence. He argues that this sense of aesthetic value requires some kind of imaginative under-

Normative	
Doctrinal	– doctrine-based criticism (most modernist criticism).
Systematic	– criteria or element based, e.g. 'commodity, firmness, delight'.
Typal	– compared against standard or classic types.
Measured	– evaluation of performance, e.g. user studies.
Interpretive	
Subjective	– personal criticism.
Advocatory	– engendering appreciation.
Evocative	– arousing feelings to recreate the personal experience.
Impressionistic	– criticism only loosely based on observation; critic constructs a new edifice.
Descriptive	
Depictive	– seeing what is there; fabric, use, or design process.
Biographical	– the designer and his career; influences.
Contextual	– socio-political explanations of design and its physical impact.

Figure 3.4   A typology of architectural criticism (after Attoe 1979)

standing whereby social, intellectual and moral meanings derived from everyday experience are attached to perceptions of architectural qualities. Scruton argues that individuals develop powers of discrimination from primitive choices and justified preferences, developing them into aesthetic standards and, eventually, sustained critical judgement. He conceives of aesthetic pleasure as a mode of understanding, with the connoisseur and the person who simply 'knows what he likes' being at either end of a continuum of aesthetic education.

But Scruton recognises the whole difficulty of distilling aesthetic values and of distinguishing the personal and the cultural, arguing that

> the whole structure of aesthetic judgement belies ... facile subjectivism. Indeed it is precisely because of the intellectual complexity of taste, and its deep connection with all the preferences that matter most to us, that we seem condemned to pursue an ideal of objectivity in the face of the most persistent disappointment. (Scruton 1979, p.132)

Scruton rescues a relative autonomy of aesthetic experience from Marxist, sociological, psychoanalytic, structuralist and semiotic schools of thought, while nevertheless recognising the existence of a common culture or system of shared beliefs (Fuller 1984, pp. 94–5). But he also reveals the political Right's general advocacy of classicism against modernism, particularly opposing the latter's attempt to make art accessible to the masses. The classicists, who value visual order, styles, ornament and authority, tend to give precedence to the visual qualities of built form and consider it necessary to develop a special elite sensitivity to appreciate architecture. Modernists are committed to questioning authority and the social order, seeking honesty and minimalism and emphasising the process and progress of design and technological skill (Holgate 1992, pp. 185–90). These contrasting perspectives may be found in much contemporary criticism.

FORMAL AESTHETICS

Much of what has been said thus far is implicitly dismissive of the study of the formal qualities of landscapes and townscapes as a means of progressing our understanding of aesthetics. It has been argued that to treat landscapes as if they were art objects is to ignore both artifact and nature and to impose a very limited and specialised perspective. Furthermore, it should be stated that formal qualities are only the stimuli to a variety of human responses, and that therefore they offer only limited understanding of aesthetic experience. However, there is a great deal of writing about the formal qualities of architecture that is of interest, though rather less about landscape and townscape. This is important because much town and country planning work – such as landscape evaluation and designation, site analysis and development briefing, townscape analysis and design policy prescription, and land allocation for development – necessarily involves some kind of formal analysis of the perceptible qualities of the location under consideration.

Some of this work takes into account aesthetic experience, but often only in a secondary and rather unacknowledged way. For example, the analyses of townscape quality and architectural character that are necessary for design briefing, development control or the development of conservation policy are usually based upon a variety of techniques of stylistic classification, morphological analysis, visual and spatial definition, identification of functional character and patterns of movement (Cullen 1961; Brolin 1980; Tugnutt & Robertson 1987). Increasingly such studies are taking on board analyses of the natural world in terms of topography, landscape, ecology, microclimate and even hydrology (Owen 1991; Beer 1990).

Much of this work is predicated upon a key finding in experimental aesthetics, the public's desire for 'harmonious', 'in character' or 'neighbourly' development, particularly where the townscape/landscape is highly valued (Groat 1986). So a good deal of planning analysis attempts to define the parameters of such development, whether it be volumetrically – as in many European local plans or US zoning plans – or stylistically/elevationally – as in many British and US design guides. The question of an appropriate style has often been a bone of contention in development/design control, particularly with the architectural profession, some of whom see any questioning of style as an invasion of their province by those untrained in design. This only serves to reassert the symbolic importance of style as an expression of competing identities and aesthetic theories.

As we have seen, debates continue over the relative merits of modernism, post-modernism and even classicism, although these are generally more animated within the architectural profession and amongst architectural critics than within planning circles (Harris & Lipman 1986). Expansive claims are made for the aesthetic validity of particular styles. To examine these, Geoffrey Scott's study, *The Architecture of Humanism* (1914), is indispensable because he exposes a particularly virulent set of historical-architectural ideas, which he terms fallacies. These include the romantic fallacy (complete emphasis upon the symbolic, poetic and associative values of styles), the mechanical fallacy (emphasis upon honesty of construction), the ethical fallacy (the association of styles with morality) and the biological fallacy (the belief in the idealist conception of evolution). Scott's fallacies had a prophetic relevance for modernism's embrace of the mechanical and ethical fallacies, though it did not anticipate the functional fallacy (form follows function). To Scott's eighty-year-old list we might also add the contextual fallacy, to express the current preoccupation, very evident in design control circles, that all buildings must be designed to be similar to, or in keeping with, their surroundings.

Many commentators have argued that contemporary architecture cannot rely on any one of these 'fallacies' but must exploit all of them in the search for rich, pluralistic and popular forms (Buchanan 1988; Glancey 1990; Mordaunt-Crook 1989). Many urban designers have argued that planners should not attempt to regulate style at all, arguing that it creates too rigid a framework for design, that an 'appropriate' style cannot be found, and that by focusing on style the controller is likely to miss environmental issues that are much more important to the general public (Southworth 1989; Habe 1989). The most thoughtful design control documents prescribe particular styles only in the most uniform and architecturally pure environments, reserving thoroughgoing contextualism for less uniform but historically important environments, while allowing freedom of expression in less sensitive locations (Gould 1991). However, there remains a problem in that styles carry powerful meanings, associations and memories. Scruton (1979, p.202) argues that 'style is the natural crystallisation of all aesthetic endeavour' and roots the meanings which are suggested to the aesthetic understanding, while Scott (1914) sees it as a principle of permanence and a set of themes to be varied by future generations of architects. Against that, research has shown that the general public have a general understanding of what might constitute harmonious development, but a limited awareness of stylistic or historic integrity (Groat 1986), even though it is difficult to see how an appreciation of even a fake architectural style is independent of its historical and cultural associations (Whitehand 1992, p.630).

But environments cannot be conceived as purely aesthetic artifacts, and the conflation of design control with elevation control has been particularly damaging and limiting, certainly in the UK. Perhaps that very preoccupation emphasises the 'architecture as art' bias in design education. Recent research, for example into residential environments, has shown that the preoccupation of planners with questions of elevations and house style is not shared by the general public. Here the difference between insiders and expert-outsiders is particularly pronounced.

Clare Cooper Marcus's work, in particular, reveals the importance to residents of greenery, long-distance and open views, intimate spaces, high levels of maintenance and quality of pedestrian pathways, as opposed to strictly architectural or townscape considerations, while a recent architect-housebuilder research project in the UK underlines the primacy of layout and landscaping considerations (Marcus & Sarkissan 1986; Marcus & Francis 1991; HBF/RIBA 1990). Such analyses only serve to emphasise the necessity to broaden the range of sensory considerations beyond architecture or style to the environment at large.

Recent design writing has tried to distill such sensory considerations into a set of criteria to aid design. One such attempt, *Responsive Environments: A Manual for Designers*, is organised around the principle of democratic choice in the urban environment (Bentley et al. 1985). The seven principles – permeability, legibility, variety, robustness, visual appropriateness, richness and personalisation (see Figure 3.1), have become part of the consensus of urban design, and they have the advantage of keeping a broad conception of aesthetics, where matters of architectural detail can be treated alongside key aspects of site planning and layout (Punter 1990). Christopher Alexander's *A Pattern Language* (1977) is a much more ambitious, multi-scale, cross-cultural, and correspondingly more controversial attempt to provide similarly useful principles, and Clare Cooper Marcus's work on housing and open spaces takes these ideas to a much more detailed level (Marcus & Sarkissan 1986; Marcus & Francis 1991). This search for principles is a welcome relief from the traditional reliance upon precedent in urban design, or the more abstract – and difficult to realise – but holistic concept of place.

CONCLUSIONS

Having explored competing conceptions of aesthetics, the nature of aesthetic experience, and the different bases of aesthetic values – particularly the important role of urban meanings – what practical applications might be made of these ideas? Such are the demands for generality in planning education and practice, such is the shortage of skilled designers in planning authorities, and such are the difficulties of attracting those already skilled in design awareness into the profession, that aesthetic education needs to be a personal quest throughout a professional career. As the quotation from Roger Scruton at the beginning of this chapter

59

implies, there must be an obligation on those concerned with regulating environmental quality to cultivate their discrimination, to develop clear ideas of what is appropriate and how it can be achieved, and to develop the ability to imagine future landscapes and aesthetic experiences. Various practical means of achieving this have been spelt out by the author of this chapter elsewhere (Punter 1993), and they involve a combination of wide-ranging reading of contemporary theory and criticism, gathering public comment and observing human behaviour, critically examining a wide variety of new and old developments, developing appropriate techniques for locality analysis and development briefing, monitoring the results of practice, and continually interrogating one's own preferences and aesthetic sensibilities.

A broader conception of aesthetics has been postulated which can be easily integrated into everyday experience of the built environment (urban and rural), whereby aesthetic experience is a 'particularly intense, engaged or heightened form of everyday experience'. In this way aesthetic experience can be set alongside the more practical concerns of finding and using facilities, meeting and watching people, and going about everyday life. Particular modes of perception – responsive, operational, inferential – and their attendant bodies of writing, can then be seen as different forms of urban experience with a distinct, but not exclusive, relevance to planning practice. Cognitive/aesthetic needs within the built and natural environment can then be seen as one extreme of a hierarchy of needs. Since each of these needs is the subject of environmental planning and urban design, it is possible to begin by re-prioritising concerns, re-ordering the various checklists or principles of urban design, to create a new agenda.

Narrow conceptions of aesthetics, based upon selective concepts of beauty and relying upon art criticism, tend to focus upon architecture as an art object, and are often obsessed with architectural guidelines on style and elevations. Broader concepts of aesthetics, set within the framework of wider sensory experience, tend to focus upon the qualities of the public realm and the development of urbanistic guidelines as creating the necessary conditions for more of the population to enjoy townscapes and landscapes (RFAC 1985; Widdowson 1992). Detailed design control will be able to draw on the former tradition for inspiration, and may occasionally contribute to the creation of a particularly high-grade townscape, but more general improvements in environmental quality, and more opportunities for the 'aesthetic moment', will be created by concentrating initially upon the qualities and treatment of public space.

This would suggest something of a de-emphasis upon the qualities of architecture and building, and the placing of progressively more emphasis upon opportunities for people to shape their environment and neighbourhood identity, to provide safe, secure, healthy and unpolluted environments, good-quality shelter and convenient essential services. Such priorities are consistent with the shifting emphasis in design control in most progressive cities from elevational control towards the broader agenda for urban design, looking at opportunities for personalisation, developing community facilities and area management, creating a lively public realm and safe, clean and comfortable spaces. It is consistent with the green agenda which places environmental sustainability at the core of planning and design and looks at energy conservation, resource consumption, pollution and nature conservation as key considerations in land-use planning and strategic urban design. It does not move elevational control or questions of design detail off the agenda, and these will remain of critical importance in highly-valued townscape and landscape settings, but it accords priority to questions about the environmental impact of development, and its contribution to the public realm. It looks at the everyday experience of moving around the environment – safety, cleanliness, comfort and accessibility – before it considers architectural treatment or design detailing. Such preoccupations are more in tune with the environmental needs of the general public – particularly, perhaps, women – who continually prioritise these concerns. They might be seen as prerequisites for the appreciation of architectural quality and the enjoyment of the subtler pleasures of townscape and landscape.

In looking at the cultural basis of aesthetics, the role of interpretation and the derivation of meanings in environmental experience, particular attention needs to be paid to the gap between professional and lay tastes, the benefits (and dangers) of acquiring greater expertise and design awareness, and the potential loss of touch with the users of places and spaces who possess an unselfconscious insider's familiarity with the environment. The uncomfortably close relationship between the 'tourist gaze' (Urry 1990) and the urban designer's perspective needs to be borne in mind, along with the dangers of a rarefied approach to aesthetics evident in the discussion of aesthetic theory.

Throughout the last seventy years experts have commented upon the need for mass design education, conceiving this as a need to give expert tuition to the masses to raise the standard of 'public taste'. But quality education is a two-way process, and there remains much to be learned about what people enjoy in their experience of built environments, and how and why they do so. So there is a need to ensure that planning policies and design control grow out of expressed preferences and community aspirations, and are soundly based upon public consultation. This means rediscovering the idea of urban and landscape design as participative processes where a dialogue is possible between the different professionals (planners, engineers, architects, landscape architects and urban designers) and the different users of the environment. No one would pretend that such participation is unproblematic, particularly when dealing with an excessive NIMBYism and an opposition to necessary change, with the difficulties of ensuring that the needs of future generations are properly heard, and reconciling lay and professional aesthetic values. Kevin Lynch (1982) reminded all urban designers that among all the design principles there were two meta-criteria that had always to be considered – the issues of social equity and economic efficiency, the latter broadly construed. Lynch also noted that the resolution of planning and design controversies often leads to decisions which are unpopular in the locality, a point reiterated in the recent Audit Commission Report (Audit Commission 1992). Furthermore, planners must encourage creativity and imagination in design, encouraging innovation wherever possible in the interests of technological progress, and cultural pluralism, for otherwise the current generation will make a lesser contribution to posterity, and contemporary and future environments will be impoverished.

Finally, it has to be recognised that planners play only a mediating role in the production of the built environment, and that their role is very much circumscribed by government and the legal system. More powers are accorded to planners to influence environmental quality and aesthetics where the landscape or townscape are deemed to be environmentally sensitive and/or of historic interest, often serving the interests of more affluent members of the community in the process. But even here planners are largely dependent upon the aspirations of householders and businesses, and the profit and investment motives of developers and funding institutions. Planning may be able to improve the quality of development in a host of ways, but it also finds itself acting as a legitimising mechanism for the largely profit-oriented activities of developers. Aesthetic arguments about design quality often obscure more fundamental questions about exploitation, expropriation, social need and environmental sustainability, and in a market economy there is often little that planners – or indeed local government – can do to change these factors fundamentally. Indeed, they often themselves become the target of criticism for allowing such developments to take place (as do the architects, largely for following their clients' instructions). Questions of morality remain central to questions of aesthetics, but in a post-modern age, where appearances are apparently everything, they are frequently neglected. The task for planners is to work with other design professionals and the general public to articulate an aesthetic based on community needs, social equity, environmental sustainability and the efficient use of resources, and to seek political support for these aspirations (Frampton 1985, pp. 313–27; Wates 1989).[1]

NOTES

1   I wish to acknowledge the helpful comments of Huw Thomas, Lyn Davies, Steve Gould, Graham King, and especially Nigel Taylor, on a draft of this paper.

REFERENCES

Abercrombie, S., 1984, *Architecture as Art: an aesthetic analysis*, New York, NY: Van Nostrand Reinhold.

Alexander, C. et al., 1977, *A Pattern Language*, Oxford: Oxford University Press.

Appleton, J. H., 1975, *The Experience of Landscape*, London: Wiley.

Appleyard, D., 1979, *Planning a Pluralist City*, Cambridge MA: MIT Press, especially pp. 104–232.

Appleyard, D., 1979, 'The environment as a social system within a theory of environmental action and perception', *Journal of the American Planning Association*, Vol. 45(2), pp. 143–53.

Attoe, W., 1979, *Architecture and Critical Imagination*, New York, NY: John Wiley.

Audit Commission, 1992, *Building in Quality: A Study of Development Control*, London: HMSO.

Beardsley, M., 1966, *Aesthetics from Classical Greece to the Present: a short history*, New York, NY: Macmillan.

Beer, A. R., 1990, *Environmental Planning for Site Development*, London: Spon.

BDOR (Bishop Davison O'Rourke Ltd), 1992, *The Design of Building and Settlements in the Countryside*, Bristol: BDOR (unpublished tender document for Countryside Commission).

Bentley, I. et al., 1985, *Responsive Environments: A Manual for Designers*, London: Architectural Press.

Bourassa, S. C., 1991, *The Aesthetics of Landscape*, London: Belhaven Press.

Bourdieu, P., 1984, *Distinction: A Social Critique of the Judgment of Taste*, Cambridge, MA: Harvard University Press.

Broadbent, G., 1990, *Emerging Concepts in Urban Space Design*, New York, NY: Van Nostrand Reinhold.

Brolin, B. C., 1980, *Architecture in context: fitting new buildings with old*, New York, NY: Van Nostrand Reinhold.

Brower, S., 1988, *Design in Familiar Places: What makes home environments look good*, New York, NY: Praeger.

Buchanan, P., 1988, 'Facing up to Façades', *Architects' Journal*, Vol. 188, 21 and 28 December, pp. 21–56.

Coleman, A., 1985, *Utopia on Trial*, London: Hilary Shipman.

Costonis, J., 1989, *Icons and Aliens: law, aesthetics and environmental change*, Urbana, IL: University of Illinois Press.

Craik, K. H., 1970, 'The environmental dispositions of environmental decision-makers', *Annals of the American Academy of Political and Social Science*, Vol. 389, May, pp. 87–94.

Cullen, G., 1961, *Townscape*, London: Architectural Press.

Cullingworth, J. B., 1976, 'Amenity' in *Town and Country Planning in Britain*, (6th edn), London: Allen and Unwin.

Dewey, J., 1929, *Experience and Nature*, London: Allen and Unwin.

DoE (Department of the Environment), 1989, *Planning Control in Western Europe*, London: HMSO.

Dovey, K., 1993, 'Corporate Towers and Symbolic Capital', *Environment and Planning D: Society and Space*, forthcoming.

Duerksen, C. J., 1986, *Aesthetics and Land Use Controls: Beyond Ecology and Economics*, Chicago, IL: American Planning Association, Planning Advisory Service Report No. 399.

Featherstone, M., 1991, *Consumer Culture and Post Modernism*, London: Sage.

Forrest, J., 1988, *Lord I'm Coming Home: Everyday Aesthetics in Tidewater North Carolina*, London: Cornell University Press.

Forty, A. and Moss, H., 1980, 'A Housing Style for Troubled Consumers: The Success of Pseudo-Vernacular', *Architectural Review*, Vol. 167 (996), pp. 73–8.

Frampton, K., 1985, *Modern Architecture: A Critical History*, London: Thames and Hudson.

Fuller, P., 1984, 'The Right Idea', *New Society*, 19 January, pp. 94–5.

Gans, H. J., 1968, *People and Plans: essays on urban problems and solutions*, New York, NY: Basic Books.

Gibson, E., 1989, 'Traditions of Landscape Aesthetics 1700–1985', in Dearden, P. and Sadler, B. (eds), *Landscape Evaluation: Approaches and Applications*, Western Geographical Series, Victoria, BC: University of Victoria, Vol. 25, pp. 23–35.

Glancey, J., 1990, *New Directions in British Architecture*, London: Thames and Hudson.

Goodey, B. and Gold, J. R., 1987, 'Environmental Perception: The Relationship with Urban Design', *Progress in Human Geography*, Vol. 11(1), pp. 126–33.

Gould, S., 1991, *London's Unitary Development Plans: Design Policy and Content*, Reading: University of Reading School of Planning Studies, MPhil thesis.

Groat, L. N., 1986, 'Contextual compatibility in Architecture', in Nasar, J. (ed.), *Environmental Aesthetics: Theory, Research and Applications*, Cambridge: Cambridge University Press.

Habe, R., 1989, 'Public Design Control in American Communities: Design Guidelines/Design Review', *Town Planning Review*, Vol. 62(2), pp. 195–219.

Hall, E. T., 1966, *The Hidden Dimension*, New York, NY: Doubleday.

Harries, P., Lipman, A. and Purden, S., 1982, 'The Marketing of Meaning', *Environment and Planning B*, Vol. 9, pp. 457–66.

Harris, H. and Lipman, A., 1986, 'A Culture of Despair: Reflections on a Post Modern Architecture', *Sociological Review*, Vol. 34(4), pp. 837–54.

Harvey, D., 1989, *The Condition of Post Modernity*, Oxford: Basil Blackwell.

HBF/RIBA (Housebuilders Federation/Royal Institute of British Architects), 1990, *Good Design in Housing*, London: HBF/RIBA.

Hesselgren, S., 1975, *Man's Perception of the Man-Made Environment*, Stroudsburg, PA: Dowden Hutchinson and Ross.

Hewison, R., 1988, *The Heritage Industry*, London: Methuen.

Holgate, A., 1992, *Aesthetics of Built Form*, Oxford: Oxford University Press.

Jacobs, J., 1961, *The Death and Life of Great American Cities*, New York, NY: Vintage Books.

Jager, M., 1986, 'Class Definition and the Esthetics of Gentrification: Victoriana in Melbourne', in Williams, P. and Smith, N. (eds), *Gentrification of the City*, London: Allen and Unwin, pp. 78–91.

Jarvis, B., 1980, 'Urban Environments as Visual Art or Social Settings? A Review', *Town Planning Review*, Vol. 51(1), pp. 51–66.

Jarvis, B., 1991, 'Too Many Words: Recent Developments in Studies of the Visual Environment, a review article', *Town Planning Review*, Vol. 62(1), pp. 109–15.

Jencks, C., 1988, *The Prince, The Architects and New Wave Monarchy*, London: Academy Editions.

Jencks, C., 1989, *The Language of Post-Modern Architecture* (3rd edn), London: Academy Editions.

Kaplan, R. and S., 1989, *The Experience of Nature: a psychological perspective*, New York, NY: Cambridge University Press.

Knox, P. L., 1984, 'Symbolism Styles and Settings: The Built Environment and the Imperatives of Urbanised Capitalism', *Architecture and Behaviour*, Vol. 2(2), pp. 107–122.

Lynch, K., 1958, 'A Walk Around the Block', *Landscape*, Vol. 8(3), pp. 24–34.

Lynch, K., 1961, *The Image of the City*, Cambridge, MA: MIT Press.

Lynch, K., 1982, *A Theory of Good City Form*, Cambridge, MA: MIT Press.

Marcus, C. C., 1982, 'The Aesthetics of Family Housing: The Resident's Viewpoint', *Landscape Research*, Winter, pp. 9–13.

Marcus, C. C. and Sarkissan, W., 1986, *Housing as if People Mattered: Site Design Guidelines for Medium Density Family Housing*, Berkeley: University of California Press.

Marcus, C. C. and Francis, C., 1991, *People Places: Design Guidelines for Urban Open Space*, New York, NY: Van Nostrand Reinhold.

Maslow, A. H., 1954, *Motivation and Personality*, New York, NY: Harper and Row.

Maxwell, R., 1976, 'An Eye for an Eye: The Failure of the Townscape School', *Architectural Design*, Vol. 46(9), pp. 534–6.

Mordaunt-Crook, J. M., 1989, *The Dilemma of Style: Architectural Ideas from the Picturesque to the Post Modern*, London: John Murray.

Morris, A. E. J., 1979, *History of Urban Form: before the industrial revolutions*, London: Godwin.

Newby, H., 1979, *Green and Pleasant Land? Social Change in Rural England*, Harmondsworth: Penguin.

Newman, O., 1973, *Defensible Space*, London: Architectural Press.

Owen, S., 1991, *Planning Settlements Naturally*, Chichester: Packard.

Prak, N. L., 1977, *The Visual Perception of the Built Environment*, Delft, The Netherlands: Delft University Press.

Punter, J. V., 1981, 'Landscape Aesthetics: Synthesis and Critique' in Gould, J. and Burgess, J. (eds), *Valued Environments*, London: Allen and Unwin, pp. 100–23.

Punter, J. V., 1986, 'The Contradictions of Aesthetic Control under the Conservatives', *Planning Practice and Research*, 1(1), pp. 8–13.

Punter, J. V., 1986-7, 'A History of Aesthetic Control 1909–1953; 1954–1985', *Town Planning Review*, Vol. 57(4), pp. 351–81 and Vol. 58(1), pp. 29–62.

Punter, J. V., 1990, 'The Ten Commandments of Urban Design', *The Planner*, Vol. 76(39), pp. 10–14.

Punter, J. V., 1993, 'Developing Design Skills for Development Controllers', in Oxford Polytechnic Joint Centre for Urban Design, *Making Better Places: Urban Design Now*, forthcoming.

Raban, J., 1974, *Soft City*, London: Fontana.

Rapoport, A., 1977, *Human Aspects of Urban Form*, Oxford: Pergamon.

Rees, R., 1975, 'The Taste for Mountain Scenery', *History Today*, Vol. 35(5), pp. 305–12.

Relph, E. C., 1981, *Place and Placelessness*, London: Pion.

Relph, E. C., 1985, *Rational Landscapes and Humanistic Geography*, London: Croom Helm.

Relph, E. C., 1987, *The Modern Urban Landscape*, London: Croom Helm.

RFAC (Royal Fine Art Commission), 1985, *Twenty-Second Report, October 1971–December 1984*, London: HMSO, House of Commons, Cmnd 9498.

Scott, G., 1914, *The Architecture of Humanism*, London: Constable.

Scruton, R., 1979, *The Aesthetics of Architecture*, London: Methuen.

Shields, R., 1989, 'Social Spatialisation and the Built Environment: The West Edmonton Mall', *Environment and Planning D: Society and Space*, Vol. 7(2), pp. 147–64.

Shoard, M., 1979, *The Theft of the Countryside*, London: Temple Smith.

Smith, P., 1977, *The Dynamics of Urbanism*, London: Hutchinson.

Southworth, M., 1989, 'Theory and Practice of Contemporary Urban Design: A Review of Urban Design Plans in the United States', *Town Planning Review*, Vol. 60(4), pp. 389–402.

Tuan, Y-F, 1976, review of 'The Experience of Landscape' by Jay Appleton, in *Professional Geographer*, Vol. 28(1), pp. 103–4.

Tugnutt, A. and Robertson, M., 1987, *Making Townscape, A contextual approach to building in an urban setting*, London: Mitchell.

Turner, T., 1986, *English Garden Design: History and Styles since 1650*, Woodbridge: Antique Collectors Club.

Urry, J., 1990, *The Tourist Gaze: Leisure and Travel in Contemporary Societies*, London: Sage.

Venturi, R. and Brown, D. S., 1972, *Learning from Las Vegas*, Cambridge, MA: MIT Press.

Walmsley, D. J., 1988, *Urban Living: The Individual in the City*, London: Longman.

Wates, N., 1989, 'Ten Green Commandments', *Environment Now*, February, p. 10.

Watkin, D., 1982, *The English Vision: The Picturesque in Architecture, Landscape and Garden Design*, London: John Murray.

Weekend Guardian, 1989, 'Six Buildings in Search of an Architect', 25–26 February.

Whitehand, J. W. R., 1992, 'Recent Advances in Urban Morphology', *Urban Studies*, Vol. 29(4), pp. 619–36.

Widdowson, W., 1992, 'The Structure of Esthetics and the Workings of Design Review', in *Proceedings of the International Symposium on Design Review*, Cincinnati, OH: University of Cincinnati.

Wiener, M. J., 1981, *English Culture and the Decline of the Industrial Spirit*, Cambridge: Cambridge University Press, especially Chapter 3.

Williams, R., 1973, *The Country and the City*, London: Chatto and Windus.

Williams, R., 1979, *Keywords*, London: Fontana, pp. 31–2.

Wolff, J., 1983, *Aesthetics and the Sociology of Art*, London: Allen and Unwin.

Wright, P., 1985, *On Living in an Old Country*, London: Verso.

Chapter 4

Values in the past: Conserving heritage

Michael J. Thomas

The English today have been described as:

> A nation of collectors, we are afraid to throw anything away, we are famed for our train spotters, for potty hoarders who are expert in anything that can realistically be collected. We cling to the wreckage of our past whether that past be made up of old stamps, street-lamp numbers, classic cars, rock'n'roll regalia or the architecture of the fifties and sixties. (Glancey 1992)

It is not an exaggeration to say that this interest in the past has become a national obsession. The obsession is promoted and exploited by specialist publications which service groups of cognoscenti, and retail outlets, usually operated by experts who are engaged full-time in talking up the esteem and values of the objects which are conserved and/or collected.

An obvious result of this collecting mania is that the range of objects designated as worthy of collecting is continuously expanding. As the range expands, it becomes codified into fields, new categories develop, and expert knowledge grows like an exotic forest. Respectability for new areas of collecting arrives when the objects appear as cohesive groups in museums, when catalogues are written and scholarship in the new area becomes legitimate. By this stage the collectors have handed over responsibility to the curators.

It may seem unrealistic to use this rather sketchy picture of how collecting begets museums to introduce a discussion of conservation of the environment. The environment cannot be collected in the normal sense of objects being brought together to form a collection. Most environmental objects have to remain fixed in location. This is not always true. Open-air museums of buildings have been established in many countries to preserve buildings removed from their original site. But in England a collection has been created without relocation. Perhaps the size of the national collection of buildings is only known in the total number of listed buildings, scheduled ancient monuments, or designated Conservation Areas. If the collection of environmental objects nationally is very large and growing all the time, is it also true that the environment is being converted into a museum in order to ensure the preservation of the collection? It is a frequently-heard accusation that certain cities are becoming museums where the mainstay of the economy is to attract visitors to their historic environment. Thus the economic imperative is to remain *looking* authentically old, even if there is modern plumbing in Ye Olde Charles Inn. But in general, curating old environmental objects involves operating in a 'normal' economic situation, because continual use is the key to preservation. The preservation of empty buildings is not usually possible, except in the few cases where visitors will pay for a building, ruin or landscape to be insulated from normal economic usage. In fact, this insulation is often a transfer of an environmental object from general economic use to become the physical capital for the tourist or leisure industry.

The more usual environmental curating process is to impose controls on the way owners and occupiers use buildings and landscape. In this way, environmental conservation challenges the rights of property-owners to do what they will with their property. In a more general way, environmental conservation inhibits the process through which land and buildings are developed and redeveloped to satisfy economic and community demands for space and location. Under an environmental curatorial regime, the use of space must be subservient to, and facilitate, its conservation. So the curatorial management of the environment is in conflict with the basic conditions of a capitalist-run market by proposing limits on property rights and inhibiting the pursuit of the highest rent for such pieces of land – which, in 'normal' conditions, is the process which structures spatial development.

The imposing of limitations on property rights and the maximisation of rent capital leaves property-owners with the burden of conservation. Such limitations – or, more positively, the duty to conserve – can be reconciled with older concepts of land ownership than the limited form of ownership used so far. This limited, essentially capitalist, form corresponds almost exactly to the category created by Massey and Catalano (1978) to identify land ownership solely driven by the pursuit of maximum rent, which they called 'financial land ownership'. This category is applied to owners who supply land for others to use, and who are indifferent to the buildings themselves or the uses made of their land.

Conservation limitations imposed by a public authority can be seen to represent a modern version of the concept of landowners holding land in trust for future generations, or that owners had a duty of stewardship in relationship to their land. Good stewardship meant that current exploitation must not reduce its value (e.g. agricultural productivity) to the subsequent generations who would inherit it. Modern conservation regimes draw heavily on the stewardship principles to justify the limitations of property rights, while at the same time massively extending the number to whom the duty of stewardship is owed. The duty now is owed to the whole population and its future generations. This extension of a duty also implies that a new interest in land has been created, which is held by the public at large against landowners.

The idea of a publicly-held interest or right in land (including buildings) resonates with the dominant idea in conservation – that conservation is a practice which strives to maintain and inspire our heritage. But applied in this field, heritage is a slippery concept. The word alludes to ownership being passed on, but it is perhaps more accurate and useful to recast the heritage idea to stand for things created, maintained and held within a community which it wants to continue to maintain and hold. What marks things as heritage is the view that they somehow embody and express something significant in a community's experience. The Polish sociologist Alexander Wallis (1979) argued that, for a community to survive, it must control a space in which it can embody and manifest its experience. Wallis identified three basic communities with their parallel spaces thus:

Family   – Dwelling
Congregation   – Temple
Town   – Centre

Without a permanent space of embodiment and manifestation it is difficult to hold a community together. To apply this idea – of heritage as a community's experience embodied and manifested in a controlled space

– to as large and varied a nation as the English is to invite difficulties. But it is at this level that the heritage concept is increasingly applied. But, of course, the size of the English as a group means that those experiences which become embodied and manifested as marking the identity of the nation are likely to reflect the perceptions and interests of the powerful and the well-established. More recent times have seen a counter-tendency, working as democratisation of culture and/or the exploitation of the leisure time now available to the working-class population has occurred, while non-elite tastes, backed by spending power, have expanded the range of conserved items and environments which are created as heritage. Heritage has become an industry: an industry which is increasingly focused on marketing history-based tourism and entertainment, rather than being a minor part of the educational sector of the economy. Nevertheless, although the scope of what is included in heritage has broadened (a 1930 semi-detached house with original furnishing and décor was opened to the public by the National Trust in 1993) the core remains fairly constant, and might be represented by the Tower of London, cathedrals and the country house. Democracy has a marginal, if substantial, effect: the houses of the rich remain powerful attractions for visitors who, in previous times, would not have been allowed to pass through the park gates unless it was to work in the servants' hall, the stables, or on the farm.

Of Wallis's three places, the temple, and maybe sometimes the dwelling, can be considered sacred places which are sheltered from non-members of the congregation and family to act as repositories of faith, memory and experiences. The expansion of the modern heritage inventory of objects and environments is not located in exclusive zones but must coexist with everyday life in multi-layered and multi-functional environments. Protection is given to some buildings and areas, but it can never be total. Nevertheless, the more intense the heritage significance of something, the more it demands an environment of separateness.

In a well-known passage from Patrick Cormack (1976, pp. 11–12) core elements of the heritage ensemble are readily apparent:

When I am asked to define our heritage I do not think in dictionary terms, but instead reflect on certain sights and sounds. I think of a morning mist on the Tweed at Dryburgh when the magic of Turner and the romance of Scott both come fleetingly to life; of a celebration of the Eucharist in a quiet Norfolk church with the medieval glass filter-

71

ing the colours, and the early noise of the harvesting coming through the open door; or of standing at any time before the Wilton Diptych. Each scene recalls aspects of an indivisible heritage and is part of the fabric and expression of our civilisation.

Cormack writes of an elegiac mood engendered in places separated from everyday life in modern society, of elitist values of a predominantly rural and pre-industrial character. History and place are powerfully conjoined to convey an image of a time and place of beauty and peace. It is a powerfully seductive image of another place to set against the ugly, stressful and mundane places in which we live our lives. But the image has a reality, if under threat. The political programme for conservation which flows from this romantic image is to see that the image remains real in ever more protected places.

This type of conservation practice is a relatively new phenomenon. In England it took just over one hundred years to achieve the transition from small active bands of campaigners pressing for legislation to protect a small number of uninhabited ruins, and lobbying to stop what they saw as the desecration of churches by modern adaptations and decoration (the 'Anti-Scrape' campaign led by William Morris), to a situation characterised by a comprehensive code of environmental conservation legislation and a conservation lobby with massive public support.

WHY CONSERVE?

The argument which this part of the chapter develops is based on a distinction between a conservation practice based on economic and resource considerations and one which is driven by cultural values. It is the latter type which is the focus of attention, since it is this practice which is defined in relationship to an inventory of buildings and objects collectively known as 'our heritage'. Although this culturally-defined conservation process is a comparatively recent arrival on the social and political scene, in popular perception it dominates the debate about conservation. For most of the period of human history, culturally-defined conservation would not have been a significant factor in the attitude taken to the physical world, for reasons that can be classified as concerning the status of the objects or conditions which an economic form of conservation values, and the prevailing sense of time and the understanding of the process of change held by the community. Culturally-defined conservation directed towards a heritage inventory seems to achieve the importance it enjoys currently only when the past becomes viewed as a lost space (a foreign country) and the future is seen as a threat.

Conservation in its practical/economic form is based on four imperatives:

(1) To maintain the natural resource base for future use.
(2) To reduce the rate of exhaustion of non-renewable resources.
(3) To re-use resources incorporated in expended objects (e.g. recycling glass, paper and metals).
(4) To continue to extract value from objects while they remain useful.

For the most part, conservation characterised by these four imperatives has been a continuous feature of human activity. Before the development during the last 200 years of industrial technology, land and land-based resources were not substantially endangered by human activity. Particularly in relation to imperatives 1 and 2, the impact of human activity on the physical environment before the industrial period was marginal, and the slow rate of change allowed learning and adjustment to take place. In this way the human/land relationship could be maintained.

Imperatives 3 and 4 represent value placed on the conservation of human work, which could be lost, with a consequential effect on living conditions. The extended use of man-made objects up to the point of breakdown and the recovery or re-use of materials used in their manufacture were logical responses to the issue of the conservation of human energy.

There is, therefore, a need to discuss heritage conservation in the context of time structures. The contemporary importance of heritage conservation must be seen in the context of the way in which time is understood. Pasi Falk (1988) argues that modern time structures are basically versions of linearity combined with 'progress thinking', so that typically three phases – past, present and future – are in a linear (i.e. non-recurrent) sequence. Three versions of linear time can be identified according to the extent to which a break is posited between the phases. The first version is a naturalistic concept of the flow of time. No major dysfunction is recognised in the flow from past through present into the future. The present is the space we inhabit, but within it both the past and the future exist. The present can be either a narrow or a broad space: its dimensions depend to a large extent on expectation about the future. Generally, within the naturalistic concept of time, the future is conceived of as likely to be similar to the present, and in most senses a desirable state of affairs. In any case there exists no great sense of disruption between the past and the future which would give rise in the present to deep feelings of anxiety or heightened expectations about the future.

In the other two versions of time sequence, a separation between two of the three phases is fundamental, but the gap is located differently in each of the two versions. The second version argues that the past has gone and is separated from the present, which represents the first stage of the future. This version is a characterisation of what we might call 'progress thinking'.

Progress thinking can be said to be the dominant ideology of planning in Europe, especially in its 'Heroic period' from the beginning of this century until the mid-1970s. The past was there to be transcended through planned action constructing a better society. Some varieties of this type of thought had very little place for any part of the past in the future. For example, when T. Marinetti proclaimed Futurism in 1909 he poured contempt on the historic achievements of Italy represented by the museum. The past had to be swept aside. War was a cleansing process, to set Italy free from the dead weight of the past: 'We stand on the last promontory of the centuries! ... Why should we look back, when what we want is to break down the mysterious doors of the Impossible?' (Marinetti 1909). Similarly H. Read (1935) argued that Dada and abstract art had different historic functions in relation to the transformation project in the Soviet Union. Dada would kill off bourgeois art, clearing the space for revolutionary art and design, but abstract art, through its rediscovery of basic forms, would provide the vocabulary for communist design. However, the communist version of design – constructivism – did not survive the onslaught of the conservatives' style of socialist realism.

Other less revolutionary movements drew on the past to formulate a pattern for the future. Ebeneser Howard's 'A peaceful path to Reform' (Howard 1946) drew on an English tradition of building to create a new form of settlement. Frank Lloyd Wright (1963) based his new city design, Broadacre City, on the tradition and myth of the frontier-colonising farmer.

What is common to these positions is the emphasis on planning as action which took place in the present but which was dedicated to making the future. Pasi Falk (1988) speaks about these views as having a

74

concept of spatialised time: the present is a vacant site on which to build the future.

Confidence in the ability to create a new future is the dominant value of the modern project (Thomas 1990). The decay of this vision, particularly in the collapse of the East European communist regimes, leaves the political arena without a grand narrative of the future (Bauman 1990). But perhaps, given the tyranny which the future held over the present for those societies, the loss is not to be regretted. The sense of optimism which disappeared long before the collapse of communism leaves a situation where the future has not been created but a heritage might have been destroyed.

The combined attack on the inherited built and natural environment from simplistic functional planning, the rush for industrial development without consideration of its ecological impacts, and finally, economic failure, has left most of the former communist states in Europe with an enormous task of environmental recovery.

The third version of the linear time structure places the break between present and future. In this version the future is largely unknown and determined by forces which are not policy-controlled. Alternatively, if the policy and its postulated future is rejected by, or threatens, the interests of a social group, they may adopt this view by expressing an understanding of time sequence in which past and present are part of a continuing process leading to the edge of an unknown or unwanted future. In this case, values are situated in the past, and they are directed to be extended into the future. But this can only be achieved either by delaying the undirected future or replacing it with a development process based on continuity – in effect, replacing version 3 with version 1.

With the collapse of the future in politics (that is, version 2), and the prevailing sense of change without direction, version 3 has become dominant. Version 3 occurs in those political positions which reject modernisation and industrialisation but also, interestingly, can be seen as a theme within modernism itself, even at an early stage.

Jochan Schalte-Sasse (1989) seeks to distinguish between two modes of aesthetic modernism, and argues that both modes presuppose a radical critique of social modernity – that is, the political and social programme of the modern project (Habermas 1985). This critique includes the instrumentation of reason and language, alienation of people from one another, and the development of increasingly agonistic identities (such as class?).

75

One reaction – typified by the invention of Cubism by Braque and Picasso – leads to the possibility of an art, as suggested by H. Read (1935), purged of its bourgeois background, which could be employed in the process of social modernity. It therefore fits in as part of the process allied to version 2. The second aesthetic reaction 'intersperses nostalgic, utopian images of a better reconciled world into its critique of civilisation' (Schalte-Sasse 1989, p.36). This work, says Lyotard (1984, p.80), is on the side of melancholia, and he cites as an example the work of the German Expressionists. T. S. Eliot's 'The Waste Land' could be evidenced as a consummate example of a modernist critique of modern civilisation, but significantly without 'utopian images'. Excluding pessimistic modern masters like Eliot and Edward Hopper, the general tendency of this trend, as Schalte-Sasse (1989) argues, is to 'offer merely compensatory aesthetic experiences in the functionally differentiated world of capitalism'. This remark echoes almost exactly Kenneth Frampton's (1983) criticism of regionalism in contemporary architecture, which he sees as providing only a compensating façade covering a universal form of building.

Whilst these strands exist within modernism itself in its attitude towards the political, social and economic impact of the modern project, the politically influential positions within the third version of linear time have been deeply critical of the whole edifice of modernity. This position has been legitimised by the collapse of communism. What has not usually been articulated by the anti-modernists is a critical position in relationship to capitalism. If we accept Bauman's view (1990, pp. 20–25) that modernity is the child of capitalism and socialism, and that socialism played a vital role in tempering the excesses and civilising the process of transformation led by capital, then the removal of the socialist grand narrative may produce a more dangerous scenario for the future.

The anti-modernists of the third version develop their position on the two bases of rejection of modernity – most publicly in the architecture of a classicist like Quinlan Terry – and the pain of loss. Consequently, the desired state, in both the environment and social affairs, is to be found in the past. The future must be resisted by defending what remains of the past, and recovering continuity, to allow the projection of the best of the past into the future. Consequently, the work of the present is both defensive and recuperative.

It is this position as a source of operative values which largely informs popular attitudes towards conservation. Conservation is a movement which opposes modernism, usually in the name of the defence of the heritage.

The mass membership of organisations like the National Trust testifies to the popularity of this cause. There can be little doubt that it is deeply embedded in the mood of the times.

Of course, the confrontation between conservation and modernisation, or development, takes many forms depending on the values which are embodied in or represented by the particular artifact or environment which is at risk.

Obviously there are economic interests at stake in the process of environmental change. There is an inherent tension between what Lipietz (1980) calls the 'inherited urban space' and the 'projected urban space'. Projected urban space is the implicit spatial expression of the development tendencies of economic and social forces. Inherited space represents a barrier to continued development which is not easy to overcome. The economic stakes involved in the inherited space can be compensated in most cases if the gains from development are sufficient. The problems become critical where the losers are not economic stakeholders, or when the loss of the inherited space is not seen primarily in economic terms but is represented in other values, such as culture, history and symbolism. The dual role of buildings and environments as both real estate and cultural objects, and the fact that environmental change occurs almost entirely within the structure of the land market, gives many opportunities for unresolvable conflicts. The various schemes promoted to redevelop the Paternoster Square area, which is immediately north of St Paul's Cathedral in the City of London, illustrate the point. The modernist office blocks in the overall design of Sir William Holford were constructed in the 1960s, and largely ignored the pre-existing medieval street pattern. This generally unloved ensemble is regarded as not providing an appropriate setting for Wren's cathedral, and the windswept open spans within Holford's scheme are compared unfavourably to the urban quality of the previous morphology. Conservationists – including the Prince of Wales, who took a close interest in the proposals for the Paternoster Square redevelopment – are very much in favour of limiting the height of new buildings, the use of classic styles, and the recovery of the old street pattern. The problem for the designers of the new scheme is that financing requires the creation of more rentable space than the conservationist objectives would allow. John Punter (1992) says that the brief given to the designers 'proposed a 9.5:1 plot ratio, nearly twice that permissible in the City, and nearly three times that of the existing post-war development'.

St Paul's is a conflict about recuperation: if the conservationist impulse is successful – that is, if the favoured scheme is constructed – it
would replace a disliked modernist development with buildings in a
classical style, broadly arranged according to the 1870s street pattern. It
could be argued that the urban tradition of the past had been reapplied,
but it could also be argued that a compensating façade had been erected.
The space is likely to be occupied by the offices of multi-national companies and the branches of national retailers. The small firms and inter-
dependent retailers who occupied the premises in the late nineteenth
century would not reappear.

The sense of loss that results from the process of destruction and
redevelopment which has transformed large areas of towns and cities,
and the seemingly relentless urbanisation of the countryside, have been
the subject of many accounts (see Marris 1982). Memories are fixed on
places and buildings, so that when an urban quarter is faced with the
prospect of redevelopment the whole community can experience a poign-
ant mixture of outrage, powerlessness, loss and displacement. The extent
to which these feelings can be channelled into effective opposition depends usually on whether leadership is located within the community.

However, this tendency to see development threats to valued buildings
and environments as occasions for confrontation is perhaps better seen as
the sharp edge of a much deeper and longer established self-image of the
English and their country. Whilst it might be more properly thought of as
a mood which developed and is strongest in southern England, given the
cultural and political hegemony of the South, and particularly London
and the Home Counties, within English culture, it has permeated throughout the country. It is useful to quote Martin J. Wiener (1981, pp. 158–9)
at length on this aspect.

In particular the later nineteenth century saw the consolidation of a
national elite that, by virtue of its power and prestige, played a central
role both in Britain's modern achievements and its failures. It adminis-
tered the most extensive empire in human history with reasonable
effectiveness and humanity, and it maintained a remarkable degree of
political and social stability at home while presiding over a redistribu-
tion of power and an expansion of equality and security. It also pre-
sided over the steady and continued erosion of the nation's economic
position in the world. The standards of value of this new elite of civil
servants, professionals, financiers, and landed proprietors, inculcated

by a common education in public schools and ancient universities and reflected in the literary culture it patronized, permeated by their prestige much of British society beyond the elite itself. These standards did little to support, and much to discourage, economic dynamism. They threw earlier enthusiasms for technology into disrepute, emphasised the social ills brought by the industrial revolution, directed attention to issues of the 'quality of life' in preference to the quantitive concerns of production and expansion, and disparaged the restlessness and acquisitiveness of industrial capitalism. Hand in hand with this disparagement went the growth of an alternative set of social values embodied in a new vision of the nation.

The dominant collective self-image in English culture became less and less that of the world's workshop. Instead, this image was challenged by the counter image of an ancient, little-disturbed 'green and pleasant land'. 'Our England is a garden', averred the greatest poet of Imperialism; another Imperialist, a poet laureate, celebrated England at the height of Imperial fervour for its 'haunts of ancient peace'; and an anti-Imperialist socialist has inspired his readers with the aim of making England once again, as it had been before the industrial revolution, the 'fair green garden of Northern Europe'. The past, and the countryside – seen as inseparable – were invested with an almost irresistible aura. These standards and images supported a very attractive way of life, geared to maintenance of a status quo rather than innovation, comfort rather than attainment, the civilised enjoyment, rather than the creation, of wealth.

The paradox is that it is increasingly obvious that, as the image and goal of the attainment of civilised enjoyment – or at least comfortable living – was democratised through the struggle between capital and organised labour, the necessity for efficient, productive economy was underlined.

As the total of Conservation Areas (CAs) designated by English local authorities approaches 10,000 it is obvious that areas designated have long ago gone beyond the limited, but albeit considerable, number of 'sacred places' of national or regional importance in terms of history and architecture. Because the declaration of CAs is purely a local decision, the justification for individual declarations is not bound by rigorous rules. In general, areas now being created as CAs are increasingly marginal cases, except in a few instances where there has been adventurous use of the category, for example the designation of the route of the

Carlisle–Settle railway line in northern England. The haphazard process of extension of what must be admitted is a weak form of protection to areas is nevertheless evidence of a process of building barriers to change in areas which are increasingly places of everyday life. However, it is argued by Larkin and Jones (1993) that frequently designations are not supported by comprehensive statements justifying the action, identifying what are the important features which are to be protected and outlining what policy measures will be applied to bring about enhancement of the area. It is possible to read into this progressive inventory of CAs a number of motives. It is true, as Morton (1991) observed, that this level of designation cannot be matched by any publicly-funded programme of improvement or enhancement. Even if local authorities wanted to adopt an active improvement and management programme for the areas they are designated, the present resource position of English local government would prevent this. Funds devoted to area conservation constitute 'voluntary' expenditure over and above that required to discharge statutory duties in respect of services like education, social services, and refuse collection and disposal. So, apart from the desire on the part of local authorities to establish a map register of local historical and architectural assets, there is little doubt that the growing number of CAs is partly the result of the growth of an institutionalised conservation bureaucracy in local government, with full-time conservation officials often holding formal, specialised educational/professional qualifications and belonging to professional associations. Conservation Area designations and the listing of buildings of historic interest or architectural merit gives these professionals a legal framework within which to develop their practice and to justify their intervention. Being a Conservation Area gives a status and character to the way in which change to that area is treated. One of the major reasons given by local authorities for designation is not that they themselves will become more active in directly enhancing an area – because money is short and there are now too many areas, so any money spent will tend to be spread so thinly as to not make much of an impact – but that such designation will give the authority greater power to control change than that provided by the normal planning legislation. Applications for planning permission inside a CA can be viewed with greater attention to the effect of the proposed development on the surroundings. The designation is limited in this respect to concerns about the physical context rather than the social and economic character of an area. This bias can result in changes to the use of buildings being approved primarily because they will provide for the conservation of the building. However, the problem of finding economic uses for old buildings remains one of the most difficult tasks facing conservators. Employing conservation legislation gives a higher profile to development control decisions. It gives conservation lobbies greater access to planning processes.

If local planning authorities use CA designation as a means of gaining greater control over change, communities faced with the consequences of changes similarly welcome any possibility of greater effectiveness. In higher-class residential neighbourhoods the visual/physical focus of conservation legislation resonates with the underlying political ground which structures their relationship with the local authority. The residential market has already constructed the social base for defensive action. The personal investment in older – probably larger – property, usually accompanied by restoration work, represents in some favoured urban locations (such as parts of Islington in London), in aggregate, a massive collective investment in urban fabric. Such communities of wealth and lifestyle know that their investment, both in finance and time, is validated by the maintenance of the neighbourhood character – that is, the quality of the public space (streets, squares, etc.), its servicing by the local authority, and the condition and use of surrounding properties.

Conservation Area designation provides the conduit and legitimisation to conduct the neighbourhood's defensive and enhancement strategy. The recent change back to a property value-based local taxation system (the Council Tax replaced the standard charge per capita under the short-lived Community Charge in April 1993) revives one of the more disreputable arguments sometimes used in these defensive and enhancement political strategies by the residents of better neighbourhoods (that is, as higher than average local tax-payers they feel entitled to a higher than average level of expenditure in their area). But the usual, and more legitimate, argument is for policies which protect important physical assets which are available for all to enjoy as part of the city's built environment. Protection of the best areas has obvious attractions based on the quality which is recognisable, even if the enjoyment of it is in reality controlled by the residential market.

Any success which well-placed neighbourhoods have can result in costs being transferred to other areas. In the management of traffic, for example, moving or parked vehicles which are excluded from the better areas are likely to find their way into other areas. The defensive strategies of higher-class residential neighbourhoods are likely to be successful in

protecting their environment from unwanted change because their existing base in class and interest is sufficiently strong and articulate to form a
common political ground from which community response to threats can
be organised. Because there are rules, procedures and an attentive
professionalised bureaucracy established at the local level, these can be
used to promote and legitimise the neighbourhood's interests.

Other areas of lower-class residential and mixed land use will not
create a political terrain so conducive to action. For the communities
living and working in such areas, the experience of change and the threat
which it represents may not be so easily focused on the built environment
and its conservation. Changes to buildings are a manifestation of deeper
socio-economic restructuring – the loss of small independent retailers
and manufacturing and/or skilled manual jobs in the inner areas of cities,
to give some obvious instances, leads to abandonment of buildings which
may or may not find alternative users. If there is a case for conservation
in these types of areas it is likely to be for the conservation of the
community as a viable, employed (and therefore consuming) local social
system with a sense of its own future existence. The recent history of
community activism in the coal mining villages or towns experiencing
the effects of a rapidly contracting industry shows how difficult it is to
establish a claim for conservation for a community with no physical
assets to protect.

If the attitudes appropriate to the third version of time sequence are
dominant within heritage conservation, this has profound implications.
This position was characterised above as defensive and recuperative. The
uses to which heritage is put range along a spectrum from protective at
one end – the ultimate protection being to put heritage objects into a
museum – to being made into a theme park at the other. Both extremes
have something in common: heritage is located in a place which can be
visited, the museum in hushed reverence and the theme park expecting to
enjoy a day's outing. Both these experiences are, in the main, non-
interactive, and reflect a view which values preservation above use (by
'use' is meant the incorporation of heritage into the mainstream of current practice). Now this looks like a strange notion in the face of a
heritage which predominantly assumes the form of environments or buildings. The natural and built environment is involved in all human activity,
but involvement may only involve locations and accommodation. The
more active involvement of a broadly conceived concept of heritage
across many fields can be seen in the role of this historic environment as

an accumulated social resource of thought and practice available to architects, builders and town planners.

If the term 'heritage' were replaced by 'tradition' then the practical
possibilities of past achievements being made central to current practice
become clearer. Tradition suggests not just things (building and landscape) but a much wider range of human creativity and practice (e.g.
music, philosophy, medicine, the theatre). Tradition carries the idea of
continuing activities that have a history which contributes to present
forms.

An example of tradition being used by modern practitioners is seen in
the way that visual artists relate to art galleries. In a very revealing series
of small exhibitions at the National Gallery, London, a number of practising artists were invited to present some of their recent work and to select
pictures from the Gallery's collection to illustrate themes and concerns in
their work.

For a modern abstract artist like Bridget Riley the collection of the
National Gallery, which excludes twentieth-century art, is vital resource
which she can use (Riley 1988). Only if you take the view that art's
history is the development of techniques to render ever more naturalistic
representations of the external world can you see the history of painting
as movements towards a form of perfection. Such a view would, of
course, create many problems for the art of the twentieth century, which
has been dominated by the turn away from naturalistic representation.
The art gallery is the manifestation of the way artists feed off the long
tradition of visual art to develop their work by reworking, transposing,
extending and subverting the work of earlier artists. In any case there are
values which reside in the built environment which go beyond the usual
justifications (Age, Beauty and Significance) offered by conservationists.

The potential of the conserved built environment as a social resource
to support a version of urban life at variance with that projected upon the
interplay of economic forces is a belief which lies at the heart of the
Bologna Conservation Programme. The historic environment is designated to have the ability to preserve certain traditions of urban life –
essentially the idea of a densely connected, largely face-to-face social
system.

So, in a broad sense, the conservation of the built environment can
assist the maintenance of traditions or urban life and urban culture by
keeping the physical framework of an urban society intact, with the
communication possibilities that it implies. On the other hand, physical

conservation can represent a threat if the energy and resources devoted to it are gained at the expense of other areas of historically-derived activities which could also be said to be part of our heritage. It would seem a misplaced emphasis, for example, if the physical conservation of pre-war cinemas took precedence over public support for the film industry.

CONCLUSION

Conservation of the built and natural environment has, within the space of just over one hundred years, become a major responsibility of government at national and local level, with a concomitant development of legal rules and procedures, and a technical/professional bureaucracy to apply the rules and formulate policy. What is significant is the values and concerns which surround and structure each policy area. Conservation in the current period – which is marked by a fully institutionalised presence within government – has emerged as a policy area enjoying immense public support. Yet this support could also be read as a sign of our sense of anxiety about the future, and sense of ill-being towards the modern world. It has been argued that the underlying concept of time sequence behind conservation is one which emphasises a disjunction between a closely-related past and present, and the future which is unpredictable and potentially undesirable.

The general loss of credibility of optimistic progressive thinking further strengthens the feeling that the past was/is a good place which should not be violated by development. The regulatory framework provides for a number of ways in which duties are laid on owners to preserve old buildings and landscape, and means are available to protect designated parts of the environment. The general anti-modernist attitude running through conservation thought and policy is itself a threat to the conserved object, 'the heritage'. Anxiety about the future leads to excessive protectiveness – the museum may yet become the favoured location for heritage environment but, because environmental objects are difficult to move, the museum must move to the objects – thus the creation of museum towns. Alternatively, heritage can be accommodated into objects of the tourists' gaze. Tourism and leisure use heritage as their stock-in-trade. The result is that heritage is isolated from those who might make use of it to understand and rework their experience.

But another practice is possible. Paula Rego was invited to be the first artist-in-residence at London's National Gallery. The paintings she did there drew inspiration from paintings in the Gallery's collection, but also changed the way we look, through her, at the Gallery's paintings. She said of the Gallery, that it is: 'A treasure house ... it's all treasure of the greatest kind, the richest treasure in the world' (Greer & Wiggins 1991). With such a model in mind it should be possible to re-establish the past in the present, not for the purpose of banishing the future, but to enrich the future by historically-informed human endeavours.

REFERENCES

Bauman, Z., 1990, 'From Pillars to Post', *Marxism Today*, February, pp. 20–25.

Cormack, P., 1976, *Heritage in Danger*, London: New English Library.

Falk, P., 1988, 'The Past to Come', *Economy and Society*, Vol. 17(2).

Frampton, K., 1983, 'Towards a Critical Regionalism: Six Points for an Architecture of Resistance', in Foster, H. (ed.), *The Anti-Aesthetic: Essays on Postmodern Culture*, Washington DC: Bay Press.

Glancey, J., 1992, 'A Bridge Too Far?', *Independent Magazine*, 11 July.

Greer, G. and Wiggins, C., 1991, *Paula Rego: Tales from the National Gallery*, London: National Gallery.

Habermas, J., 1985, 'Modernity – An Incomplete Project', in Foster, H. (ed.), *Post-modern Culture*, London: Pluto, pp. 3–15.

Howard, E., 1946, *Garden Cities of Tomorrow*, London: Faber and Faber.

Larkin, P. J. and Jones, A., 1993, 'Conservation and Conservation Areas in the UK: A Growing Problem', *Planning Practice and Research*, 9(2), pp. 19–29.

Lipietz, A., 1980, 'The Structuration of Space, the Problem of Land and Spatial Policy', in Carney, J., Hudson, R. and Lewis, J. (eds), *Regions in Crisis*, London: Croom Helm.

Lloyd Wright, F., 1963, *The Living City*, New York, NY: Mentor Books.

Lyotard, J.-F., 1984, *The Postmodern Condition*, Minneapolis: University of Minnesota Press.

Marinetti, T., 1909, 'The Founding and Manifesto of Futurism', reprinted in Apollonis, U. (ed.), 1973, *Futurist Manifestos*, London: Thames and Hudson, pp. 19–24.

Marris, J., 1982, *Community Planning and Conceptions of Change*, London: Routledge and Kegan Paul.

Massey, D. and Catalano, A., 1978, *Capital and Land*, London: Edward Arnold.

Morton, D., 1991, 'Conservation Areas: Has Saturation Point been Reached?', *The Planner*, 77(17), pp. 5–8.

Punter, J., 1992, 'Classical Carbuncles and Mean Streets: Contemporary Urban Design and Architecture in Central London', in Thornley, A. (ed.), *The Crisis of London*, London: Routledge, pp. 69–89.

Read, H., 1935, 'What is Revolutionary Art?', in *Five on Revolutionary Art*, London: Wishart, pp. 11–22.

Riley, B., 1988, *The Artist's Eye*, London: National Gallery.

Schalte-Sasse, J., 1989, 'Carl Einstein; or, The Postmodern Transformation of Modernism', in Auyssen, A. and Bathrick, D. (eds), *Modernity and the Text*, New York, NY: Columbia University Press, pp. 36–59.

Thomas, M., 1990, 'The Planning Project', paper given at Oxford Planning Theory Conference, Oxford Polytechnic.

Wallis, A., 1979, *Informacja i Gwar*, Warsaw: Państwowy Instytut Wydawniczy.

Wiener, M. J., 1981, *English Culture and the Decline of the Industrial Spirit 1850–1980*, Cambridge: Cambridge University Press.

Chapter 5

Environmental issues and the public interest

Nigel Taylor

PLANNING AND THE PUBLIC INTEREST: A CONTENTIOUS ISSUE

It may be that many (if not most) of the established professions end up serving the interests of some, generally more powerful, groups in society rather than other, generally weaker, groups. Whether or not this is so is an empirical question. But even if it is so, few if any professionals themselves would regard this as desirable – as something which *ought* to occur. And certainly no professional body that I can think of *claims*, or *expresses the intention*, to serve only – or even primarily – the interests of some particular section or group within society. Rather, the established professions proclaim their intention of serving the interests of the public as a whole. To be sure, doctors serve the interests of the sick, teachers the interests of students, and so on, and the sick or students, etc., might be thought of as particular groups within society. But the point is that *anybody* in society may become sick, or anybody may at some stage in their life become a student, and hence in their professional practice doctors or teachers may find themselves treating or teaching anybody in the public – be they rich or poor, old or young, male or female, black or white. And it is in this sense that these professions claim to be serving the interests of the public in general, rather than particular sectional groups within the public.

The town planning profession is no exception to this general rule. Thus, in the opening sentence of their code of professional conduct, the Royal

Town Planning Institute (the RTPI) states that: 'The object of the Royal Town Planning Institute ... is to advance the art and science of town planning in all its aspects ... for the benefit of the public' (RTPI 1991, p.7).

However, it may be asked whether this talk of the *public* interest carries, or could in principle carry, any meaningful sense at all, or whether, alternatively, it is merely empty rhetoric – a high-sounding phrase which is used to justify, or legitimise, this or that occupation as a 'profession' but which, in fact, is utterly meaningless.

In the 1960s and 1970s the iconoclastic dismissal of the idea of the public interest was widely accepted, especially by sociologists wedded to a conflict model of society which held that societies – or at least contemporary capitalist societies – are composed of different groups with different, and very often conflicting, interests. Given this, it seemed to some to follow that there was not any over-arching or supervenient interests which all groups (or everybody) in society shared in common. As the sociologist planner James Simmie (1974, p.125) put it: 'there is no such thing as THE public interest. Rather there are a number of different and competing interests'.

Although, in the planning field, there have remained a few who have continued to proclaim the meaningfulness and centrality of the idea of the public interest – most notably the North Americans Friedmann (1973) and Klosterman (1980) – much of the literature on people's interests in relation to planning has turned away from talk of the public interest and examined, instead, the interests of specific groups in relation to planning and the land development process (e.g. Ambrose 1986; Rydin 1986; Healey et al. 1988).

The suggestion that there is no such thing as an overall public interest did not just arise in the 1960s and 1970s. It goes back at least to the beginning of this century, when Arthur Bentley, the 'father' of interest-group theory in political science, proclaimed that 'We shall never find a group interest of ... society as a whole', and this because, according to Bentley (1908, pp. 222 and 208–9):

We shall always find that the political interests and activities of any group – and there are no political phenomena except group phenomena – are directed against other activities of men, who appear in other groups ... society is nothing other than the complex of the groups that compose it ... When the groups are adequately stated, everything is stated. When I say everything, I mean everything.

Writing fifty years later, the political theorist David Truman (1951, p.51) followed Bentley exactly in claiming that the interests of different groups in society often conflict, so that 'in developing a group interpretation of politics ... we do not need to account for a totally inclusive interest, because one does not exist'.

The fallacy in these arguments lies in the twin assumptions that society is composed *only* of groups with conflicting interests, and that where conflicts of interest exist between groups there cannot also be areas of consensus co-existing with the conflicts. Both these assumptions can be contested. Thus, while it may be true that different interest groups possess (by virtue of the different properties which constitute and distinguish them) *different* interests, it does not follow from this that such groups will necessarily or always possess *incompatible or conflicting* interests. On occasions there may be a happy coincidence of interests. For example, teachers, parents and children may be distinct interest groups, but each may share a common interest in good teacher training and facilities for children's education. Moreover, even where two or more interest groups do possess different and conflicting interests, it does not follow that there are no interests that they share in common. For example, although the respective interests of employers and employees can often generate conflict (e.g. over wages), they can at the same time share an interest in resolving such conflicts (e.g. by agreeing on *some* wage settlement). Thus the existence of conflicts of interest between groups does not necessarily also rule out the possibility of consensus, and in this respect the conception of society as being constituted *only* by conflicting interest groups is misleading – as misleading, in fact, as the contrary idea of society constituted only by consensus.

It is, of course, an altogether bigger step to go from these observations about the possibilities of consensus between *some* interest groups to the claim that there can be areas of consensus between *all* interest groups and thus all individuals, which is what is required for something to be in the public interest as I conceive it. But the possibility of such universal consensus cannot be discounted out of hand. Thus Barry (1965, pp. 194–5) contends that the argument of Bentley and Truman that there are no interests common to all members of society:

is superficial because it ignores the question: why are some logically possible proposals never advocated by anyone at all? Why, for example, is nobody in the USA in favour of having the Strategic Air Command take off and drop all its bombs on the USA? Obviously, because nobody at all believes this would be in his interests.

In the same vein, Graham (1984, p.55) suggests that:

> certain interests are so fundamental that they must be recognised to some degree in any community, and it is the obligation to observe the protection of such interests that gives rise to social morality. Demands may be made of an individual in matters such as the infliction of injury and the deceiving of others, where some standards are necessary if there is to be any society at all.

There is another argument that is sometimes raised against the idea of the public interest – that there is no conceptually coherent theory of the public interest. Schubert (1962) advances this view, as does Sorauf (1962), who describes the idea of the public interest as a 'conceptual muddle'. Both Schubert's and Sorauf's main ground for saying this derives from an analysis of the way the concept of the public interest has been used by some political theorists and, more especially, in everyday political discourse by politicians, pressure groups, and the like. Now, it may well be that the concept is sometimes used incoherently. It may also be true that, in everyday political debate, the notion of the public interest is sometimes used to legitimise all kinds of claims, including sectional ones. As Sorauf (1962, p.188) observes: 'in political debate public interest serves as little more than rationalisation for some particular group's interest'. However, this appeal to ordinary discourse does not necessarily prove anything. For the fact that the concept of interest has been and continues to be used in some quarters in incoherent or partisan ways does not show that it is impossible to provide a coherent and impartial account of the concept.

In this essay I hope to show that it is possible to provide a coherent and non-partisan account of the public interest, and to demonstrate the relevance of this to environmental planning. I shall set out and discuss this account later in this essay. But before that, in the following section, I shall set down a number of points about the concept of interest in general which I presuppose in my account of the public interest. There have, it has to be admitted, been other conceptions of the public interest which differ from the one I shall be advancing. I shall also deal briefly with two of these and, I hope, demonstrate their shortcomings in comparison with my favoured conception. I will conclude by indicating the importance of the idea of the public interest in thinking about environmental issues and planning.

SOME PRELIMINARY POINTS ABOUT THE CONCEPT OF INTEREST

It has been claimed (e.g. by Connolly 1974; Lukes 1974) that the concept of interest is an example of what Gallie (1956) has called an 'essentially contested concept'. Although I have insufficient space here to argue this, I dispute this claim, at least in the strong sense which holds that the concept is, literally, *essentially* contested. For it seems to me that there is at least a core concept of interest which is generally accepted – that for x to be in N's interest x must yield more benefit than harm for N (or, if a net gain in benefit is impossible, because the circumstances facing N are particularly adverse, then x must at least maximise the *ratio* of benefit to harm to be in N's interest). In other words, talk of things being in or against a person's or group's interest is talk of what *benefits and harms* them. Even Connolly (who suggests that the concept of interest is essentially contested) grants this when he says that 'To say that a policy or practice is in the interests of an individual or group is to assert ... that the recipient would somehow benefit from it' (Connolly 1974, p.46).

Given this, a number of points follow about the nature of interest judgements. Once again, I have not space to argue all of these points fully here, so I shall list and describe them only briefly:

(1) There are some things which would seem to be so obviously beneficial or harmful to human beings that, on occasions, it appears that what is in or against a person's or group's interest is a matter of empirical fact. Thus it seems an incontrovertible fact that starvation, or grinding poverty, homelessness, breathing poisoned air, etc., are all objectively harmful to people and therefore against their interests. If this is so, then immediately we reach the interesting conclusion that some judgements of interest may not be value or normative judgements, but rather, descriptive or empirical judgements.

There is, however, a strong argument against this conclusion. Even in the examples just mentioned there are certain fundamental (if seemingly self-evident) value judgements, underpinning the interest judgements – concerning the value of life, the well-being that attaches to a degree of material comfort or to living in a healthy environment, etc. And although values about these matters may sometimes be well-nigh universally shared, we should be wary of assuming that they always are. For different people who subscribe to (say) different religious beliefs, or who inhabit or have been socialised into different cultures, can subscribe to quite different normative conceptions of what constitutes a good life for a person to lead, and this in turn can generate correspondingly different values and views about what is beneficial and harmful in life. For example, the theist may not regard her/his own death as a harm in the same way that an atheist might, the ascetic would not regard the amassing of material wealth as beneficial as would an oil magnate, and so on (cf. Strawson 1961). So, although it may not be contestable that judgements of interest (and thus the *concept* of interest) are about benefits and harms, what constitutes benefits and harms in human life may be disputed, because judgements of benefit and harm (and therefore of interests) rest upon more fundamental value judgements about the ideal life for a person to lead. This makes interest judgements normative or evaluative and not simply descriptive or empirical.

(2) Even if we allow that interest judgements are normative and thus evaluative, this does not make them *moral* judgements. On the contrary, interest judgements are typically non-moral, and so distinct from moral judgements. This is shown by the fact that what is in a person's or group's interest may not be something of which we morally approve. For example, it may be in my interest to pocket the £10 note I have just seen somebody drop, or it may be in some group's interest to earn huge profits from speculating in real estate, but morality may demand that I return the £10 to its owner, that groups do not earn huge profits from land deals, etc. It is useful, then, to distinguish between interest and moral judgements as two distinct kinds of evaluative or normative judgement, so if we speak of what is good for a person or group in terms of their interests we are here using the term 'good' in a non-moral sense.

It does not follow from this that what is in a person's or group's interest need always conflict with what that person or group ought, morally, to do. This, again, depends upon one's normative conception of the ideal life for a person to lead or aspire to, but, according to some conceptions, the best kind of life for a person to lead in terms of their interests is a morally good life (cf. Griffin 1986, p.68; Parfit 1984, p.12). Moreover, even if we grant that interest judgements are, in themselves, non-moral evaluative judgements, interest judgements remain highly relevant to – indeed, are absolutely central to – moral deliberation and judgement. For, as Bernard Harrison (1989) has pointed out, usually what we believe it is morally right to do (either as individuals in our behaviour towards others, or in expressing views about collective political action) bears some relation to the furthering of *some* people's interests and well-being, if not humanity in general, so the identification of those people's interests is part and parcel of deciding how we ought, morally, to act.

(3)   The previous point leads naturally on to the question of how we can best (i.e. most accurately) identify – or judge – a person's or group's interest (including our own interests). And directly allied to this is the question of *who* is best placed to judge people's interests. Needless to say, this is a matter of high controversy, especially when it is suggested that some people might be better judges of *other people's* interests, and even more when it is further suggested that these third-person judges should *act* on their assessment of other people's interests. Clearly, such suggestions raise the spectre of political authoritarianism, if not oppression (see e.g. Benton 1981, 1982). It is partly from fear of this that many writers within the tradition of political liberalism have insisted that people are generally the best judges of their own interests (e.g. Mill 1848, Ch.XI, p.957), and this assumption is, of course, central to democracy.

Nevertheless, even the most trenchant liberals have allowed that persons may sometimes make mistaken judgements about their interests, and especially if they clearly lack the capacity to make reasoned judgements (e.g. young children, people suffering from brain damage, etc.). What this shows is that, even for liberals, there are certain preconditions of being a competent judge of one's interests, and these preconditions are mainly to do with being a rational, 'relatively autonomous' agent (see e.g. Lukes 1974, Ch.5 and 6). And since a person's capacity to be rational and autonomous may be enhanced by being well-informed (both about oneself and the external world), this connects directly with important questions about the preconditions for effective democracy or – in relation to plan-

93

ning – effective public participation. Thus a central reason for ensuring that people in a democracy are well-informed, and that there is free and open discussion, etc., is that it is by these means that people may be brought to make better judgements about their interests and so exercise their democratic rights (such as the opportunity to participate in planning) more intelligently.

(4)   It is not just individuals *as* individuals who possess interests. Groups can also possess interests, or – to put this another way – individuals possess interests as members of groups, and not just as lone, individual selves. Thus, for example, the members of occupational groups (e.g. nurses, teachers, construction workers, etc.), the members of age groups (e.g. children, the elderly, etc.), the members of different client or consumer groups (e.g. the sick, students, etc.), and so on – all these can possess distinct interests *as* nurses, teachers, children and students.

What makes a *group*, as distinct from a random collection of individuals, is that all the individuals in the group bear, and share in common, some distinguishing property (e.g. an occupation, age, etc.); it is this property, indeed, which distinguishes the group from other groups, as well as from random collections of individuals. And what makes a group an *interest group* is that the relevant individuals share an interest in common which is directly associated with the property they bear as members of that group (cf. Graham 1986a, Ch.6, and 1986b). Thus, it is by virtue of her/his occupation as (say) a construction worker that a person possesses certain distinct interests in the conditions of work in the construction industry; it is by virtue of age that the elderly acquire an interest in such things as the level of state pensions and the accessibility of local shops, and so on.

Clearly, in any moderately complex society there will be very many different interest groups, though some of these may be socially more significant (e.g. in terms of their power) than others. And, equally clearly, any individual will be a member of many different interest groups at any one time in their lives, though again – in terms of their overall interests as an individual – their membership of some of these may be more significant than others (e.g. being a member of the unemployed may affect a person's interests more detrimentally than, say, being a member of a football team whose playing field is threatened with housing development).

One way of viewing society, then, is as a 'patchwork' of different interest groups, each with some distinct interests, but where, on occasions, the interests of different groups can overlap and concur, or alternatively come into conflict. And this interplay between the interests of different groups has its counterpart in the life of individuals, in which their various social identities (as imparted by their membership of different groups) can generate inner conflicts (as well as concurrences) of motives and interests.

With this picture in mind, the question arises whether, in relation to some things at least, there are interests which *all* individuals share. Or, to put this in the language I have employed above, the question arises whether there is one interest group of which everybody in the public is a member. It is exactly this suggestion which brings me to the idea of the public interest that I shall develop in the following section.

A COMMON INTEREST CONCEPTION OF THE PUBLIC INTEREST

I shall take it that for something (x) to be in the public interest, x cannot be only, or even primarily, in the interests of some particular group in society. In other words, the public interest – if it exists – cannot be a *sectional* interest. If there are any things in the public interest, then they must be in the interests of *all* groups of society or (to put this another way) in the interests of individuals *regardless* of their membership of particular sectional interest groups. It follows that for something to be in the public interest it must be in the interest of *any* individual or group *taken at random*, or, as I shall henceforth put it, in the interest of 'anyone'.

It is this idea which is captured by Benn (1960, p.134) when he says that: 'The public interest ... is, in the strictest sense, the interest of no one *special*.' It is this idea, too, which is advanced by Benditt (1973, p.301) when he says that: 'something is a public interest if, and only if, it is an interest of anyone who is a member of the public'. Likewise Barry (1965, p.192), when he equates the public interest with the interest of 'non-assignable individuals'. And, if we think of the public as one large interest group, and of individuals as members of the public as a group, then, according to Barry (1965, p.192) again, the public interest is synonymous with 'those interests which people have in common *qua* members of the public'.

If there are interests which any person, taken at random, possesses, then (as Barry says) these are interests which are shared in common by anyone, just as the members of more particular groups share interests in common, and, in fact, Held (1970) calls the view of the public interest described above a 'common interest' conception of the public interest. Further, to be shared in common, the interests in question must be general, not particular to specific individuals, and also not just a summation or aggregate of particular individual interests which are not shared in common (this latter 'individualist' conception of the public interest I shall discuss later). In this respect, the idea of the public interest sketched here is analogous to Rousseau's idea of the 'general will' which he, too, was at pains to distinguish from people's particular private wills or interests, or some sum of these which he called the 'will of all'. As he put it:

> There is ... a great difference between the will of all (what all individuals want) and the general will; the general will studies only the common interest while the will of all studies private interest, and is indeed no more than the sum of individual desires. ... the general will, to be truly what it is, must be general in its purpose as well as its nature; ... it should spring from all and apply to all. (Rousseau 1762, II, pp. 72 and 75)

I raise here two further points by way of clarification of this 'common interest' conception of the public interest.

First, it is important to stress that 'anyone' might not, in practice, be 'everybody'. To be sure, for something (*x*) to be in the interest of anyone in the public (and thereby, on my account, in the public interest), it follows that *x* must be *potentially* in the interest of everybody in the public. However, it does not follow from this that everybody will *in fact* benefit from *x*, or even if they do so, that they will in fact benefit to the same degree (i.e. equally). For example, a public facility such as a national park or a public library may be in the public interest in that it is open to anyone in the public, and so, potentially, everybody in the public may use and benefit from that park or library. But it is a contingent empirical matter whether everybody in the public will use, and therefore benefit from, these facilities, and in fact (of course) it is extremely unlikely that everybody will use the given park or library. Thus some people may not visit a national park because they do not live near it, or because they would prefer to visit another park instead, or because there are other things that they prefer doing anyway.

This fact might be exploited by some to suggest that, after all, these facilities are not in the public interest because not everybody actually benefits from them. But this is not sufficient to weigh against the idea of the public interest, for the point is that anybody, and thus potentially everybody, *could* (in principle) use the facility, and so may benefit from it. If one were to accede to the foregoing anti-public interest argument, then, by the same reasoning, one would have to conclude that there are also no group interests either, for not everybody in a given group will necessarily use and benefit (or use and benefit to the same extent) from a facility provided for members of that group. For example, not every blind person will necessarily use and so benefit from a Braille library, or certain books which are published in Braille, and so, according to the above argument, one would have to conclude that the provision of a Braille library (or the publications of certain books in Braille) is not in the interests of the blind as a group, and that is obviously absurd. And likewise, it is absurd to suppose that one can refute the suggestion that something is in the public interest simply because somebody (even one person) does not use and benefit from it. So, in assessing whether some *x* might be in the public interest it is necessary to assess whether *x* might be in the interest of (i.e. benefit) *potentially* everybody, but not *literally* everybody.

However, something may be *more or less* in some group's interest, and likewise, something may be more or less in the interest of the public conceived as a group (thus we distinguish between what is in a person's or group's interest *simpliciter*, and what is in a person's or group's *best* interest). And the relevant measures here are two: first, how *many* persons in the relevant group may benefit from the policy or action under consideration, and second, to what *degree* those people will benefit from the given policy or action compared with some other policy or action. Thus, whilst the provision of a Braille library in a building at a certain place may be in the interests of blind people as a group, the provision of a *mobile* Braille library may be *more* in the interests of the blind, because it would enable more blind people to gain access to the benefits of reading. Likewise with the public interest: a single town park may be in the interests of the public of that town, but the provision of several comparable parks located evenly throughout the town would be more in that

97

public's interest because they would serve and so benefit more people. It is this, of course, which permits comparisons and choices between different things, all of which may be in the public interest, but not all to the same extent.

This talk of the public of a particular locality, such as a town, brings me to my second point of clarification. In thinking about 'the public' as a group (or, relatedly, who 'the public' is, who is in 'the public', etc.) it can be quite reasonable to define the public more or less widely for different purposes. Thus, if we are assessing a piece of national legislation in terms of the public interest, then the relevant public is anyone in that nation; if we are assessing a plan for a city, then the relevant public would be the inhabitants (and/or the users) of that city; if we are assessing a piece of internationally binding environmental legislation, then the relevant public would be humanity in general; and so on. But note that in any narrower or wider interpretation of 'the public' the same conception of the public interest still applies – namely that, in assessing whether something may or may not be in the public interest, one would assess whether that thing benefits *anyone* in the relevant public.

Already I have, I hope, warded off some criticisms which might be levelled against the conception of the public interest advanced earlier in this section. But even if we adopt this conception in theory, the real critical question does arise: *are* there any things which are in the interests of anyone (i.e. potentially everybody) in the public (or some given public)? For if there are not, then however appealing the foregoing formulation of the *idea* of the public interest may be, it would turn out that there are, after all, no things which are in the public interest in practice. But in fact it is, I submit, relatively easy to think of a number of things which are, in practice, in the public interest, and precisely because these things do benefit anybody in the public indiscriminately.

For example, policies or laws which are designed to protect the safety of anyone in the public indiscriminately are in the public interest as I have described it – for example laws against the assault and abuse of persons; laws and regulations to ensure that certain standards of cleanliness and non-contamination are met in food, water, medicines, etc., sold for public consumption; laws and regulations to protect the safety of the public in transit (e.g. traffic lights and pedestrian crossings, clear road signals, similar measures on or adjacent to railways, airports, etc., safety standards in vehicles – cars, bicycles, aircraft, ships, etc., standards for the licensing of individuals to drive potentially dangerous vehicles such as motor vehicles, trains, aeroplanes, etc.); laws against dangerous structures, including fire precautions in buildings and other enclosed public spaces; laws forbidding or controlling the pollution of air, land and water; and so on. In short, all measures designed for public safety are in the public interest according to the conception outlined earlier.

Another example is provided by laws and procedures to ensure that no one is unjustifiably held in custody, mistreated or punished, and hence, too, laws and regulations pertaining to the grounds for arrest, the right to a fair trial if one is accused of an offence, rights to compensation for any false accusation or punishment which adversely affects one, etc. – in short, all aspects of procedural justice.

The above are examples of what Barry has called 'negative' applications of the public interest in which 'what is said to be "in the public interest" is preventing someone from doing something which will have adverse effects on an indefinite group of people' (Barry 1965, p.208). And Barry himself cites, as another example of this 'negative' application of the public interest, environmental planning controls: '"Negative" planning, which has as its aim the prevention of eyesores such as ... flashing neon lights in the Cotswolds, is a perfect example of action of a negative kind based on "the public interest"' (Barry 1965, p.208). By contrast, a 'positive' application of the public interest occurs where, according to Barry (1965, p.208), 'a facility is actually provided for an indefinite group of people. A local authority, for example, acts positively in the public interest when it provides such things as parks.' Likewise, universal systems of welfare provision, such as public health care and education, are examples of positive applications of the public interest in that they benefit, and so further the interests of, anyone in the public, without discrimination.

Of course, some things can be both positively and negatively in the public interest, in that they can be deliberately provided to benefit the public at large and, at the same time, certain restrictions can be attached to their provision to ensure that the benefits they provide are not destroyed. Here again environmental planning provides vivid examples. Thus the designation and management of national parks provides areas of beautiful open countryside for the enjoyment of anyone in the public, and this positive benefit is simultaneously protected by planning controls against new development which might spoil the parks. Likewise, arguably, the designation and control of development in 'Areas of Outstanding Natural Beauty' (AONBs in the UK); 'Sites of Special Scientific

Interest' (SSSIs); Conservation Areas of historic and/or architectural interest in towns or cities (such as in Venice, Florence, Paris, etc.); and 'green belts', 'urban forests' and all manner of public open spaces provided for the benefit of anyone in the public who wishes to use them.

But now, these last examples from the field of environmental planning might be seized upon by some to re-state a criticism of the whole idea of the public interest which I touched on earlier. For the aforementioned policies (such as Conservation Areas, green belts, etc.) have, when implemented, had the effect of benefiting, or harming, some groups in the public more than others, and – our critic may remind us – something that is in the public interest must not favour or disadvantage some groups more than others – it must not be a sectional interest.

The following might be cited by our critic as an example. In their study of British land-use planning policy between the end of the Second World War and the late 1960s, Peter Hall and his colleagues (Hall et al. 1973, Vol. 2) claimed that policies such as green belts – which were put in place to restrict and 'contain' urban expansion – did, by limiting the supply of land for new housing, contribute to increases in the price of land and property. And this, in turn, favoured existing (and especially wealthier) property-owners whilst simultaneously imposing greater hardship on poorer groups who wished to buy a house of their own, and were either unable to afford to do so or incurred greater costs in doing so (Hall et al. 1973, Ch.12). Similar distributive effects against poorer communities have been claimed in respect of other environmental policies, such as the provision of improvement grants for the renovation of dilapidated housing in inner city areas which has contributed to the 'gentrification' of these areas, or the designation of attractive townscapes – often already inhabited by better-off middle-class people – as urban Conservation Areas. But do such distributive effects necessarily show that these policies are not in the public interest?

Such a conclusion does not necessarily follow. For, from the fact that a policy designed to further the public interest has, when implemented, had effects which benefit some groups more than others, it does not necessarily follow that the policy – or at least the *aim* which the policy is trying to realise – is not in the public interest. For example, the regressive distributive effects of green belt policy, or of Conservation Area policy, does not necessarily show that it is not, in principle, in the public interest (i.e. in the interest of anybody) to have *some* restrictions on urban sprawl, or to protect architecturally attractive or historically interesting townscapes. It is, then, the *aim*, *objective* or *intention* of a policy which must be addressed when assessing the public interest, and which our critic, too, must address in seeking to refute the idea of the public interest. And if our critic does concede that the intention of, say, limiting the size of cities, or of protecting valued areas within cities, is desirable because it is in the interests of people in general, our critic thereby concedes that there are some things which are in the public interest.

To be sure, if some policy which aims to satisfy some general public interest does, when enacted, generate discriminating effects against certain groups, this itself may become a legitimate matter of public concern. But again, this does not show that the public interest which the policy aims at should be abandoned. It may show, instead, that the particular policies chosen to achieve the desired end should be revised, or replaced by other policies which achieve the desired end without discriminating effects, or that the original policies should be backed up with others which offset the former's discriminating effects by, say, compensating those groups who turn out to be disadvantaged by the policies in question. In the case of British planning policy, for example, if (the aim of) controlling urban growth is indeed in the public interest, and yet if restrictive planning policies to achieve this end inevitably have discriminatory effects on particular groups in society, then there is a case for additional policies to, say, control land and property prices (e.g. by 'betterment' or development taxes which tax away land and property price increases attributable to planning policies), to compensate those who are adversely affected by property price increases, or to subsidise that group's housing costs, and so on. Indeed, the principle of compensating people who are adversely affected by public planning (and other) policies is itself another principle which is in the public interest. For there is no way of telling precisely to whom such compensation may be due in the future, so such a principle or policy of compensation applies to anyone in the public, without discrimination.

It must be admitted, however, that practically any policy which serves the public interest will inevitably have *some* differential effects on different groups, and sometimes little or nothing can reasonably be done to compensate those who benefit least from such policies. This is inevitably the case, for example, with spatial policies – that is, policies which involve providing facilities in particular locations, such as public parks, libraries, etc. Here, it will usually be the case that those living nearer to these facilities will benefit from them more than those living further away, simply because they have easier access. It is by virtue of this inevitable discriminatory effect that attempts are made by public authorities to secure as even a distribution of these facilities as possible (even by providing mobile libraries, etc.), but clearly there are practical limits to this, and especially in the case of space-consuming facilities such as parks (this, indeed, may be a key reason why controlling the size and shape of urban areas is in the public interest). Be this as it may, this still does not show that the provision of public parks, or libraries, etc., is not in the public interest. Indeed, if one were to suggest this simply because some people do benefit from easier access to these facilities than others, then – as I pointed out earlier – one would be logically committed to arguing that the provision of a Braille library is not in the interests of the blind simply because some blind people will inevitably live nearer to it than others, or that the provision of cycleways is not in the interests of cyclists because some cyclists will have easier access to them than others. In other words (as, again, I argued earlier), one would be logically committed to the view that there are no *group* interests at all – and that position is clearly untenable.

In this section I have advanced a conception of the public interest and sought to defend it against those who dispute the notion of the public interest altogether. According to this conception, an action or policy would have to satisfy two criteria to be in the public interest. First, in accordance with my definition of the concept of interest, the effects of the given policy or action (e.g. clean air, safe travel, uncontaminated food, safe buildings, recreational open space, etc.) would have to be experienced as beneficial. And second, the effects should be beneficial to *anyone* (and thus potentially everybody), without discrimination; in Barry's (1965, p.192) words, policies and actions which are in the public interest benefit 'non-assignable' individuals, or an 'indefinite group'. If a policy or action meets both these conditions then, on my account, it is in the public interest.

TWO OTHER CONCEPTIONS OF THE PUBLIC INTEREST

The conception of the public interest described in the previous section holds that there are some interests which all persons (and thus 'anyone') share in common, and that it is precisely these common interests which constitute the public interest (hence my description of this – *pace* Held

1970 – as a 'common interest' conception of the public interest). It is important to appreciate that this is not the only conception of the public interest which has been advanced, and in this section I describe, and criticise, two other conceptions which have each had some influence in environmental planning: one, a utilitarian, individualistic conception, and the other a Hegelian, holistic conception.

Utilitarian individualistic conceptions of the public interest

There is a conception which sees the public interest as an aggregation or 'sum' of the interests of all the relevant individuals in the public. The classic exposition of this is given by the utilitarian philosopher Jeremy Bentham when writing of the 'community' interest: 'The interest of the community then is, what? – the sum of the interests of the several members who compose it. It is in vain to talk of the interest of the community, without understanding what is in the interest of the individual' (Bentham 1789, Ch.1, paras 4–5).

If the public (or, for that matter, some other group) interest is the sum of individuals' interests, then there is a sense in which the *public* does not exist as a collective entity distinct from individuals, and likewise there is no public *interest* distinct from the interests of individuals (the public interest is 'merely' the sum of individual interests). As Bentham (1789, para. 4) again put it with regard to the community: 'The community is a fictitious body, composed of ... individual persons', and 'the public interest ... is only an abstract term; it represents nothing but the mass of individual interests' (quoted in Benn 1960, p.131). Clearly, then, this Benthamite conception is an individualistic conception of the public interest. And it is a conception which has been widely influential in public policy-making generally and in environmental planning in particular (see e.g. Allison 1975, Ch.7; Lichfield et al. 1975; Hampshire 1972).

The most widespread application of this conception of the public interest has been in cost-benefit analysis, which has been developed as a 'technique' for identifying whether or not some policy or action is in the public interest, and no better illustration of this can be found than the attempt of the Roskill Commission in the UK to find, by means of cost-benefit analysis, the best site for London's third airport (see Commission on the Third London Airport 1971; and, for brief accounts, Lichfield et al. 1975, Ch.11; Hall 1980, Ch.2). In this, and most cost-benefit exercises, the analysis typically proceeds by first assessing what effects – in terms of benefits and costs (harms) – a given policy (e.g. for an airport) is likely to have on all the individuals who stand to be affected by that policy, and generally some 'weight' (often in terms of cash values) is ascribed to these to indicate the *degrees* of benefit or harm likely to be experienced by the relevant individuals. These weights are then summed in a balance sheet of benefits and harms, and if the result shows a net gain in benefits the policy is deemed to be in the public interest, not otherwise (and clearly, this procedure can be employed, as it was by the Roskill Commission, to evaluate which of a series of alternatives is *most* in the public interest).

There are two aspects of cost-benefit analysis which have attracted considerable attention and controversy: first, how individual benefits and harms are to be identified and weighted (subjectively – by asking the relevant people themselves? or objectively – but then how?); and second, whether it is legitimate to aggregate or *sum* different individuals' benefits and harms to arrive at some *total* of benefit and harm for all individuals taken together (the questionableness of this is compounded if the benefits and harms to be summed are of different *kinds* – as they were when the Roskill Commission tried to add together such harms as the losses of a Saxon church, a wildlife habitat, a person's lifelong home, and the time spent travelling from the airport to London itself). Nevertheless, these problems are by no means peculiar to cost-benefit analysis, for they arise in relation to any attempt to identify and weight benefits and harms to persons (including mixtures of different kinds of benefits and harms which issue from most actions), so these controversies would arise in identifying benefits and harms under my (or any other) conception of the public interest.

But even if we set aside these methodological problems, cost-benefit analysis – and variations on it such as Lichfield's planning balance sheet – may still be questioned as a means of identifying the *public* interest, for two reasons. First, what cost-benefit analysis does is to identify, weight and total *any* interest that an individual has with respect to a policy or action under consideration, so that what results as being in or against the public interest represents a summation of all manner of potentially very particular, personal and *private* interests held by individuals, rather than (as in my conception) those interests which individuals *share in common* as members of the public. And it is questionable whether interests which are particular to just some individuals should count at all – or are at all relevant – in assessing the *public* interest. For example, I may have a

104

particular interest, shared only by *some* other people, in aeroplane spotting, and so think it a positive benefit to live near an international airport. But, precisely because this is not an interest shared by the public at large (by 'anyone'), there is a strong case for discounting this in assessing whether or not an airport is in the public interest. Yet individualistic approaches to identifying the public interest do count such interests because, after all, they regard the public interest as nothing more than the sum of the relevant individuals' interests, whatever these interests happen to be.

A second criticism is that, with the method of cost-benefit analysis described earlier, it is possible to arrive at the conclusion that a policy which is only in some group's (or some people's) interest is, because of the superior weight of benefits which that group will enjoy from the policy, also in the public interest. In other words, something which is only a sectional interest can, because of the weight of that interest, also be described as in the interests of the public as a whole. And this seems wrong for, as we noted earlier, whatever the public interest may be it surely cannot be equated with a particular sectional interest. Suppose, for example, that a proposed policy P (e.g. for an airport at site C) benefits individuals in group A, and harms individuals in group B, but that the benefits to A outweigh the harms to B (because, say, there are more people in A than B). Then, under a utilitarian individualistic conception of the public interest, we would have to conclude that P is in the public interest. But it is surely more accurate to say, simply, that P is *in* the interests of group A, and *against* the interests of group B. To be sure, it may be necessary to make a decision about the policy, and we may – because, say, we support majoritarian democracy – decide in favour of group A. But this is quite separate from saying that P is in the public interest as a whole; indeed, on my account, P would not be a policy that could be said to be in (and so justified in terms of) the public interest, even if it could be justified on other grounds (such as the will of the majority).

Like many environmental planning policies, airports do typically benefit some groups and harm others. But if they *only* do this then, on my account, such policies cannot be described as in the public interest. However, a policy for an international airport *could* be in the public interest if it could be shown to be in the interests of anyone in the public taken at random by, say, being essential for the economic well-being of a nation (and thus a nation's public) as a whole. But this is to employ precisely the conception of the public interest I advanced in the previous section, not an individualistic conception. To be sure, my favoured conception of the public interest does relate the latter to interests which real, live individuals possess, but it does not equate the public interest with *any* interest they have, only with those interests which all individuals share in common. For, to be in the public interest, something must be in the interests of all individuals (or 'anyone') in the public, not just some individuals.

It might be thought that one of the great advantages of utilitarian methods of assessing the public interest (such as cost-benefit analysis) is that they permit a clear comparison of, and thus facilitate choice between, alternative possibilities. But, as I made clear earlier, my common interest conception of the public interest also enables us to compare alternatives in terms of whether they are more, or less, in the public interest by, for example, assessing how many, and to what degree, members of the public may benefit from (or be harmed by) the available alternatives. To be sure, this assessment may involve something akin to utilitarian methods of identifying and weighing benefits and harms. But the difference is that, under my conception, it would only be those benefits and harms (and thus interests) which members of the public share in common which would count in such assessments, rather than, as occurs under strict utilitarianism, any interests which individuals happen to possess. Thus – to return to the airport example – if (and only if) the degree of aircraft noise, or the risk of accidents, the loss of beautiful countryside, the convenience of access to the town served by an airport, etc. – if these are matters which are potentially harmful and/or beneficial to *any* person, and thus interests which are shared in common by anyone, only then would they count in assessing which of various alternatives is most in the public interest. But consequences which are only potentially beneficial or harmful to *certain* individuals, and thus sections of the public (such as aircraft fanatics), would not, on my account, be relevant in assessing the public interest – either in general, or in evaluating specific alternatives.

Hegelian holistic conceptions of the public interest

There is another non-individualistic way of thinking about the public interest which is rooted in Hegelian philosophy, and which identifies the public interest of a particular nation or society with some overall ideal or purpose which, it is claimed, is good for (in the interest of) that society as a whole. Meyerson and Banfield (1955, p.289) have described this model of the public interest as 'unitary', and according to Hall and his colleagues, something like this unitary Hegelian conception of the public interest guided British town and country planning in the years after the Second World War, where:

> decision-takers have an organismic view of the public interest; all other interests are subordinated to that of the social 'organism'. This is opposed to a *utilitarian* view, which would essentially consist of trying to compare and sum up individual pleasures and pains ... Such an approach tends to an extremely lofty yet imprecise definition of the public good in terms of ends with infinite values ... in terms of the absolute virtue of a concrete set of policy measures. (Hall et al. 1973, Vol. 2, pp. 69–70)

As an illustration of this conception of the public interest, Hall et al. cite Lord Reith's view that 'There are few in this country who would increase existing conurbations; there are few in this country who would not feel that the suburban sprawl of the past hundred years is deplorable from every point of view' (Hall et al. 1973, p.70). It was from this sweeping judgement that Lord Reith held that the planning of free-standing new towns was in the public interest.

Another version of this unitary conception of the public interest which derives directly from Hegelian philosophy is that which equates the public interest with the 'essence', character, or 'spirit' of a particular nation or society. This character or spirit of a nation may not be viewed as fixed for all time; rather, it is often seen as evolving and developing in certain directions, often under the guidance of some assumed laws of social development which govern a nation's history. Beliefs of this kind have been described by Popper (1957) as 'historicist'.

In everyday parlance we meet this historicist conception of the public interest when people say 'you can't stop progress', and thereby imply that, firstly, whatever is 'progressive' in a given society is readily identifiable, and secondly, since one can't stop or avoid this progress, it is in the general public interest of that society to accept and accommodate itself to it or, even better, put itself at the forefront of such progressive social development.

We hear this view of what is in the public's interest bandied about every day in the rhetoric of politicians to justify, for example, the UK's joining –

or playing a more 'positive' role in – the European Community; the need to 'bring things up to date' to fit in with the 'dynamic competitive world within which we live', and so on. But, in relation to environmental planning, this historicist view of the public interest was most vividly expressed in justifications of modern architecture, as Watkin (1977) has made clear. Thus the protagonists of modern architecture – such as Walter Gropius, Mies van der Rohe and Le Corbusier – typically justified plain, geometrical, 'functional' architecture, using modern industrial materials, as the only 'true' or 'genuine' architecture for our age, as the only architecture which accorded with and expressed the 'spirit' of the modern age, and which, accordingly, it was in the general public interest to adopt. As Watkin (1977, pp. 1–6) observes, modern architecture was put forward as 'not just a style but a rational way of building evolved inevitably in response to the needs of what society really is or ought to be', as an '"expression" of the "collective unconscious"', and which, therefore, has 'an authority and an inevitability which it would be improper to question'.

As we now know, this kind of justification of modern architecture was widely influential in the planning and design of huge areas of towns and cities throughout Europe and North America in the years following the Second World War. And as we also now know, the kind of development that resulted, especially in high-rise housing estates, has been almost uniformly disastrous, and thus *anything but* in the public interest. And this, in turn, should make us wary of this whole conception of the public interest. Two points, in particular, weigh forcibly against it.

First, if the weakness of individualistic accounts of the public interest is that they put too much emphasis on individuals by counting as relevant *any* interest an individual possesses with respect to a given policy or action, the weakness of Hegelian conceptions is that they go to the opposite extreme and advance views of what is in the public interest whose relationship to the interests of real live individuals in the public is often quite unclear; these conceptions are, as it were, too 'holistic'. Thus what has often been proposed as being in the public interest is not generally (as it would have to be under my conception) tested against the interests of any individual taken at random in a given public; for example, the benefits of building modern high-rise housing estates, or (for that matter) new towns, were not so tested. Which brings me to the second criticism. The examples of the public interest touched on in this section often represented the views, and values, of only particular groups or individuals in a society, so they were not shared by everybody (or 'anyone') in the public. This was especially so

with respect to the policy of comprehensive redevelopment and the building of high-rise housing estates in post-war Europe and the USA, where,
from the earliest days when these planning ideas were mooted, there were
many (including many of those who were to be rehoused in these estates)
who objected that this policy was *against* their interest (see e.g. Dennis
1970). What we find too often with this conception of the public interest is
that what is proposed as being in the public interest is nothing other than a
partial view of what is good for a society or nation, often held by (and
often, because of their power, imposed by) a particular elite group in that
society, and, moreover, this view is typically not tested against the interests
of anyone in the society (as it would have to be to qualify under my
common interest conception of the public interest).

CONCLUSION: PLANNING, VALUES AND THE PUBLIC INTEREST

I began this essay by describing the views of those who hold that society
is typically composed – and *only* composed – of different interest groups,
who, from this, have drawn the conclusion that there can be no over-
arching general or public interest in society. This argument leads to the
view that public planning authorities can only, at best, seek to mediate
between the interests of different groups and, further, that this is all that
planning authorities *ought* to be trying to do (see e.g. Reade 1987, Ch.6;
Kitchen 1991).

Two questions arise from this: first, what interests do, as a matter of
fact, reside 'out there' in society? And second, what interests (if any)
should environmental planning seek to promote?

Concerning the first of these questions, I must stress that I do not
dispute that in any society imaginable – and certainly in contemporary
industrialised societies – there are different interest groups with different,
and sometimes conflicting, interests. It has been no part of the analysis of
this essay to dispute that proposition. What I hope I have shown is that,
notwithstanding this, there can be *some* things (some policies, actions,
states of affairs, etc.) over which *any* group, and thus any person taken at
random, shares interests in common. Thus, whilst two (or more) groups
may have conflicting interests over some things, they may at the same
time share interests in common over some other things; indeed, they may
share an interest in finding some resolution (some compromise) of the

very issues over which they come into conflict. It is precisely these interests shared in common by any group or person which, I submit, constitute the public interest. And, in case anyone still doubts that there can be such public interests, I need only remind them of some of the environmental problems facing all our societies at present, for it is not in anybody's interest to inhabit a world with a depleted (or, still worse, non-existent) ozone layer, or to breathe poisoned air, eat contaminated food, and so on.

As to the second question noted above, concerning which interests planning *ought* to promote, it does not necessarily follow that planning ought always to promote only – or even always primarily – those things which are in the public interest. As I stressed in point 2 on page 92, when discussing the concept of interest in general, interest judgements are, in themselves, non-moral judgements about what benefits or harms some-one or some group, and from the fact that something benefits somebody (e.g. acquiring stolen goods) it does not follow that we should, morally, supply that thing to the person in question. The same applies to things which are in the public interest. Thus, there may be occasions where some action might be in the public interest but where, because (say) of limited resources, we think it morally right (or think it a greater moral priority) to do something instead which promotes the interests of a par-ticular group – say, a group which is especially disadvantaged, such as the mentally or physically handicapped, or the unemployed, or refugees in flight from war or tyranny. As Benditt (1973, p.300) has written:

> not even the fact that a policy x is in the best interest of the public is conclusive on the question of whether or not x should be adopted. The public interest is just one consideration among many that go into deciding what to do. Considerations such as fairness, equality, and others compete with considerations of the public interest in determin-ing what to do.

In environmental planning as elsewhere, then, questions of the public interest do not exhaust questions of what ought, morally, to be done, or (therefore) of whose interests ought, morally, to be promoted. There may therefore be occasions when we think we ought to promote a sectional interest over the public interest – such as, for example, providing a park for the blind, ensuring that built environments are accessible to the physi-cally handicapped, providing sites for Gypsies, etc. (see e.g. Bennett

1990). It is here, then, that questions of moral values come face to face with questions of interest – including the public interest.

The foregoing considerations might seem to present a problem for *professional* ethics (in environmental planning or in other professions), for (as I noted at the very beginning of this essay) it would seem to be a central part of the ethics of professions to support the public interest over and above any particular sectional interest; indeed, if a profession were to be seen to be deliberately serving some 'narrow' sectional interest this would typically also be seen as impugning its 'professionalism' (or its ethical credibility as a 'profession'). This *may* be a problem for professional ethics, but it need not necessarily be a problem where, for example, the sectional interest which is occasionally favoured over the general public interest is that of a disadvantaged individual or group.

Consider, for example, medical treatment. It is part of any medical practitioners' professional ethics to provide health care for anyone in the public, without discrimination, and in this they are serving the public interest as I have described it. However, in pursuance of this goal, in a world where there are limited resources, and thus where hard decisions have to be made between different kinds of medical treatment for different clients, there is a strong argument to the effect that medics should attend to the most needy first (hence the priority given to 'emergencies' in hospitals), and the most needy will typically be those who are most disadvantaged with respect to health.

The same might be said in relation to town planning, concerning those sections of society who are particularly disadvantaged with respect to their environmental conditions. Indeed, in the UK the town planning movement in the nineteenth century was fuelled by a simultaneous concern for the health of the public in general and the appalling living conditions of the poor in particular, and many town planners have seen no incompatibility between these two commitments.

It is possible, then, to construct an argument comparable to that employed by Rawls (1972) with respect to social justice which would square a commitment to the public interest with a simultaneous commitment to the needs of the most disadvantaged in society.

But even if, on occasions, there is some moral tension between a commitment to the public interest and a commitment to the interests of a particular needy group, in general the fact that some policy or action would benefit anybody (and thus potentially everybody) in the public can constitute a compelling moral reason for implementing that policy or action. And this is especially so if the benefits of enacting the policy (or the harms of not doing so) have a *significant* bearing on anybody's interests. Here, to conclude, I shall mention two such matters which are surely publicly significant, and which, therefore, should engage the attention of all those concerned with planning and managing the physical environment.

The first of these are those environmental issues (such as ozone depletion, global warming, and pollution and resource depletion generally) which, if not addressed, threaten the very survival – and certainly the healthy survival – of anybody on the planet. Planning for what is now called 'sustainability' is certainly in the public interest, and it is such a fundamental interest – which we all share – that the moral case for planning, and planning urgently, to realise this goal is surely incontestable (see here: Underwood 1991).

Second, there is the issue of what has come to be called the 'public realm' – that is, those spaces (such as streets and squares, plazas and parks, etc.) which are open to anybody in the public and which, therefore, it is in anybody's (and therefore the public) interest to maintain and enhance. In most contemporary Western societies a number of forces have contributed to a general deterioration in the quality of public spaces, for example, the pollution, noise, danger, and visual intrusion of motor vehicles; social disintegration and rising crime rates; cuts in public spending to enhance, maintain and police public spaces, etc. (see e.g. Punter 1990). Yet we all, at some time or another, need to use public spaces, so we all have an interest in them being as safe, congenial, even as beautiful as possible. Here, then, is another great task facing environmental planning which it is in the public interest to address.[1]

NOTES

1   I am grateful to Huw Thomas for his very perceptive comments on an earlier draft of this essay.

REFERENCES

Alexander, P. and Gill, R. (eds), 1984, *Utopias*, London: Duckworth.
Allison, L., 1975, *Environmental Planning: A Political and Philosophical Analysis*, London: Allen and Unwin.

Ambrose, P., 1986, *Whatever Happened to Planning?*, London: Methuen.

Barry, B., 1965, *Political Argument*, 1st edn, London: Routledge and Kegan Paul; 2nd edn, 1990, Hemel Hempstead: Harvester/Wheatsheaf.

Benditt, T., 1973, 'The Public Interest', *Philosophy and Public Affairs*, Vol. 2, pp. 291–311.

Benn, S. I., 1960, '"Interests" in Politics', *Proceedings of the Aristotelian Society*, Vol. 60, pp. 123–40.

Bennett, T., 1990, 'Planning and People with Disabilities', in Montgomery, J. and Thornley, A. (eds), *Radical Planning Initiatives*, 1990, Aldershot: Gower, pp. 259–69.

Bentham, J., 1789, *An Introduction to the Principles of Morals and Legislation*, in Bowring, J. (ed.), 1843, *The Works of Jeremy Bentham*, Vol. 1, Edinburgh: William Tait.

Bentley, A. F., 1908, *The Process of Government* (1967 edition, Odegard, P. H. (ed.)), Cambridge, MA: Harvard University Press.

Benton, T., 1981, '"Objective" Interests and the Sociology of Power', *Sociology*, Vol. 15, pp. 161–84.

Benton, T., 1982, 'Realism, Power and Objective Interests', in Graham, K. (ed.), *Contemporary Political Philosophy*, Cambridge: Cambridge University Press, pp. 7–33.

Bowring, J. (ed.), 1843, *The Works of Jeremy Bentham*, Edinburgh: William Tait.

Commission on the Third London Airport, 1971, *Report*, London: HMSO (the Roskill Report).

Connolly, W. E., 1974, *The Terms of Political Discourse* (2nd edn) , Oxford: Martin Robertson.

Dennis, N., 1970, *People and Planning: The Sociology of Housing in Sunderland*, London: Faber and Faber.

Friedmann, J., 1973, 'The Public Interest and Community Participation: Toward a Reconstruction of Public Philosophy', *Journal of the American Institute of Planners*, Vol. 39, pp. 2–7.

Friedrich, C. J. (ed.), 1962, *The Public Interest*, New York, NY: Atherton Press.

Gallie, W. B., 1956, 'Essentially Contested Concepts', *Proceedings of the Aristotelian Society*, Vol. 56, pp. 167–98.

Graham, K. (ed.), 1982, *Contemporary Political Philosophy*, Cambridge: Cambridge University Press.

Graham, K., 1984, 'Consensus in Social Decision-Making: Why is it Utopian?', in Alexander, P. and Gill, R. (eds), *Utopias*, London: Duckworth, pp. 49–60.

Graham, K., 1986a, *The Battle of Democracy: Conflict, Consensus and the Individual*, Brighton: Wheatsheaf.

Graham, K., 1986b, 'Morality and Abstract Individualism', *Proceedings of the Aristotelian Society*, Vol. 87, pp. 21–33.

Griffin, J., 1986, *Well-being: Its Meaning, Measurement and Moral Importance*, Oxford: Clarendon Press.

Hall, P., 1980, *Great Planning Disasters*, Harmondsworth: Penguin.

Hall, P., Gracey, H., Drewett, R. and Thomas, R., 1973, *The Containment of Urban England*, London: Allen and Unwin.

Hampshire, S., 1972, 'Morality and Pessimism', in Hampshire, S. (ed.), 1978, *Public and Private Morality*, Cambridge: Cambridge University Press.

Harrison, B., 1989, 'Morality and Interest', *Philosophy*, Vol. 64, July, pp. 302–22.

Healey, P., McNamara, P., Elson, M. and Doak, A., 1988, *Land Use Planning and the Mediation of Urban Change*, Cambridge: Cambridge University Press.

Held, V., 1970, *The Public Interest and Individual Interests*, New York, NY: Basic Books.

Kitchen, T., 1991, 'A Client-based View of the Planning Service', in Thomas, H. and Healey, P. (eds), *Dilemmas of Planning Practice*, Aldershot: Avebury Technical, pp. 115–42.

Klosterman, R. E., 1980, 'A Public Interest Criterion', *Journal of the American Planning Association*, Vol. 46, pp. 323–33.

Lichfield, N., Kettle, P. and Whitbread, M., 1975, *Evaluation in the Planning Process*, Oxford: Pergamon.

Lukes, S., 1974, *Power: A Radical View*, London: Macmillan.

Meyerson, M. and Banfield, E. C., 1955, *Politics, Planning and the Public Interest: The Case of Public Housing in Chicago*, Glencoe, Ill.: The Free Press.

Mill, J. S., 1848, *Principles of Political Economy*, (1976 edn), Fairfield, NJ: Augustus Kelly.

Montgomery, J. and Thornley, A. (eds), 1990, *Radical Planning Initiatives*, Aldershot: Gower.

Parfit, D., 1984, *Reasons and Persons*, Oxford: Oxford University Press.

Popper, K. R., 1957, *The Poverty of Historicism*, London: Routledge and Kegan Paul.

Punter, J. V., 1990, 'The Privatisation of the Public Realm', *Planning Practice and Research*, Vol. 5(3), pp. 9–16.

Rawls, J., 1972, *A Theory of Justice*, Oxford: Oxford University Press.

Reade, E., 1987, *British Town and Country Planning*, Milton Keynes: Open University Press.

Rousseau, J. J., 1762, *The Social Contract* (1968 edn, translated by Maurice Cranston), Harmondsworth: Penguin.

RTPI (Royal Town Planning Institute), 1991, 'Code of Professional Conduct', *The Planner*, 1 March.

Rydin, Y., 1986, *Housing Land Policy*, Aldershot: Gower.

Schubert, G., 1962, 'Is there a Public Interest Theory?', in Friedrich, C. J. (ed.), *The Public Interest*, New York, NY: Atherton Press, pp. 162–76.

Simmie, J., 1974, *Citizens in Conflict: The Sociology of Town Planning*, London: Hutchinson.

Sorauf, F. J., 1962, 'The Conceptual Muddle', in Friedrich, C. J. (ed.), *The Public Interest*, New York, NY: Atherton Press, pp. 183–90.

Strawson, P. F., 1961, 'Social Morality and Individual Ideal', *Philosophy*, Vol. 36, pp. 1–17.

Truman, D. B., 1951, *The Governmental Process*, New York, NY: Knopf.

Underwood, J., 1991, 'What is really Material? Rising above Interest Group Politics', in Thomas, H. and Healey, P. (eds), *Dilemmas of Planning Practice*, Aldershot: Avebury Technical, pp. 147–55.

Watkin, D., 1977, *Morality and Architecture*, Oxford: Clarendon Press.

Chapter 6

Planning and justice

Nicholas Low

INTRODUCTION

Why should planners concern themselves with justice? Although the subject is today unfashionable, it is not hard to find in the literature of planning a thread of concern for justice – being fair to people who seem to have suffered hardship through no fault of their own; putting right the unfair consequences of market transactions; a concern with the poor, old people, disabled people, aborigines, black people, migrants, young children and, in so far as they are discriminated against by market society, women (Mazziotti 1974; Gans 1975; Davidoff 1965, 1975; Donnison & Soto 1980; Katznelson 1981; Forester 1982a, 1982b; Best & Bowser 1986; Friedmann 1987; Krumholz & Forester 1990; Low 1991). Social justice is one of a number of values to which good planning aspires.

Here, however, I shall not look at justice from the point of view of planning, but planning from the point of view of justice. An ethical conception of the planning task is necessary, as Krumholz and Forester (1990, p.233) point out, not to provide ready solutions but to enable the planner to take part in political practice, to 'argue about what to do ... to think about, evaluate, and judge alternative courses of action'. I shall argue for a conception of justice which demands that planners work actively to achieve a better deal for the poor and vulnerable than the market provides. I believe that planners have an obligation to take part in political practice because that is how the cause of justice is served. In short, I propose that planning for justice ('equity planning') should not be regarded as an *optional* but a *necessary* position for planning.[1]

I want to focus the discussion further by posing the question: on grounds of justice, should land-use planners seek to improve the life chances and living standards of the poor? This is, of course, by no means the only question of interest to planners which involves considerations of justice (see Miller 1992). Justice among generations (Barry 1977, 1978), justice among nations (Beitz 1979; Barry 1989b), justice to women (Okin 1989), justice to the environment (Stretton 1976; Goodin 1991, 1992) and justice to animals (Feinberg 1974; Singer & Regan 1976) are all important matters. Consideration of each reveals core questions of justice from a different angle. The angle I shall take here is that of justice within one human generation (of men and women) and within one nation. I do so with the political aim of keeping the question of poverty alive. The question really has two parts:

(1)   On grounds of justice, should there be action by the state to improve the life chances of the poor?
(2)   What role, if any, can land-use planning play in such action?

In the bulk of this essay I explore two opposing philosophies of justice which yield different answers – those of Rawls and of Nozick.[2] I shall discuss the implications for planning of the two theories. I then want to consider the direction of more recent thought on the subject, and I shall try to show why Rawls is to be preferred to Nozick.[3] Needless to say, a great deal has been written since Rawls and Nozick produced their seminal works but, in order to explore the foundations of the debates in sufficient depth, the discussion of subsequent work will have to be curtailed.

Two further introductory points should be made. First, I shall assume that capitalism with all its faults is the best available existing economic system, and that the primary political task is to improve its operation. In order to improve it we may have to transform it, but 'capitalism today' must be the starting point. Second, I shall be dealing here with what is usually termed 'social justice' or 'distributive justice' as opposed to 'legal justice':

Social justice … concerns the distribution of benefits and burdens throughout a society, as it results from the major social institutions – property systems, public organizations, etc. It deals with such matters as the regulation of wages and (where they exist) profits, the protection of persons' rights through the legal system, the allocation of housing, medicine, welfare benefits etc. (Miller 1976, p.22)

'Social justice' does not embody principles which are fundamentally different from legal justice, though the links between the two need to be further clarified (see Campbell 1988). All legitimate institutions – whether they are legal, economic or something else – refer back to principles of justice.

PLURALISM, MONISM, PHILOSOPHY AND POLITICS

David Miller (1976, p.24) explains that commentators on justice fall into two camps:

> those who believe that there is a single concept of justice – i.e. that the same criterion is always used when the concept is applied – and those who believe that there are several concepts, each encapsulating a different way of distinguishing between just and unjust states of affairs.

Miller himself believes that there are three concepts of justice which can be summarised in the three principles: 'to each according to his rights', 'to each according to his deserts', and 'to each according to his needs' (Miller 1976, p.27).[4]

Planning to meet needs and planning to preserve rights will be familiar ideas to most planners. For example, plans are made to ensure that the necessary physical and social infrastructure is provided in the right place at the right time. A great deal of 'town planning' is also about arbitrating between conflicting property rights, and apportioning the costs that neighbouring land uses impose on one another and on the wider community. Planning to meet needs routinely conflicts with property rights – as when the location of a hostel for homeless youths is the subject of protest by local homeowners on the grounds that property values in the area will fall. Numerous examples exist in the literature of planning. But 'planning for desert' is another matter. Planning to give people what they deserve has two features with which one feels uncomfortable. The idea appears to arrogate to planners (or their political superiors) the judgement about what people deserve, and it has the added implication that people should

118

not get *more* than they deserve. Yet, before we dismiss 'desert' as a criterion of use in planning, we should perhaps ask whether, in many cases, planning for need is, in fact, planning for desert in disguise. In practice, planners frequently have to make judgements about what counts as 'need'. From the point of view of the recipients of services this might seem little different from a judgement about what they deserve. Moreover, in times of economic stringency, the deployment of public resources so that certain people do not get more than they deserve makes a certain amount of sense. It is not that a judgement about 'who deserves what' is so very repugnant, but that it is difficult, or perhaps impossible, to agree on an appropriate judge or procedure for judging. Perhaps an open recognition that planners make desert-based judgements would at least bring such judgements more clearly into the political arena where they can be debated. The issue, however, requires fuller treatment than I can give it in this essay, and I shall not take it further.

The concepts of need, rights and desert are, in Miller's (1976) view, irreconcilable as principles of justice. Although each may be true in its own way, each does not encompass or dispose of the others. There is nothing more than a plurality of true definitions of justice. Such also seems to be the conclusion of Campbell (1988, p.3), who says that the belief that there is a 'true' meaning of justice is 'naive'. Herein lies a problem (I shall refer to it later as 'the problem of pluralism') whose implications I am also unable to pursue for reasons of space, but which seems to me very important. A course of planned action may be based on a conception of justice. If there are several *true* but *incompatible* conceptions of justice, and the truth of each of these incompatible conceptions is recognised by the planner, what guide can the philosophy of 'justice' provide to the choice of conception? Is the matter to be decided by subjective preference alone, by mere ideology, by the material interest of the planner, or by throw of the dice? Or is there some higher criterion on which we can base the choice between incompatible conceptions? If there *is* a higher criterion, might not such a criterion – which, say, provides a way of giving weight to different principles of justice, or a means of choosing between them – itself *be* a principle of justice? If this is the case, and we are able to specify such a principle, then we would have moved beyond a pure pluralist approach to the problem, or so I would argue. Such a principle would, I think, refer to a 'just politics'. John Rawls seeks such a principle in his conception of the social contract; arguably Nozick does the same with a principle of individual free-

119

dom from social coercion. Neither seems an entirely satisfactory way of specifying a 'just politics'.[5]

RAWLS AND NOZICK

The liberal thought of the Enlightenment is built on the assumption that each person must be regarded as of equal intrinsic value. People are ends in themselves. This is axiomatic: a principle of 'self-ownership' and equal citizenship. It is inequality in actual societies which has to be explained.

Rawls, from a contractarian perspective, wants to show that actual people – with normal knowledge of one another and of their society, reasonably equal in their endowments, without envy but with a desire for co-operation (that is, in 'circumstances of justice') – would elect to decide upon principles of justice on the basis of those which would be selected by people in the 'original position'. In this 'original position' we are asked to suppose that the group of people devising the contract has yet to be born into a particular position in a particular society at a particular time. They exist, therefore, under a 'veil of ignorance'. Each person has an even chance of finding himself or herself in the position of being most or least well-off, or anywhere in between. Barry argues that the purpose of this device is to ensure impartiality: 'He [Rawls] objected to bargaining power playing any role in determining the adjudicated outcome. And it is precisely in order to achieve this elimination of power relations that the original position is introduced' (Barry 1989a, p.183). Rawls takes the view that individuals cannot be said to 'deserve' their place in society or the 'assets' with which they come into the world: abilities, traits and talents. This is entailed by the presumption of intrinsic equality. Further, if people do not deserve their 'natural assets', then no more do they deserve the advantages that those assets make possible – wealth, status and so forth. So Rawls's theory is opposed to the concept of 'desert' as a principle of justice. Sher (1987, pp. 22–36), however, attempts to refute Rawls on this point. I accept Taylor's view that not only are 'talents' to a large degree socially created (through education, parentage and the like) but so also is the context in which the skilful application of talents becomes useful to society: 'Someone with great mathematical gifts is much in demand in an age of computers, not at all perhaps in prescientific society!' (Taylor 1986, p.58).

Rawls elaborates his theory through a process of seeking what he calls 'reflective equilibrium'. Such equilibrium is reached when our intuitive judgements about what is just coincide with the principles which we put into words and sentences to express such judgement. There is a process of writing something down, then reflectively working out its implications, then modifying what is written down and so on, until an answer with which one feels satisfied is reached. To remind readers of Rawls's final position it is worth setting it out in his own words:

1. Each person is to have an equal right to the most extensive total system of equal basic liberties compatible with a similar system of liberty for all.
2. Social and economic inequalities are to be arranged so that they are both:

   a) to the greatest benefit of the least advantaged, consistent with the just savings principle, and
   b) attached to offices and positions open to all under conditions of fair equality of opportunity.

First priority rule (the priority of liberty)

The principles of justice are to be ranked in lexical order and therefore liberty can be restricted only for the sake of liberty. There are two cases:

a) a less extensive liberty must strengthen the total system of liberty shared by all;
b) a less than equal liberty must be acceptable to those with the lesser liberty.

Second priority rule (the priority of justice over efficiency and welfare)

The second principle of justice is lexically prior to the principle of efficiency and to that of maximizing the sum of advantages; and fair opportunity is prior to the difference principle. There are two cases:

a) an inequality of opportunity must enhance the opportunities of those with lesser opportunity;
b) an excessive rate of saving must on balance mitigate the burden of those bearing this hardship.

General conception

All social primary goods – liberty and opportunity, income and wealth, and the bases of self-respect – are to be distributed equally unless an unequal distribution of any or all of these goods is to the advantage of the least favoured. (Rawls 1972, pp. 302–3)

The core of Rawls's position is the 'difference principle' (2a above). In a condition where the participants to the contract cannot predict where they will end up, they will want to protect themselves should they end up at the bottom. Projecting themselves into the position of the least advantaged, they will agree to others being in a better position only as long as an improvement in the position of others also leads to an improvement in their own position. Rawls (1972, p.78) illustrates the point in the following terms:

Those starting out as members of the entrepreneurial class in property-owning democracy, say, have a better prospect than those who begin in the class of unskilled labourers. It seems likely that this will be true even when the social injustices which now exist are removed. What, then, can possibly justify this kind of initial inequality in life prospects? According to the difference principle, it is justifiable only if the difference in expectation is to the advantage of the representative man who is worse off, in this case the representative unskilled worker. The inequality in expectation is permissible only if lowering it would make the working class even more worse off.

It is important to stress that the difference principle is severely constrained by the priority of liberty and freedom of thought and choice on the one hand, and by the principle of fair opportunity on the other. The one guarantees free markets, and the other fair organisations and 'procedural justice'.[6] Inter-generational justice is guaranteed, Rawls thought, by the 'just savings principle' (a point disputed by Barry, 1978). Rawls combines the just savings principle with the difference principle by arguing that it is representatives from the least advantaged in any generation who are to decide on the rate of accumulation. It is also important to note that Rawls is only talking about the accumulation required to attain a *just* society. Accumulation for other purposes is permissible, but irrelevant to the argument. However, Rawls (1972, p.290) expresses quite a strong view of the accumulation of wealth for its own sake:

What men want is meaningful work in free association with others, these associations regulating their relations to one another within a framework of just basic institutions. To achieve this state of things great wealth is not required. In fact, beyond some point it is more likely to be a positive hindrance, a meaningless distraction at best if not a temptation to indulgence and emptiness.

Let us turn now to a different view about wealth. To use his own expression, though out of context, Nozick 'backs into' a theory of justice in the course of his critique of the welfare state. He is principally concerned to make the case for the minimal state and against the view that poverty is unjust. Nozick writes:

In a free society, diverse persons control different resources, and new holdings arise out of the voluntary exchanges and actions of persons. There is no more a distributing or distribution of shares than there is a distributing of mates in a society in which persons choose whom they will marry. The total result is the product of many individual decisions which the different individuals are entitled to make. (Nozick 1974, pp. 149–50)

Nozick calls his view of justice 'the entitlement theory'. His theory contains the following principles:

(1)   A person who acquires a holding in accordance with the principle of justice in acquisition is entitled to that holding.
(2)   A person who acquires a holding in accordance with the principle of justice in transfer, from someone else entitled to the holding, is entitled to the holding.
(3)   No one is entitled to a holding except by (repeated) applications of 1 and 2. (Nozick 1974, p.151)

Nozick elaborates Hayek's (1944) point that to attempt to arrange society in accordance with a pattern interferes with the liberty of individuals to arrange their lives according to their own preferred patterns. Liberty, Nozick says, upsets patterns. Those who seek to redistribute resources by, say, taxation undermine each person's liberty to spend their own resources on themselves or others. Inequality, and thus riches and poverty, arises from people being free to choose to whom they transfer the resources they have legitimately acquired either by production or exchange. People are entitled *only* to what they produce or acquire through a contract of exchange, and they are entitled to dispose of their property as they wish. This is the principle of entitlement which underwrites both justice in acquisition and justice in transfer. Nozick (1974, p.160) states the principle thus: 'From each as they choose, to each as they are chosen.'

However, that is not the end of the matter, for the justice of a series of transfers depends on how private property came into existence in the first place. Nozick repeatedly states that his theory is a *historical* theory. And it has to be, because the history of the ownership of property is always relevant to the justice of a particular transfer. If his theory were to depend only on justice in transfer he would have to ignore the possibility that property was acquired by the unjust use of force or deception at some time in the past (theft, for example). He could, of course, argue for some 'statute of limitations' such that unjust acquisition several generations back can legitimately be ignored. And, in fact, he comes close to this position when he says: 'Things come into the world already attached to people having entitlements over them' (Nozick 1974, p.160). But he does not pursue this line, because to do so would fatally weaken his case for the absolute *justice* of the *existing* distribution of property and thus for the minimal state.

'The crucial point', Nozick (1974, p.175) writes, 'is whether appropriation of an unowned object worsens the situation of others.' Nozick enters into a discussion of the proviso made by Locke (1690) on appropriation – namely, that any original private appropriation (presumably made by people in a state of nature) should leave 'enough and as good for others'. Nozick then arrives at a refined definition of his position: 'A process normally giving rise to a permanent bequeathable property right in a previously unowned thing will not do so if the position of others no longer at liberty to use the thing is thereby worsened' (1974, p.178). Despite his failure to discuss the actual history of property in capitalist societies, it is clear that he believes that – with the exception of criminal acquisition, which can be rectified by the criminal justice system – the existing distribution of property stems from a process which meets the above condition. The condition, however, as we shall see, is faulty.

Comparing the two theories, we can see that Rawls's theory, and in particular the difference principle, leads to a positive answer to the first question posed in the introduction. The state *should* intervene to guarantee employment and equal opportunity to all by, for example, providing for education, health and housing, and by regulating markets to produce outcomes in accordance with the difference principle (see Rawls 1972, pp. 274–83). Although 'need' is not the foundation of Rawls's theory, in practice governments would have to base their interventions on needs-related criteria. Nozick's theory is, of course, founded on the principle 'each according to his rights'. In Nozick's view, no action by the state is permissible other than action to protect property rights. All taxation, for example, is 'on a par with forced labour' (Nozick 1974, p.169). Nozick (1974, p.209) insists that Rawls's difference principle is 'an especially strong kind of patterned end-state principle'. This, it seems to me, cannot be denied but, in Rawls's defence, it must be noted again that Rawls gives precedence to procedural justice over the difference principle. Moreover, Rawls does not seem to want to stake all on linear logic. The aim is rather to arrive at an *institutional* structure which embodies a mixture of intuitively correct principles (see Rawls 1972, p.89).

Herein lies a key difference between Rawls's and Nozick's perceptions of how society is constituted. Nozick (1974, p.186) agrees that people co-operate in making things, but, he says, they work separately; each person is a miniature firm. Likewise, one might add, each firm is a macro-individual. Rawls (1972, p.84), by contrast, says:

> Society is interpreted as a cooperative venture for mutual advantage. The basic structure is *a public system of rules* defining a scheme of activities that leads men to act together so as to produce a greater sum of benefits and assigns to each certain recognized claims to a share in the proceeds. What a person does depends on what the public rules say he is entitled to, and what a person is entitled to depends on what he does. [my emphasis]

Rawls views society as a set of institutions, Nozick as an aggregate of individuals.

IMPLICATIONS FOR PLANNING

Plainly these two views of the constitution of justice have widely differing implications for land-use planning. But they do converge on one point. In neither case is a concept of planning acceptable in which a physical plan is drawn up and implemented by professionals regardless

125

of the preferences of citizens expressed through markets and political processes. Markets and politics are not inconveniences in the way of good planning: in a democratic society they are a condition of good planning (see also Lindblom's brilliant analysis, 1977). Note, however, that this is no argument against planners and designers drawing up imaginative proposals for the future of cities – indeed, the more the better, since they increase the choices available (see Davidoff & Reiner 1962).

Where the two conceptions of justice diverge is in what they have to say about the purposes for which the state may intervene in land markets. If Rawls's theory is accepted, land-use planning can be seen as part of the fabric of institutions designed to uphold the principles of justice, including, of course, the difference principle. Rawls (1972, pp. 27–83) identifies four legitimate functions of government: allocation, stabilisation, transfer, and distribution. Under the 'allocation' function, state intervention prevents the formation of unreasonable market power and corrects departures from efficiency caused by the failure of the price system to take account of social costs and benefits. Under 'stabilisation', the state strives to bring about reasonably full employment such that those who want work can find it, and 'the free choice of occupation and the deployment of finance is supported by strong effective demand' (Rawls 1972, p.276). The purpose of the 'transfer' function is to provide for a 'social minimum' (i.e. income or wealth) to enable all competent people to participate in markets. Under the 'distribution' function, the state raises taxes in order 'gradually and continually to correct the distribution of wealth and to prevent concentrations of power detrimental to the fair value of political liberty and fair equality of opportunity' (Rawls 1972, p.277).

Rawls's theory leads to the conclusion that the role of land-use planning is to ensure the fairness of land markets in accordance with the ordered principles of liberty (freedom of choice), equality of opportunity, and the difference principle. The target for action is not the land, nor even the people who occupy it, but the *institution of the market* as it manifests itself in particular places and at particular times. Planners must facilitate balanced investment in the urban environment to supply needs and to ensure work. They must try to stabilise markets so that violent booms and busts do not occur, leading to wasteful oversupply in some areas and undersupply in others. They must guarantee the maximum choice of access to places for all people for all legitimate purposes. They must not erect discriminatory barriers (e.g. exclusionary zoning) and they must

126

guard against the formation of severe socio-economic spatial polarisa-
tion. Stretton's analysis contains a host of specific recommendations on
how planners might manage the land market to achieve greater equality.[7]

> Land and housing should be traded in managed markets, with public
> agents operating wherever possible as competitive rather than
> monopolist suppliers, and using their tougher powers sparingly, under
> legal and political safeguards. They should work to distribute land and
> housing first, money second; but both equitably. Their dealing should
> aim to make owner-occupation of houses, workshops, small shops and
> other smallholdings as secure and widely available as possible, at
> prices as close as possible to building costs; and to make absent
> ownership and business investment in land as such less attractive than
> productive investment in building, manufacture, commerce or serv-
> ices. Most of the unequalizing type of capital gain and rent-taking
> from property should cease. (Stretton 1976, pp. 241–2).

The best-known and probably the best-documented example of planning
practice in the pursuit of justice is the work of Krumholz and his team in
Cleveland, Ohio (Krumholz et al. 1975; Krumholz 1982; Krumholz &
Forester 1990).[8] The point particularly stressed by Krumholz and Forester is that, in the pursuit of justice, planners must take the initiative and
seek out the opportunities for action which exist within the complex web
of political relationships in an urban polity. Their message is that, while
the scope for action by planners is always limited, openings exist, allies
can be found, support can be nurtured, and networks can be developed
for a set of projects 'that pay particular attention to the needs of the poor
and vulnerable populations, populations also likely to suffer the burdens
of racial and sexual discrimination, both institutional and personal'
(Krumholz & Forester 1990, p.210). While political engagement and a
highly entrepreneurial attitude was a key part of the style of Krumholz
and his team, the focus of their policy-making was the institutional level:

> In Cleveland the planners found institutional opportunities in several
> places: the non-monolithic character of urban politics, the ambiguity
> of planning mandates and problems, the needs of the powerful for
> planners' analyses, the nature of publicity and problem formulation in
> planning and the organization of planning itself. (Krumholz & For-
> ester 1990, p.212)

127

There are, however, two pragmatic objections to the Rawlsian view of the aims of planning. The first is the argument that markets cannot be made to operate more fairly without striking at the foundations of capitalism. Paradoxically, in view of its concern with the injustice of capitalism, this is a conclusion one might be tempted to draw from some Marxist work. If unfairness and exploitation is what supports capitalism, then action to reduce unfairness may be detrimental to capitalist urbanisation. Uneven development is the very essence of market behaviour (Smith 1984). 'Scarcity is actually a precondition for markets to operate' (Griffiths 1990, p.30). Harvey (1974) showed how struggles between unequal classes of landlords and land users drive the urban development process. Although, as a Marxist, he is concerned about the injustice of capitalism in general, he seems to regard such unfairness as necessary to capitalist operations. Indeed he writes:

> The realization of a class-monopoly return depends, however, on the existence of a class of speculator-developers who have the power to capture it … Since the urbanization process relates to economic growth in general, the speculator-developer who is, in effect, the promoter of urbanization, plays a vital role in promoting economic growth. (Harvey 1974, p.243)

If capitalism in general is unjust, then there is nothing in particular that the planner can do to reduce injustice. This objection to a Rawlsian reformism can be countered by pointing out that we really do not know how much inequality and/or unfairness *is* necessary to capitalism. Economic success does not appear to be positively correlated with crude power differentials between capitalists and workers (see Badcock 1984, p.329). The experience of recent attempts to empower the capitalist class by curbing union power, reducing regulation, and privatising government enterprises has not yet succeeded in projecting post-industrial capitalism into a new phase of growth.

The second pragmatic objection is more difficult to counter. A land market and its institutional envelope is such a wide-ranging and complex creation that there is no existing arm of government, even in central governmental agencies, able to act on it as a whole. The corporate concentration of power needed to restructure a whole land market is politically distasteful and probably unworkable. Territorial boundaries, the powers of local authorities defined by such boundaries, the planning

legislation, bureaucratic structures administering the legislation, financial institutions, their mode of interaction with the state, professional
associations, global developments affecting interest rates, and many other
factors structure particular markets in particular locations which provide
serviced land and buildings. The point was very well made by Ball
(1985). Land-use planners play a bit part in this market. Often they
confront the symptoms of its malfunctioning, and the public expects
them to put it all to rights. Planners at any level should understand that
they cannot do this. Yet that does not mean that they can do nothing. The
opportunities for restructuring markets will always occur sporadically
and in parts. Being effective as a planner means recognising the opportunities and exploiting to the full the avenues for improvement which exist,
and perhaps even more important, distinguishing correctly between matters which can be changed and those which cannot, and on which, therefore, it is pointless to waste energy.

Nozick's objection to state interference in market distribution is, of
course, fundamental. The market is a paradigm of the interactions among
an aggregate of individuals. Institutions develop out of the interactions,
and they must be structured to ensure that the interactions proceed
smoothly and with maximum efficiency. Outcomes must reflect inputs as
closely as possible. Thus cities will have rich and poor areas which
correspond with the distribution of wealth in the population. It follows
that planners have no role to play in distribution. In fact, the task of
government is to remove all regulation – including planning regulation –
which gets in the way of the efficient operation of the market. Even basic
services to property, such as sewerage, electricity and transport, are best
provided by the private sector and co-ordinated by the market. However,
there is a problem with this simple view of the world once one turns from
the market as an abstraction to actual functioning markets. The exchange
value of a plot of land is affected by the uses of all neighbouring land.
This is not just a Marxist perception (Harvey 1974; Roweis 1983), it was
also perceived by Hayek (1960, pp. 340–57).

If it is true that land markets cannot be separated from their politico-
institutional envelope, then even Hayek and Nozick would have to agree
that there is a role for planning in regulating markets – though this
regulation need not be undertaken by the state; for example, a consortium
of owners on a housing estate would be preferred by Hayek (1960,
p.352). Neither Hayek nor Nozick, in regarding land primarily as a trade-
able commodity, would have any objection to increasing inequality re-

129

sulting from its trading (cf. Stretton 1976, p.217). The overriding purpose of planning must be the protection of property rights and their means of exchange.

BEYOND RAWLS AND NOZICK

Rawls's theory is to some degree a pluralist theory which contains a solution to the problem of pluralism. He seems to be saying: 'There are many different conceptions of justice, all of which have some truth in them. But there is only one right way of combining them.'[9] That position leads to a complex argument, in keeping with the complex reality of human society. But it is possible to find inconsistencies in Rawls. He has been particularly criticised – from both the Right and the Left – for choosing a method of arriving at a view of justice which gives him the distributional patterns he intuitively approved of (Goldman 1980, pp. 373–4; Heller 1987, p.233). Rawls is unable to demonstrate that the method he proposes for the selection of a theory of justice (the contract, initial position and 'veil of ignorance') is the only right method. His critics argue that the method was chosen because it tends to lead to the 'difference principle'.

Nozick's theory is entirely monist in conception. The justice of the 'minimal state' rests on the truth of the postulate that owners of property are absolutely and incontrovertibly entitled to it. Now this postulate gives Nozick's theory much political dynamism and provides the rationale, in terms of justice, for 'rolling back the state'. But Nozick's theory rests on a single argument which in many ways goes against intuition. If that logic is faulty, then the theory collapses. G.A. Cohen (1986), in a much-discussed essay, demonstrates why Nozick's conception of the initial appropriation cannot sustain a theory of justice.

Nozick's case is as follows: assume a two-person world of person *A* and person *B* existing on a plot of land which neither own. Person *A* is a good organiser. Person *A* now appropriates all of the land and offers *B* a salary of more than (or at least as much of) the produce that *B* could have gained by working by himself on the common land. No one is worse off. But, Cohen asks, worse off than what? Because Nozick asserts that people are always made better off by privatisation, we can consider various alternative situations. Cohen shows that these alternatives are all *better* than the one Nozick assumes. Compared with them, one or both of the two people are made *worse off* by privatisation:

(1) Suppose that B is an even better organiser than A. B appropriates the land ahead of A, and in B's hands the land yields much more than in A's. In Nozick's case B would be worse off than in this case. Justice seems to depend on the rule of 'first come, first served'.

(2) Suppose now that B is such a good organiser that if B had appropriated the land first, both A and B would have been better off. It would not be true to say that the total benefit is increased without anyone being made worse off.

(3) Suppose now that B has the organisational talent and A force of arms. A, therefore, appropriates the land and pays B to design an optimal division of labour and then play his role in it. B, preferring exploitation to starvation, accepts. A's appropriation is still justified under Nozick's assumption, even though all the productivity gain is brought about by B. Nozick's theory leads to a simple justification of the right of the stronger.

Cohen further points out that Nozick ignores the possibility that property may originally be *jointly owned* rather than merely *not owned*. Joint owners would not act unilaterally, but would discuss together what was to be done, and not act until agreement had been reached. Mutual accommodation among equals through negotiation is today a real alternative to the resolution of conflict through market mechanisms. Both means in their proper place – as Walzer (1983) argues – may be used in a modern society.

Cohen's argument thus refutes Nozick's monist claim that entitlement is the sole basis of justice. Nozick himself has recently accepted that his position of 1974 was flawed in certain respects, and he contributes an interesting auto-critique. He says that the social aspect of the human condition finds expression in the value of 'human solidarity'. This value is just as important as the value of individual liberty on which the theory propounded in *Anarchy, State and Utopia* (Nozick 1974) was based. The way we express the value of solidarity is through the 'public realm', government, the state. This is an important part of the meaning of 'statehood': 'Joint political action does not merely symbolically express our ties of concern, it also *constitutes* a relational tie itself. The relational stance, in the political realm, leads us to want to express and instantiate ties of concern to our fellows' (Nozick 1989, p.288).

Is Rawls's or Nozick's position to be preferred? The conclusion I draw is that Nozick's monist position is untenable. Not only are monist logics dangerous in themselves because they tend to totalitarianism, but the logical ground of Nozick's argument is itself at fault. Rawls, on the other hand, has not demonstrated incontrovertibly that his way of combining the several different concepts of justice to be found in his theory is the one best way.

The conclusion towards which the debate seems to be driving is that pluralism, even in philosophical conceptions of justice, is the proper condition of a free society. However, in pluralism we encounter the problem mentioned above: that we have no way of choosing between incompatible principles of justice. This could lead to a kind of political paralysis, and might actually hinder the development of a society that is not only free but also fair. The challenge, then, is to go beyond pluralism and find that elusive 'higher criterion' which provides the basis of choice. Those who have taken up this challenge – such as Habermas (1983), Walzer (1983) and Heller (1987) – seek not so much a just *society* as a just *politics*. I want to conclude by discussing Walzer's work, which, of the three above mentioned, is most readily interpreted in terms of planning practice.

Walzer (1983, p.10) writes: 'There is no single standard. But there are standards (roughly knowable even when they are also controversial) for every social good and every distributive sphere in every particular society.' Different standards for the distribution of social goods arise out of the spheres of human activity in which such goods are produced. Walzer sets out to define these spheres and the standards which define a 'just' distribution in each sphere. The spheres he discusses are: membership, security/welfare, money/commodities, office, hard work, free time, education, kinship/love, divine grace, recognition, and political power.

Walzer's conception of how standards of justice arise is close to Wittgenstein's conception of language games and language regions.[10] Walzer, firstly, notices that one consistent and dominant set of standards tends to govern activity in one sphere. Thus, *within* a sphere, one need not encounter the problem of conflicting valid standards. Secondly, on the question of justice *between* spheres, Walzer applies what amounts to a meta-standard. Implicit in his argument is a conception of 'fitness' or 'appropriateness'. Different standards are 'fit' for different distributive activities. Walzer does not define this meta-standard, but we are led to assume that the appropriate standard is that which pragmatically and intuitively makes sense in each sphere. In effect, the standard and the sphere it governs develop together out of the experience and interpretation of human action. Standard and sphere define each other. Standards appropriate to one sphere should not 'colonise' and take over the assessment of what is just within another. Thus, for example, moral standards appropriate to the sphere of money and commodities should not take over the assessment of justice in the realm of social welfare.

There is clearly a lesson here for planning. Urban development in capitalist cities is normally a market-led process. In this 'for-profit' process, private sector planners have a role in the sphere of 'commodity exchange'. They market their services and sell their information – quite legitimately – as private sector consultants and advocates to developers. Within the sphere of commodities the standards of the market apply. Both consultants and developers are entitled to the profit they make under the rules and discipline of the market which apply at that place and time. But government planners play a role in the sphere of 'welfare'. The state exists to provide for the needs of its people. Nozick himself has recognised this. Walzer takes a very strong line on the matter. There can be no 'surplus' until 'needs' have been met.[11] 'What the surplus finances is the production and exchange of commodities outside the sphere of need. Men and women who appropriate vast sums of money for themselves, while needs are still unmet, act like tyrants, dominating and distorting the distribution of security and welfare' (Walzer 1983, p.76). The existence of current levels of poverty and wealth in capitalist nations is a matter of great immorality and injustice. It is an essential part of the government planner's job to identify the nature and location of need and, what is more, campaign for the relief of need – need for affordable housing, need for transport, need for recreational opportunities, need for the care of children, old people and the handicapped, and need for a pleasant and clean physical environment. These are the sorts of needs which urban planners in particular have to take care of. But it is also part of the governments planner's job to regulate the land and property market so that capital is invested for useful and productive purposes, and not for mere speculation. Such regulation is an example of the exercise of power in one sphere checking the exercise of power in another – just as the power of private corporations in the market checks the exercise of governmental power.

The conception of a just politics is the heart of Walzer's thesis. It is one in which the idea of checks and balances is taken very seriously. In Walzer's view, the standards we set for human behaviour are powerful. They do, in fact, govern behaviour to a considerable degree (even if not observed entirely unswervingly), and they constrain the exercise of power. If we can uphold the standards appropriate to each sphere of activity then each will constrain the exercise of power among them in society as a whole. A just politics, therefore, is one in which state power is checked by the powers of knowledge and of property, and is strong enough, in turn, to check those sources of power (see also Galbraith 1963; Mann 1986).

But Walzer wants to go further than asserting the virtue of countervailing power supported by different standards. He is not satisfied with the politics of the United States, for instance, where countervailing powers are supposed to exist. As Walzer sees it, the problem lies within the business world and the institution of the market. Here two spheres overlap – that of commodity production and exchange, and that of governance. 'Ownership', he says, 'constitutes a private government and the workers are its subjects' (Walzer 1983, p.293). Hence, the standards proper to governance must apply in business just as they apply in the sphere of politics and the state. This is an extremely important point. Not only are standards of justice appropriate to business in danger of colonising politics, but the business world contains a political sphere within it where it is appropriate for democratic political standards to prevail. This point was made even more eloquently by Robert Dahl (1985) in his thesis on economic democracy.

CONCLUSION

Ultimately, planners will concern themselves with justice if they choose to be good and honest people – that is, if they choose to live and work according to some moral code. This is not a solitary choice. What planners do will be judged by others as just or unjust, fair or unfair. If planners wish to make a case for their actions, they must refer to principles of justice.

Two specific questions were posed in the introduction to this essay:

(1) On grounds of justice, should there be action by the state to improve the life chances of the poor?
(2) What role, if any, can land-use planning play in such action?

On the first question, I conclude that welfare, as Walzer (1983) argues, is part of the function of statehood. Whatever the pragmatic political grounds for reducing the contribution of the state to the relief of poverty, there is no case on grounds of justice. On the whole, the requirements of justice oppose the greed of the economically powerful. The rich do not have justice as well as power on their side. Planning, as one branch of state regulation, must not increase, and must try to decrease, the injustice associated with market outcomes which inevitably favour those with market power.

On the second question, I conclude that planning has an important but limited role in creating fair land markets. Throughout the foregoing discussion a nested hierarchy of justice has revealed itself: the justice of particular distributions; the justice of the institutions which create those distributions, and the justice of the political process through which those institutions are created. The institutional level is that on which planning for justice can have most effect. Since the opportunities for action are never likely to be more than piecemeal, it will be important for planners to know what effect different institutional elements of the land market have on one another and on the justice of overall distributions.

However, the possibility of succeeding at this level is also limited. One must ask why Rawlsian programmes – such as that articulated by Stretton (1976) – have not been implemented by parties of the moderate Left when in power (as in Australia); why the Cleveland programme (see page 127) has not been more widely copied in the United States. As Marris (1982) has observed, the failure of action by the state to achieve its objectives, and the inherent contradictions in those objectives, led to widespread disillusionment and the collapse of the welfare state paradigm. The problem seems to lie in the political dimension of corporate power. In order to let states fulfil their compassionate function, and markets their distributive function, corporate power will have to become subject to democratic norms in a way that will not eliminate the capacity of firms for free decision- and risk-taking. To achieve such a change it will be necessary to transcend the problem of pluralism and move towards a social form supported by a single conception of a just politics, in which equal freedom and equal life chances are promoted.

NOTES

1   This may mean raising the stakes on Krumholz and Forester, since they talk about 'equity oriented planners' in a radically pluralist way as though planning for justice were a matter of individual value choice (Krumholz & Forester 1990, p.210).

2   The Nozick of the famous *Anarchy, State and Utopia* (1974). By 1989, in *The Examined Life*, though the book is about other matters, he takes a very different view of justice.

3   The debate on social justice is both deep and wide-ranging. Wellbank et al. (1982) measured the extent of the industry surrounding John Rawls's ideas alone at over 2 500 secondary sources. Many of these are substantial critiques. No doubt the corpus is much larger today. Books continue to emerge in which a discussion of Rawls is a central feature (e.g. Barry 1989a; Flew 1989). An overlapping corpus of rather smaller proportions surrounds Nozick's ideas.

4   Others have pointed out many more principles. Perelman (1963) has discovered six; Rescher (1966) enumerates seven. Walzer (1983) finds a plurality of conceptions of justice which defies enumeration in simple principles.

5   It might be said that I should bring in the utilitarian position here. I shall not do so, partly for reasons of space and partly because I agree with Miller (1976, pp. 31–40), that the utilitarian position does not really confront the issue of justice. It espouses an 'aggregative' not a 'distributive' principle. In so far as utilitarian arguments deal with justice, they must rely on ideas of entitlement, impartial judgement or mutual advantage which are most clearly exposed in Rawls and Nozick.

6   David Harvey (1973, p.109) writes: 'From Rawls's initial position it is not difficult by a fairly simple logical argument to arrive at a "dictatorship of the proletariat" type of solution.' I think that the priority of liberty argued by Rawls precludes dictatorship of any sort.

7   Stretton refers to Rawls, and also to the Fabian socialists Tawney (1964) and Titmuss (1958). See Stretton (1976, pp. 237–41).

8   Krumholz and Forester (1990, p.51) appeal to Rawls's theory of justice for support for 'equity' planning.

9   Rawls's theory contains a concept of justice formed in making a judgement about the fairest pattern of social distribution, a concept of justice formed in thinking about the fairest process of decision-making in society, a concept of justice formed by considering how best to make an impartial judgement about what is fair, and a concept of justice formed by considering what equal people would agree on if they were to pursue their own self-interest. On the whole, Rawls's theory seems to fit the principle of justice on the basis of 'each according to his need', but there is also a concept of rights in Rawls, embodied in the notion of fair process. Desert is covered by Rawls in the axiom that people deserve equal treatment.

10   For an excellent discussion of a Wittgensteinian perspective on justice see Pitkin (1972). Walzer's pragmatic position is also reminiscent of Dewey – see Hoch (1984).

11   The argument which begins 'First we must create wealth ...' is more accurately stated: 'First we must accumulate wealth...'. But accumulation, or savings, is not necessarily assisted by gross inequality of possession of wealth.

REFERENCES

Badcock, B., 1984, *Unfairly Structured Cities*, Oxford: Basil Blackwell.

Ball, M., 1985, 'The Urban Rent Question', *Environment and Planning A*, Vol. 17, pp. 503–25.

Barry, B., 1977, 'Justice Between Generations', in Hacker, P. M. S. and Raz, J. (eds), *Law, Morality and Society*, Oxford: Clarendon Press, pp. 268–84.

Barry, B., 1978, 'Circumstances of Justice and Future Generations', in Sikora, R. I. and Barry, B. (eds), *Obligations to Future Generations*, Philadelphia, PA: Temple University Press.

Barry, B., 1989a, *A Treatise on Social Justice, Volume 1: Theories of Justice*, Berkeley, CA: University of California Press.

Barry, B., 1989b, 'Humanity and Justice in Global Perspective', in Barry, B. (ed.), *Democracy, Power and Justice*, Oxford: Clarendon Press.

Beitz, C., 1979, *Political Theory and International Relations*, Princeton, NJ: Princeton University Press.

Best, J. and Bowser, L., 1986, 'A People's Plan for Newham', *The Planner*, 72(1), pp. 21–5.

Campbell, T., 1988, *Justice*, London: Macmillan.

Cohen, G. A., 1986, 'Self-ownership, World-ownership and Equality', in Lucash, F. S. et al., *Justice and Equality Here and Now*, Ithaca, NY and London: Cornell University Press, pp. 108–35.

Dahl, R. A., 1985, *A Preface to Economic Democracy*, Berkeley, CA and Los Angeles, CA: University of California Press.

Davidoff, P., 1965, 'Advocacy and Pluralism in Planning', *Journal of the American Institute of Planners*, Vol. 31, pp. 596–615.

Davidoff, P., 1975, 'Working Towards Redistributive Justice', *Journal of the American Institute of Planners*, Vol. 41, pp. 317–18.

Davidoff, P. and Reiner, T., 1962, 'A Choice Theory of Planning', *Journal of the American Institute of Planners*, Vol. 28, pp. 103–15.

Donnison, D. and Soto, P., 1980, *The Good City, A Study of Urban Development and Policy in Britain*, London: Heinemann.

Feinberg, J., 1974, 'The Rights of Animals and Unborn Generations', in Blackstone, W. T. (ed.), *Philosophy and Environmental Crisis*, Athens, GA: University of Georgia Press, pp. 43–68.

Flew, A., 1989, *Equality in Liberty and Justice*, London and New York, NY: Routledge.

Forester, J., 1982a, 'Planning in the Face of Power', *Journal of the American Association of Planners*, Vol. 48, pp. 67–80.

Forester, J., 1982b, 'Understanding Planning Practice: an Empirical, Practical and Normative Account', *Journal of Planning Education and Research*, Vol. 1, pp. 59–71.

Friedmann, J., 1987, *Planning in the Public Domain, From Knowledge to Action*, Princeton, NJ: Princeton University Press.

Galbraith, J. K., 1963, *American Capitalism, a Concept of Countervailing Power*, Harmondsworth: Penguin.

Gans, H. J., 1975, 'Planning for Declining and Poor Cities', *Journal of the American Institute of Planners*, Vol. 41, pp. 305–7.

Goldman, H. S., 1980, 'Rawls and Utilitarianism', in Blocker, H. C. and Smith, E. H. (eds), *John Rawls Theory of Justice: an Introduction*, Athens, OH: Ohio University Press.

Goodin, R. E., 1991, 'A Green Theory of Value', in Mulvaney, D. J. (ed.), *The Humanities and the Australian Environment*, Occasional Paper No. 11, Canberra: Australian Academy of the Humanities.

Goodin, R. E., 1992, *Green Political Theory*, Cambridge: Polity Press.

Griffiths, R., 1990, 'Planning in Retreat? Town Planning and the Market in the 1980s', in Montgomery, J. and Thornley, A., *Radical Planning Initiatives, New Directions for the 1990s*, Aldershot, UK and Brookfield, VT: Gower, pp. 21–33.

Habermas, J., 1983, *Moralbewußtsein und kommunikatives Handeln*, Frankfurt: Suhrkamp.

Harvey, D., 1973, *Social Justice and the City*, London: Edward Arnold.

Harvey, D., 1974, 'Class-monopoly Rent, Finance Capital and the Urban Revolution', *Regional Studies*, Vol. 8, pp. 239–55.

Hayek, F. A., 1944, *The Road to Serfdom*, Sydney, Australia: Dymock's Book Arcade.

Hayek, F. A., 1960, *The Constitution of Liberty*, London: Routledge and Kegan Paul.

Heller, A., 1987, *Beyond Justice*, Oxford and New York, NY: Basil Blackwell.

Hoch, C., 1984, 'Doing Good and Being Right, the Pragmatic Connection in Planning Theory', *Journal of the American Planning Association*, Vol. 50, pp. 335–43.

Katznelson, I., 1981, *City Trenches, Urban Politics and the Patterning of Class in the United States*, New York, NY: Pantheon Books.

Krumholz, N., 1982, 'A Retrospective View of Equity Planning, Cleveland 1969–1979', *Journal of the American Planning Association*, Vol. 48, pp. 163–74.

Krumholz, N., Cogger, J. M. and Linner, J. H., 1975, 'The Cleveland Policy Planning Report', *Journal of the American Institute of Planners*, Vol. 41, pp. 298–304.

Krumholz, N. and Forester, J., 1990, *Making Equity Planning Work: Leadership in the Public Sector*, Philadelphia, PA: Temple University Press.

Lindblom, C., 1977, *Politics and Markets*, New York, NY: Basic Books.

Locke, J., 1690, *Two Treatises of Government* (1967 edn), Laslett, P. (ed.), Cambridge: Cambridge University Press.

Low, N. P., 1991, *Planning, Politics and the State*, London: Unwin Hyman.

Mann, M., 1986, *The Sources of Social Power, Vol. 1: A History of Power from the Beginning to AD 1760*, Cambridge: Cambridge University Press.

Marris, P., 1982, *Community Planning and Conceptions of Change*, London and Boston, MA: Routledge and Kegan Paul.

Mazziotti, D. F., 1974, 'The Underlying Assumptions of Advocacy Planning:

Pluralism and Reform', *Journal of the American Institute of Planners*, Vol. 40, pp. 38–48.

Miller, D., 1976, *Social Justice*, Oxford: Clarendon Press.

Miller, D., 1992, Review Article: 'Recent Theories of Social Justice', *British Journal of Political Science*, Vol. 21, pp. 371–91.

Nozick, R., 1974, *Anarchy, State and Utopia*, Oxford: Basil Blackwell.

Nozick, R., 1989, *The Examined Life*, New York, NY and London: Simon and Schuster.

Okin, S. M., 1989, *Justice, Gender and the Family*, New York, NY: Basic Books.

Perelman, C., 1963, *The Idea of Justice and the Problem of Argument*, London: Routledge and Kegan Paul.

Pitkin, H. F., 1972, *Wittgenstein and Justice: On the Significance of Ludwig Wittgenstein for Social and Political Thought*, Berkeley, CA and London: University of California Press.

Rawls, J., 1972, *A Theory of Justice*, Oxford: Clarendon Press.

Rescher, N., 1966, *Distributive Justice*, Indianapolis, ID: Bobbs-Merrill.

Roweis, S. T., 1983, 'Urban Planning as Professional Mediation of Territorial Politics', *Environment and Planning D*, Vol. 1(1), pp. 139–62.

Sher, G., 1987, *Desert*, Princeton, NJ: Princeton University Press.

Singer, P. and Regan, T. (eds), 1976, *Animal Rights and Human Obligations*, Englewood Cliffs, NJ: Prentice-Hall.

Smith, N., 1984, *Uneven Development*, Oxford: Basil Blackwell.

Stretton, H., 1976, *Capitalism, Socialism and the Environment*, Cambridge: Cambridge University Press.

Tawney, R. H., 1964, *Equality*, Totowa, NJ: Barnes and Noble (first published 1931).

Taylor, C., 1986, 'The Nature and Scope of Distributive Justice', in Lucash, F. S. (ed.), *Justice and Equality Here and Now*, Ithaca, NY and London: Cornell University Press, pp. 34–67.

Titmuss, R., 1958, *Essays on the Welfare State*, London: Allen and Unwin.

Walzer, M., 1983, *Spheres of Justice, A Defence of Pluralism and Equality*, New York, NY: Basic Books.

Wellbank, J. H., Snook, D. and Mason, D. T., 1982, *John Rawls and his Critics, an Annotated Bibliography*, New York, NY and London: Garland Publishing.

Chapter 7

Values, subjectivity, sex

Beth Moore Milroy

INTRODUCTION

Some years ago the crisis about which values planners do or should promote seemed to be localised in planning. With hindsight, the problem appears far more deeply lodged – a symptom of questioning who, exactly, is a desiring subject able to choose values.

When the value issue arose in planning in the 1960s, it was recommended that planners drop the idea that people in a jurisdiction had common values which simply needed to be identified in order to be used to orientate planners' work. That accepted wisdom was replaced with the recognition that people with different experiences have different values. The problem therefore shifted from trying to detect commonly-held values to the more recent formulation in which one tries to elicit a plethora of values from people affected by a planning issue, and then to find common ground on which to base a plan.

For this purpose, the practice has evolved of consulting special groups whose experiences seem to deviate from a norm (yet who, politically, seem to have a legitimate claim to contribute their ideas) – for example, people whom planners associate with issues of sex/gender, race, ethnicity, poverty, and environmental activism. I am going to focus on the way sex is generally addressed in planning. Ordinarily it takes the form, first, of identifying sex with women, not with men, and second, of asking how women's interests can be incorporated in plans.[1] This, I believe, is asked in good faith and, as I hope to show, is entirely logical within the philosophical terms planners use. In turn, my reflections are made in equally good faith. The point I would like to make is that women are most emphatically *not* a sub-group in the planning subject population, a group whose interests will enrich the generic values already adduced by other means. This approach itself supposes that a more complete, generous-spirited, sympathetic set of values will emerge from such a practice. This is practising ethics on the side of men, not women.

This essay examines the reasons why women are not a sub-set of a human population, and what it will take to stop treating them as such. Two arguments are proposed. First, that the conventional, normal subject for planners is rational and disembodied, an image that coincides with the conventions of masculinity. Consequently, it seems important to invite women as 'special guests' to a process designed for a specific type of subjectivity with which they are not associated in the symbolic structures of Western culture. Second, that planning recapitulates rational disembodiment in its structure and content. That is, it leaves whatever does not fit this image either at the periphery of planning or to be picked up by other fields of practice, such as social work or community development. Not by coincidence, this residue is associated with the feminine side of the division of labour.

PART 1: THE CRISIS OF THE SUBJECT

Who is it who values or decides what is ethical? Is this an independent, free-standing individual? And if so, where does such a person 'end', as Gregory Bateson (1972, p.459) asked: at the outer skin, at the end of her spectacles, at the dialysis machine? Can it be assumed that woman-as-subject is the same as man-as-subject?

The main characteristics of the presumed subject in planning theories derive from Enlightenment thinking. Although there are several variations, it is first and foremost a pre-given, autonomous subject – the point where thought originates. Thought is conducted in one's personal consciousness. Reason is conceptualised as developing transcendentally, beyond the material base in the body, so that it exists uncontaminated by the vicissitudes of personal materiality. The unity of the subject is attained by excluding references to bodies and feelings, the kinds of factors which risk pulling one into a kind of 'thinking through the body'. One tries to stand 'outside of and above the situation about which he or she reasons', this impartiality being the hallmark of moral reason (Young 1987, p.60)

141

and a criterion for participating in the social contract (Pateman 1989a, especially pp. 45–53).

This form of metaphysics – which is common in Western philosophy – is now sometimes called 'logocentrism', following Jacques Derrida's coining of the term. Burke describes it as implying 'an attitude of nostalgia for a lost presence, or a longing for some first cause of being and meaning', and as expressing a 'desire to posit a central presence as a locus of coherence and authenticity – whether in the form of God's statement "I am that I am" or the Cartesian *"cogito, ergo sum"'* (Burke 1981, p.293). One tries to bypass mere representations of things to reach their essence, on the assumption that:

> [b]eing can be known and experienced in its immediacy; language transfers meaning neutrally without interfering in the underlying thoughts it 'expresses'; knowledge undistortedly reflects reality in truthful representations. These beliefs retain the concept as a true idea, existing independent of particular languages or forms of expression. (Grosz 1989, p.28)

This approach is aligned with the so-called 'correspondence theory of truth', which also assumes the type of unmediated, direct access to truth expressed in empiricism: true statements are 'those that "correspond" to the way the world is in itself' (Connolly 1988, p.10).

Both the subject depicted here and the correspondence theory of truth are evident in planning theories. They are also held to apply to both the planner and those for whom one plans, of course. Sovereign selves come to the process as a collection of conscious subjects, working directly and solely from conscious reasoning.[2] It is assumed that the people involved will eventually put aside their non-rational concerns and modes of expression in order to put conscious reasoning – which all people have in common – to work in the interests of finding agreement. In this process, the parties will use information developed within a correspondence theory of truth as the 'facts of the matter'. These criteria are presupposed for planning to work as an ordering but non-coercive social technology. The idea is that we will all eventually come to a broadly unified understanding of what should be done because we are all working from a common base which – if not shared experientially – can at least be discussed in rational terms and language.

Planners' experiences in recent years have illustrated, among other things, that rational beings still do not necessarily reach agreement. The collapse of the notions of *the* rational subject and 'facts are facts' are written in the history of citizen participation, and in the advice about how to negotiate, make trade-offs, and otherwise resolve quite intractable planning problems. Lately, a few planning theorists have tried to de-centre the concept of rationality underlying planning processes, although in so doing they have not given explicit attention to subjectivity.[3]

Throughout this century, a specific chain of thinking has been devoted to re-conceptualising subjectivity and the correspondence theory of truth. This chain is structuralism and post-structuralism, and the work has been centred in France, while none the less emanating from insights borrowed from Freud, Marx and Nietzsche. In the structuralist line of thinking early in the century until the 1960s, scholars – such as the linguist Ferdinand de Saussure, the anthropologist Claude Lévi-Strauss, the liter-ary theorist Roland Barthes and the psychoanalyst Jacques Lacan – ques-tioned the autonomous subject and the idea that a sign (which might be a letter, word, person, event, text, fragment of dream, and so on) is itself its own meaning (Grosz 1989, p.10). Instead they showed that a sign ac-quires its meaning and value from its relationship to and within a whole system of signs. A sign is both material and conceptual, and is arbitrary rather than a fixed essence. The systems of signs provide the contexts within which empirical objects are recognised or become objects of social science. Consciousness is not the sole determinant of a subject's intentions, but combines with the 'unconsciousness' latent in the system of signs. The study of ideology and power was thereby displaced from a focus on expressed thought to how thought is structured. In this light, socio-historical constructions which we take as utterly natural – such as consciousness, identity, reasons and logic – appear to serve Western cultural rather than ahistorical ends (Rabine 1988, p.12). It is this analy-sis that has led to the now-frequent observation that the Cartesian subject of knowledge is obsessed with mastery.

A particularly forceful challenge to the idea of a unified subject comes from Freud's elaboration of the unconscious, in which there is no subject yet there is desiring (Grosz 1989, p.19). The knowing, conscious, unified subject was thereby de-stabilised in two ways. First, consciousness was displaced from the core of subjectivity: subjectivity could no longer be coterminous with consciousness, as widely assumed, but must be recognised as mediated. Second, the immediacy of truth and the transparency of communication were necessarily brought into question:

> The subject is irremediably split, a being located in a conscious agency (which takes itself as master and knower) *and* in an unconscious agency (which is in fact the 'true' locus of [the absence of] identity). Freud, Lacan claims, demonstrated the subject's radical *inability* to know itself. Its self-certainty is a defensive ruse. The subject's identity is not given in consciousness nor in the form of an ego, but comes from being positioned by language as an 'I'. The subject is not the master of language, its controlling speaker, but its result or product. (Grosz 1989, p.19)

As Rosi Braidotti (1991, p.23) puts it, the all-seeing *cogito* 'finds its legitimacy not in the transparency of its perception of self, but rather in the fact of being able to *say* it. It is through having taken its place on the level of *enunciation* that the subject exists.' Feminists add to this insight that the place of enunciation generates 'speaking as men', which is the same as 'speaking universal', with no room left from which to speak as women (Whitford 1991, pp. 124–5). In planning, it is assumed – for the purposes of reaching a rational decision – that the unconscious can be ignored, and values can be expressed in a universal form.

Subsequently, post-structuralists (among whom are some former structuralists) ceased conceptualising structures as ordered totalities. They turned instead to examining what structures have to *exclude* in order to set themselves up as if they were organised, logical systems (Rabine 1988, p.13). This group includes, among many others, the historian/ philosophers Jacques Derrida, Michel Foucault, Michèle Le Doeuff, Jean-François Lyotard, and Gilles Deleuze. One of the dramatic outcomes has been to show what philosophy itself covers up in its own pronouncements so as not to jeopardise its status as the master field which sets the very criteria for knowledge. What it ignores, according to Le Doeuff (1989, p.2), for example, is that myth is constitutive of philosophy, not just an embellishment used to illustrate a point, or, according to Derrida, it misses how deeply metaphorical a supposedly literal text can be. It, too, like all the other fields, is an embedded discourse producing forms of power. Along the lines of this research concerning exclusion, a dramatic absence that is directly relevant to the question of women and subjectivity has been identified in psychoanalytic theory. In the process of dwelling on the difference between men and women coming to knowledge, psychoanalytic researchers in the Freudian and Lacanian traditions have reached widespread agreement that 'woman' as a subject does not exist separately and independently from 'man' or, if she exists, does so in ways that differ from 'man' as subject. 'Woman' is symbolised in social and cultural practices as the absence of man, the 'other' of man, the outside, complement, void or residue in opposition to man who is the complete and whole being in and of himself. She occurs in imaginary and symbolic structures as a function – primarily as a maternal or sexual function. It is relevant to planning because the claim would follow from this reasoning that adequate cultural images are not available for women to express values 'for themselves'. Not having images of women-for-themselves, women, when asked what they want, frame their responses in terms of the images they *do* have, mainly as complements of men, as objects to be desired, and as mothers.[4]

Few, outside of psychoanalytic theory, recognise the absence of woman as a claim. If it *is* recognised, however, the next question dividing researchers is whether to interpret it as a datum or as a problem to be investigated. I take it as a problem and, in wanting to know how this exclusion came about and how it is legitimised, I am inspired by Luce Irigaray, French philosopher, linguist and psychoanalyst, who is simultaneously developing an understanding of the absence and an alternative configuration of feminine, woman, women. This is taken up later in this essay.

A major area of feminist research, therefore, uses insights from both psychoanalysis and post-structuralism to try to understand the origin of the non-existence of woman in cultural symbolism. It must be stressed that the problem is that women are not *really* absent. Like men, they live and work – materially – in society. They are absent *symbolically*, not *materially*. By failing to distinguish between the two, and failing to symbolise woman, she can be exploited materially without having the symbolic structures to question it or to express her own desires, her own values. They are all fed through her functions in relation to man – as mother and sexual complement.

The confluence of feminism, psychoanalysis and post-structuralism results in several perspectives regarding subjectivity and values which are specific to feminists' interests in radically changing the situation. First, for example, there is insistence on sexuate, embodied subjects, because the notion of a neutral or generic subject has been a misnomer for 'masculine' in which the feminine is unrepresented. This returns us to a point made in the introduction, that sex/gender is attached to women, not to men. This is because man is seen as the universal human subject, outside of gender, while woman is inherently gendered, and the one who marks the difference from man (Rabine 1988, p.22).

Second, and in a related vein, the materiality of the body is tied to symbolic processes, refusing to give the same degree of significance to a rationality that soars above material bodies – the better to think clearly – that the Enlightenment subject has carried. The firm insistence on materiality is also a gesture against utter dispersal of the subject in so-called 'textual games', in which meaning is presumed to be adduced for its own sake, apolitically, and without material intent. Third, rather than thinking of masculine and feminine as either alike or as opposites, they can be thought of as asymmetrically different (Rabine 1988, pp. 20–22). Fourth, it is not so much the death of the subject as the potential for alterity (otherness) which interests women in the ideas of post-structuralists (Braidotti 1991, p.23). After all, the death of the subject only refers to men if it is accepted that women have not yet achieved subjectivity – the basic claim being made in this feminist elaboration. Finally, there is considerable hesitancy among feminists regarding post-structuralism, because masculine usage increasingly emphasises a 'feminine' which has nothing to do with advancing women's identity, but rather with men's interrogation of their unconscious, feminine self. This is well and good in itself; however, for women to adopt the same position as male post-structuralists from which to speak can in no way advance – and indeed would seriously retard – women's political and strategic interests in achieving identity and subjectivity. Luce Irigaray is one among several who warns against the usurpation of women's emerging discourse:

> What I am able to say without any hesitation is that when male theoreticians today employ women's discourse instead of using male discourse, that seems to me a very phallocratic gesture. It means: 'We will become and we will speak a feminine discourse in order to remain the master of discourse.' What I would want from men is that, finally, they would speak a masculine discourse and affirm that they are doing so. (Whitford 1991, p.132)

This, then, is some of the ground upon which subjectivity is being reconsidered.

PART 2: THE DISEMBODIED SUBJECT AND PLANNING

Having a few hints about an alternative perspective on subjectivity, we might think for a moment about planning's evolution in concert with the value of disembodied subjects.

To the extent that planning came out of the human sciences, it adopted their values of ordered governance based on reason. Planning as such was founded for the purpose of giving order to urban development and change, and this is the case whether one considers the Housing and Town Planning Act in the UK, the Chicago World Fair and zoning regulations in the USA, or the Commission on Conservation and the early town plans in Canada. These founding events paid attention to large-scale activities on the land – such as private and civic buildings, roads and waterworks. They were related to legislation, regulation, and large-scale design, and women had very little to do with them, barely having the right to vote (if they did at all), or to own property if married. They had few opportunities to make major things happen on the land. Their role in the process was – and largely still is – to assist and react. Cities came to be analysed in terms of money and possession – as economic engines, as things that men own and know about.

In these images of what constitutes an orderly city one also finds images of the inhabitants. The citizen-subject of concern to planners needs and uses a city primarily in the economic terms in which a city has been defined. Meanwhile, the planner-subject is concerned to use reason and abstraction to fashion money, land, design and politics into plans. For planners, citizen-subjects are as abstract as the other inputs to the plan; they are essentially reasoning beings pursuing their own interests.

The same disembodying gestures found in planners' views of the Enlightenment subject are recapitulated in planning practice and theory: sources of knowledge associated with real material bodies are cut off from planning's purview, and the lore of planning confirms in innumerable ways that the amputation is logical and reasonable. The amputation is a value judgement. It is supported by many theories and practices, one of which is the division between so-called 'public' and 'private' life. This is essentially a partriarchal division of work and other activities by sex, giving prominence to activities conducted in the sphere of reason – the public sphere.[5]

But, of course, more than public-sphere work is going on in communities. Other realms are domestic and community work, where *bodies* are looked after. This is what is cut off from planning, I am suggesting, in order to focus on things and thinkers – disembodied and disengaged selves. Needless to add, the fact that embodied selves are shielded from view does not mean they are not there.

I am in charge. But it keeps falling apart and being stuck back together again, always in different forms. Like a wholly malleable substance without its own form. Endlessly forgiving of the bits removed, the bits glued on again. Informal helping in the community turns into organised, formal community work. Reverts to an arm of domestic work. Is incorporated into traded work. Falls back again onto the community as community work. Fragmented, unstable, out of sight. Like the laundry. This is not planning. Never-ending, quotidien maintenance; not the special-occasion theatre of change. The perspiration; not the inspiration. Planning deals with strength; this other work has to do with neediness, dependence, the non-sovereign, embodied self. Ailing, mangled, incomplete bodies. Becoming. Growing up. Growing out. Growing old. Or needing help with the affective self: railing against the hand one was dealt; feeling abandoned; hurting, vulnerable. An attending subject becomes an encumbered subject, willy-nilly. Cut off. The uncharmed, and the uncharming of the charmed. Work here for social welfare, community development, volunteers, domestics, families, social activists. By cutting off this work, planning seems closer and more relevant to the power accorded to money, height, land, industry, rational development … Planners beware! These are not the bodies or subjects of abstract planning thought. But they do indeed exist. They are the residue, the unacknowledged foundation.

Cutting off allows some people to surge ahead, crediting their success to sacrifices made and self-discipline exercised. This, it is held, is good, possible and beautiful. So good, in fact, that everyone should strive for the same standard. But illogic lurks silently in this logic: the looking-after is essential. Even a power-broker has not always been invulnerable, and will not always be so. This knowledge threatens the logic of the rationally-based surging ahead. This is why it must not be brought to our attention.

Why the refusal to give full recognition to material bodies? Where does it come from? I want to suggest that the amputation of the knowing subject from her or his body is closely related both to the absence of woman from the symbolic field (mentioned in Part 1), and to the well-documented assignment of body-related tasks and characteristics to women more often than men. As a result, the image of the 'normal', valuing subject that planners adopt has a particular political and ideological agenda regarding what counts as valuable.

An opposition is set up – between masculine, transcendent rationality and feminine, symbolic sacrifice. Rosi Braidotti (1991, p.215) notes that the symbolic disqualification that takes place in scenarios such as these has its counterpart in real-life, socio-economic oppression of women. The reason why some feminists insist on keeping the material and symbolic linked in their work comes from experiencing the downside of splitting.

PART 3: BODYWORK

What are the images of women acting in a planning jurisdiction – images that help planners think out what to do about community space? Certainly, studies of the work women do in cities illustrate – through the attention women give to specific activities – that their communities are very different constructs to those prized in logocentric logic. However, it does not follow from this observation that the time women spend on these activities is an indicator of women's values. One can argue, inversely, that the amount of time spent is a function of what is *undervalued* by those with the most influence over values. The disproportionate attention women give to health, education, kin networks or poverty is not necessarily because women do not want to be inventors, politicians, astronauts and corporate presidents – or because they have a natural aptitude for or interest in the former rather than the latter. It is just as plausible that the former are activities that men tend to reject as not being their responsibility. They are left by default to women to do because, being crucial to the overall system, they cannot be left undone – in a system we claim is ethical.[6]

> 1900. House Committee of orphanage. 1902. Drinking fountain for civic square. 1905. Quilting for home burned down. 1906. Study focus is Africa, the dark continent. 1907. Bale of clothing to Alberta. Visiting sick and shut-in's. 1908. Cotton jackets for lepers; clothing and quilts to Mattawa. Quilt and some sewing for Mrs. W. For Berlin Orphanage: 3 lbs butter, sewing, gave supper, clothes made over, quilt and comforters made, boy's suit bought, two little dresses bought, sewed carpet rags, ... 1909. Study focus is China. 1913. Travellers Aid

149

to meet trains. 1914. Work among the foreign girls. Picnic for mothers and children. Christmas cheer for needy families. 1915. Quilting for Belgian Relief. Study sessions on Japan, India, Chile. Flowers to hospital and House of Refuge. Scrapbooks for wounded soldiers. Christmas program for inmates of House of Refuge. Knitted socks for soldiers. Knitted covers for amputees. School grounds secured for sports in July and August for YWCA girls. Practical nursing talks. 1916. Two pairs shoes bought for needy family. Mothers Club for general welfare of home, mother and child. Address given on Social Services. Women's Auxiliary League and Emergency Corps for war effort. 1917. Helping nurses in influenza epidemic. Prepared dinners for people ill with flu. 1919. Story Hour for children. 850 bales of clothing to Germany, and every year until 1929. Night school for new Canadians. 1923. Sewed linens for hospital. What to do about the poor family living off Albert Street South near the rubber tire factory. 1924. A ward (a boy) wants work after school. Scholarships for veterans' children. Layettes for the Northwest Territories, Yukon and overseas. Flags and portraits of the Queen for new schools. Sponsorship of school on Indian reservation. 1925. Financial aid to the Widow G. Mrs T has had to go out begging while Mr T does housework. Mrs C is cheating on charity. 1926. JB taken, pregnant, to House of Refuge. More money for Mrs G. Wood and boots for Mrs G. Another pregnant woman to House of Refuge. Three of Mrs G's children made wards of Children's Aid Society. CAS taking two of the H. children because mother taken to hospital. No support from father; can't find him. 1927. More needy families identified. Discussed a suitable place to care for children during the day while their only means of support – their mother – is at work. Mrs G not right mentally. 1929. Study circle discussions on prohibition and temperance. Community Concerts Association launched. Tea and bake sales. Card parties. Bazaars. Christmas TB sticker sales. Rummage sales. Raffles. Suppers. 1930. Swimming lessons for orphans. Quilts for city relief. Shoes and boots for children and needy families. Grocery shower for Christmas needy. Baskets for needy and flowers for invalids. 1931. Seventeen boys and fourteen girls in orphanage. Eye glasses for children. Milk. Stockings. Picture-showing lantern for orphanage. 1932. Picnic for orphans. 1933. Staff the gift cart and case at hospital. Assist in admitting, emergency, paediatrics, x-ray, diaper service distribution, clerical, flowers, making tray favours, money for education fund for nurses, books for medical library.

Suppers for 65 poor children. Suppers for another 70. Playing piano for weddings, choirs and seniors. Blood donor clinics. Red Cross loan cupboard (crutches, wheelchairs). Looking after neighbour's children while she does Red Cross work, relief work, churchwork ... Mrs P does Mrs M's housework because she crushed her fingers. Canvassing. Petitioning city council re curfew for children, and re household commodity prices. Clothes for unemployed. 1934. Visiting sick, shut-in's, newcomers. 1935. Furnishings and scholarships for new college. 1940. Ditty bags for soldiers. Knitting socks, sweaters, scarves, caps, mitts. Paper drives. 1941. National registration of women willing and able to be employed. 1942. Tea for men of #10 Basic Training Centre. Selling war stamps. Housing girls arriving to work in war industries. Wool to women internees in Kingston. 1943. Entertained international girls of #3 Basic Training Centre. Council of Friendship started. Nursery. Farm service. 1945. War Brides Club. Meeting re VD. Housing survey. Christmas entertainment for orphanage children. Stockings for sick children. Women's rally re equal pay and representation on government committees. Education re community health. Juvenile delinquency. Help for soldiers' wives. Ration duties. Community Nutrition Committee. Drivers for blood donor clinics. 1946. Canvassing re TB tests. Used clothing to Europe. Food drives for Europe. 1947. Relief to China – diapers, pyjamas, knitted wear. 20 bales of clothing to Europe. Petition for warning signs at street corner near school. 1948. Costumes made for Santa Claus parade. Sponsoring and placing displaced persons. Toy drive. 1949. 71 bales clothing to Europe. 1950. 40 boxes of clothing to Europe. Classes on child guidance. Cooking classes. Petition against beer sales in grocery stores. 1951. 81 boxes to Korea. 1952. Driving patients to hospitals for cancer treatments. 1954. Consumers association. Money to Korea. 1955. Clothes to Korea. 1956. 634 calls to sick and shut-in's. 19 charity quilts made. Layettes for Hungarian relief. Neckerchiefs for boy scouts. 1957. Scented garden for blind. Rummage sales, bazaars, suppers, socials, banquets, card evenings, free will offerings, teas, art exhibitions, concerts, musicales. 1958. Volunteering for therapy department of crippled children's centre. 1960. Club 50, for more mature women. Poise and Personality classes. 1961. Red Cross swimming tests. 41 quilts made. Choir gowns made. Layettes. Cancer dressings. Drapes for church office. 1962. 78 boxes of clothing overseas. 6 cartons to Angola. 1300 visits to sick and shut-in's. Supported a Halifax port worker assisting refugees. 1963.

Bridge classes. Cake Decorating. 1964. Baby-sitter course for young people. Discussion series on The Affluent Society and Me. Lecture series on The Feminine Mystique. Discussion about problems minority groups face. 58 cartons of clothes overseas. 1965. Two-day health fair. 1967. Drop-in centre for teens. Money and food to House of Friendship. Meals on Wheels. 1969. Programs for teens on drugs. 1970. Finding homes for people with dependencies and ugly home situations. 1971. Helping with Youth Hostel tent city. Drug policies developed for YWCA. 1973. Help for single mothers. Noon-hour program for local kids. 1975. Preparation for International Women's Year. Rape Distress Centre. Watercolour painting classes. Belly-dancing classes. Assertiveness training. 1976. Children's Aid Society groups are half-creative, half-therapeutic, for 8–12 year olds. Training programs for YWCA residence staff from university specialists and chief of crisis clinic at hospital. Diet Day Camp for overweight teens. 1977. Discussions re alcohol abuse, junk food and discrimination against women in jobs. 1980s. Quilting. Craft sales. Toy lending library. Teaching crafts. Contemplative retreats. Driving seniors to shop. Snow shovelling for elderly neighbours. Cuddles program at hospital. Bake sales. Raffles. Co-operative pre-school volunteer. Intervening with social agencies on women's behalf. Doing crisis calls for food, housing, emotional support. Able-bodied seniors entertaining and helping less able-bodied seniors.

These tasks, associated with the maternal-feminine, are entirely real; they take time and energy. They are lower-order functions, being related to bodies rather than minds. Minds are related to spirituality and godliness; bodies are not. They are body-related activities that, in the dominant philosophy, one needs to get out of doing (or at least not be detained by) in order to make significant strides in the world. To admit that these tasks are central to the survival of the system would jeopardise it. In addition, the symbolic division of labour between body and mind is simultaneously a division of labour between those people described as women and those as men. This symbolises women as 'outside', 'predicate', 'substratum' or 'residue'. The status of women and of the work they engaged in is evidenced in what is said about them and it. This work is treated – even by women themselves – as background, supplement, maybe even optional, and certainly outside the main ring. The descriptions accord with the symbolisation of this work in the culture, and how they are internalised by these women. The women speaking here are often ambivalent: they are modestly proud of what they have accomplished, yet they are aware their freedom to act was granted out of good faith; their images were assigned to them and not self-crafted; whatever image modification they achieve is so fragile it needs 'cheerleading' for reinforcement; their work is of very little consequence to powerful people.

1900–1950. Edna Augustine, speaking about her mother, Mary Kaufman, who was one of the most active women in KW affairs throughout her life, said: Mother was liberated. Father was behind her and willing to support her financially and morally.[7] 1920. 'But of course we were looking that women should have more. That was just part of any organization you belonged to. They were all "hip-hip for it". We felt women should have more say in what was going on ... we felt ... in the things we were doing we were sort of on the top crust. They were so essential. And we were so essential to them. Anything in the war ... or of that nature. This continued after the war ... You cheered for the women ... whenever there was an opportunity.'[8] 1921. The University of Toronto Alumni [sic] Association branch of KW held a social evening with 100 members and guests present. The women of the association, themselves graduates, were the refreshments committee.[9] 1925. The death of Mrs L.J.B., wife of one of the most successful industrialists in the city, 'marks the passing of one who adhered to the old-time traditions and ideals of the home as a social institution. Indifferent to the attractions of society as such, Mrs B. gave of her best to her home, her family, and the other interests dear to her heart ... As a type of true wifehood and as an ideal mother, Mrs B. was a genuine influence for good in an age that too often overlooks the virtues that are the foundations of Christian life and fellowship.'[10] 1930. The speaker, Miss R.M. Wigle, barrister from Preston, addressed the KW Business and Professional Women's Club on the subject of laws relating to women, especially married women. In conclusion she 'urged her hearers to do their part by thinking for themselves and learning to think of themselves as individuals working side by side and sharing responsibility equally with men'.[11] 1930–1980. Question: What did you get from your 50 years of service with the Red Cross, Mrs S? Answer: Well, it was something I could do. That was it. Question: What about being president of the local Women's Liberal Association? Answer: I was interested, but it was also something I should do,

153

because of Norm.[12] 1930–1980. Fortunately my husband was a very agreeable man and he gave me full leeway for those things in which I was interested like community work and entertaining.[13] 1940. Local 67 of the United Rubber Workers of America protested to city council against women working nightshifts. City council motion passed to prohibit factories employing women after 6:30 pm.[14] 1941. The Women's Association of Trinity Methodist Church 'is a band of careful housekeepers …'.[15] 1940s. We needed a women teachers' federation because the men were and are only concerned with themselves, they never did anything for the women.[16] 1944. ELB gave a report to the Local Council of Women meeting on … 'The [newspaper] reporter was here but the editor would not allow her to write-up my report because he concluded that the annual meeting in Port Arthur [about 900 kilometres away] had been well-covered by the CP [Canadian Press Wire Service].'[17] 1947. Social Committee of the YWCA and the Ladies Auxiliary of the YMCA provided dinner for 237 Federated Charities members and canvassers.[18] 1950. Letter from Federated Charities to the YWCA 'asking us to provide efficient and sufficient canvassers and that we carry out all our duties so that we can expect our full allotment.' 1950. Another letter from Federated Charities 'stating that all those not carrying out full responsibility will be penalized.'[19] 1951. Federated Charities wrote to the YWCA to request 'that as many male canvassers as possible be supplied'. This was discussed by the YWCA Board of Directors and 'it was unanimously agreed that as this is strictly a women's organization we would carry on as formerly with women canvassers.'[20] At the same meeting it was announced that the YWCA would again provide the Federated Charities dinner and '[a]ttention was called to the fact that 12 Board Members would be required to supervise the waitresses (2 for each table) and some would be called upon to help set up tables in the morning'. 1969. YWCA finds itself limited by Federated Appeal as to the money raised 'yet the Appeal is not able to meet our needs'.[21] 1900–1980. Women regularly forgot or downplayed the work they did: Mrs GRG said at the end of an interview that she did shopping for years for the Sisters of Notre Dame and for people in the neighbourhood who couldn't go out. Interviewer: Why didn't you mention this earlier? Answer: I never thought about it; it was just something I did.[22] Another example: Late in the interview, KB said: 'Oh, yes. Then I was in Scout Mothers for years. I forgot all about that … *very* involved in Scout Mothers … Cub

Camp ... Did the cooking for the cubs ... actually it was a very big involvement ... anything that the cubs or scouts needed, we'd raise money, have white elephant sales and things like that ... kept them in supplies ...'.[23] Or, Margaret Schreiter, a trained nurse: 'After my marriage [in 1920] I delivered and took care of a friend's baby, helped here and there, caring for friends, for example, going to their homes and bathing them or giving back rubs, but I did not return to nursing.'[24] On oral history tapes where husband and wife were interviewed together, the woman would occasionally add something about her work while the man would speak articulately and chronologically about his. 1900–1980. What is my name? How much of my energy has gone into getting it right? Am I Mary Jones, Mrs Edward Smith, Mrs Edward Smith (Mary), Mary (Mrs Edward) Smith, Mary Smith, Mary Jones Smith, or maybe just Mary Jones, again?

A contradiction occurs right at the core of the system such that certain activities occurring within the system are simultaneously essential to it *and* unable to be recognised. Non-recognition is backed up by ways to legitimise the blindness. Were this contradiction recognised – that minds come in bodies, and bodies are our primary locations in the world – the logic of the unified, objective, rational being would be considerably less credible. A restructuring of the rational subject would be needed, not to throw out rationality but to re-house it. Some contributions towards such a re-housing are described in Part 4.

PART 4: MATERIAL/SYMBOLIC SUBJECTIVITY

If, as suggested above, symbolic representation depends for its coherence on excluding women's material bodies, the point for women will be to change the symbolic. One cannot achieve such changes simply by calling 'foul', or even by simply changing existing social relations associated with economy, politics, or law. Those efforts need support from underlying structures which Luce Irigaray identifies as the symbolic and the imaginary. The symbolic order combines body, psyche and language (Whitford 1991, p.37) to form the structures for a person to accede to subjectivity. Symbolic forms include the linguistic, social, semiotic, structural, cultural, iconic, theoretical, mythical and religious (Whitford 1991, p.76). The imaginary is an order of unconscious fantasy and images used in creating an ego. It provides content which influences feelings toward knowledge developed in the symbolic order. Thus the two orders are linked.[25] In effect, the symbolic order is rooted in the landscape of mythology, some of which shifts from fantasy to become enshrined symbolically, thereby becoming rule-like in its function. If the material of the symbolic order presents a landscape peopled by men in strong, valued roles and women as absent or supplements to them, this is repeated in socio-cultural practices.

A line of feminist philosophy seeks to reconceptualise the body as the place where matter and symbolic forms interact, as 'the threshold of subjectivity', in Braidotti's (1991, p.282) words. Thus the body:

> is not a biological notion, but marks, rather, the non-coincidence of the subject with his/her consciousness and the non-coincidence of anatomy with sexuality. Seen in this light, the body, far from being an essentialist notion, is situated at the intersection of the biological and the symbolic; as such it marks a metaphysical surface of integrated material and symbolic elements that defy separation. (Braidotti, 1991, p.282)

Some of the elements in a strategy for changing the symbolic so that women are symbolised 'for themselves' include the following. The first element is to understand that this change cannot be realised by fiat, as I have tried to say in the preceding paragraphs. Second, symbols must be understood as unstable, as having a history, and therefore susceptible to being changed. This contrasts with the convention of assuming, for example, that the symbol of woman as 'other' (mentioned in the first section) is a datum – stable and ahistorical.

The third element makes use of the post-structuralist idea that presence is privileged in Enlightenment logic, and that this constitutes a way to mask absences which threaten the logic. Why, for example, are minds present and bodies absent in philosophical thinking? Why are women carnal representations for men? What is it about the body that urges philosophers to shun it as a proper source or housing for knowledge? Briefly, the psychoanalytic explanation given by Luce Irigaray revolves around the prominence and interpretation of the Oedipal myth which is used psychoanalytically to interpret accession to subjectivity by both boys and girls via their recognition of sexual differentiation. In the Oedipal myth, the boy symbolically effects his separation from his mother by killing and replacing his rival father, taking his mother as his wife/lover, discovering who she is, and killing her too. The myth goes on to describe

Oedipus being struck blind as punishment for his acts. The idea is that this product of the imagination – the mythical murder of the father and mother and the ensuing blindness of the son – has emerged to structure the symbolic order, being one of the imaginary fantasies that has successfully reached the symbolic. In an interview, Luce Irigaray suggested it results in symbolic structures based on the idea that 'if one touches the mother, one becomes blind'. She prefers to reverse that:

> and say that one becomes blind because one forgets and one denies the beginning, that is to say, the connection with the mother. The fundamental blindness of our culture is there. And if this denial of the connection to the mother posits in some fashion the murder of the woman who gives us life, it is necessary to understand that one doesn't dare to touch that again without fear because it would be to participate again in the same crime. (Baruch & Serrano 1988, p.158)

A further problem with the myth, from a feminist perspective, is that the girl (who is assumed to be pre-Oedipally identical to the boy) cannot effect subjectivity within the terms of such a myth because it casts her as passive and receiving, rather than active. In the myth she is transformed into the desired object, not the desiring subject. This poses problems of boundaries and generational (or genealogical) differences between the mother and the woman, and a collapsing of the one into the other. As a result, a woman can only *replace* her mother, not stand beside her. A myth conveying a girl's relationship with her mother is notably absent from the pantheon of persuasive myths in Western culture.

This is one illustration, and a crucial one, of the content and structuring of social relations via the imaginary and symbolic orders. It has material, not metaphorical, consequences (see Connell 1987, p.197).

A fourth element is to posit a systemic relationship between the imaginary (of the myths) and the symbolic (social representations of mythical content in language, iconic forms, etc.), such that a change in one entails a change in the other. Without this supposition it would be impossible to shift the existing structure so that woman-as-woman could be represented. Current myths would be ahistorical, current symbolisation without connection to myths, and any relationship between consciousness and the unconscious made doubtful.

Further elements in a strategy for changing the symbolic include a method for simultaneously understanding the current symbolisation of women without assuming it as 'the truth', of acknowledging it and changing it all at the same time; and of doing this using social rather than psychological material, because symbolisation is collective, not individual.

CONCLUSIONS

What values would be consistent with a nascent material/symbolic subjectivity on the side of women? And how might these influence the actions of planners? To summarise the main points from above, there are first the observations by feminists on subjectivity that serve as theoretical statements about subjectivity (see Part 1). These include an insistence that subjects are sexuate beings, that the materiality of the body and symbolic processes of mind are linked, and that masculinity and femininity are asymmetrically different. Part 2 contains illustrations of how these perspectives differ from existing practices in planning. In Part 3 some evidence is presented for the splitting of community activities along sex lines, and the concomitant double standard in values. Proposals for a strategy for changing the situation in keeping with the foregoing are sketched in Part 4.

The following practical work on the part of planners would help lift the brake on women acceding to a separate subjectivity and identity on the grounds presented. First, women should be invited *as women* to meet with men *as men* in planning processes. This would mean, among other things, recognising the encumbered self. Another task would be to go after (and to support going after) a feminine genealogy associated with design, community development, planning, community work, political action, and so on. This is needed because women's involvement is not just beginning. It has a history. However, we can barely imagine what it is, because it has been thought irrelevant to developments on the land. Therefore, it cannot serve as part of the background that women bring as separate subjects to the planning process. It needs to be as available as the male genealogy and history, also providing a source for reflection and implementation. A third task would be to refuse complicity in exploiting the motherhood function of women in all designs for structures and processes. Making it tougher for women to be in planned environments than men continues the exploitation of women's bodies. Finally, a major piece of work would be for planners to find a new place from which to speak, because the position of mastery (the default position within current philosophical thought and planning theory) is not an option if the lived experiences of at least two asymmetrical, non-hierarchical subjects are honoured.

In conclusion, treating women as a sub-set of the human population reinforces the idea of a generic human being, the normative image of which is male. I have argued against the notion of a generic human being altogether, because it does not represent women materially. To the extent that planners envisage unencumbered, disembodied subjects as both subjects and objects of planning, then they plan to leave the bodywork as residue – as an unacknowledged resource from which a few draw freely.

NOTES

1   Here, 'sex' refers to either men or women, without further refinement such as by age or sexual orientation.
2   For a brief discussion of 'sovereign', 'disengaged', and 'unencumbered' selves, see Benhabib and Cornell (1987, pp. 10–14).
3   For example, Christine Boyer's *Dreaming the Rational City* (1983, Cambridge, MA: MIT Press) is an excellent example of putting the rationality of city planning into question.
4   The type of problem that this poses in terms of eliciting values is posed in two ways in my 'Some Thoughts about Difference and Pluralism', in *Planning Theory*, Vol. 7/8, 1992, pp. 33–8.
5   See Carole Pateman, 'Feminist Critiques of the Public/Private Dichotomy', in Pateman (1989b, pp. 118–40); and in a planning context, Beth Moore Milroy and Susan Wismer (1994).
6   The following listing is a selection of activities taken from a research project on women and work covering the period from 1900 to the 1980s. It is merely indicative of community work undertaken, and in no sense exhaustive. The reason for including this listing in this form is (a) to remind readers of the nature of this work – its location in the day-to-day lives of everybody and its cyclical and never-ending qualities; (b) to propose that readers consider how the tasks are moved from one sector to another – domestic, community and traded (or paid) sectors – a point which was suggested by the comments on the fluidity of this work in Part 2, indicating that it is a residual; and (c) to provide a partial listing of tasks to form a background for the observations which follow about the way this work is understood. The Women and Work project was carried out between 1989 and 1992 in the cities of Kitchener (formely Berlin; renamed in 1916) and Waterloo, in Ontario, Canada (henceforth referred to as 'KW'). Using qualitative methods, we put together data from various primary sources such as diaries, letters, oral histories, minutes and records of groups, and interviews, depending on these first and foremost, with newspaper reports and published books forming a secondary line of information. The wording used in the listing reflects the way these activities were described in the primary sources.

Funding received for this research from the Social Sciences and Humanities Research Council of Canada is gratefully acknowledged, as is the help from Dr Susan Wismer and research assistance from Susan Montonen and Sabine Furino.

7   Kitchener Public Library (KPL), Grace Schmidt Room of Local History (GSR), Oral History Tape (OHT) 013, recorded 3 July 1981, side 2, @084, Edna (née Kaufman) Augustine.

8   Women and Community Work Project (WCW), interview with Margaret (née Erb) Schreiter, recorded 2 June 1989, side 2, @145.

9   KPL, GSR; Group records, University of Toronto Alumni Association for North Waterloo, Minute Book, 7 January 1921, p.17.

10   'In Society' column, *Kitchener Daily Record*, 12 June 1925.

11   Minutes, KW Business and Professional Women's Club, 10 February 1930.

12   KPL, GSR, OHT 77, side 2, @ 357 and OHT 78, side 1, @ 150, recorded 13 April 1982, Ethel (née Lapsley) Schneider. Norm Schneider, her husband, was Liberal Member of Parliament for the federal riding of Waterloo North, 1952–8.

13   KPL, GSR, OHT 103, recorded 3 June 1982, side 1, @ 683, Mabel (née Lane) Krug.

14   Kitchener City Council Minutes, 15 April 1940.

15   Dunham, M. B., 1941, *So Great a Heritage: Historical Narrative of Trinity United Church*, Kitchener, Ont.: Cober Printing Service, p.61.

16   KPL, GSR, OHT 305, recorded 16 May 1985, side 2, @ 230, Agnes Stock.

17   University of Waterloo, Doris Lewis Rare Book Room, Breithaupt Family Papers, E. L. Breithaupt to M. E. Breithaupt, 4 July 1944.

18   KW Young Women's Christian Association (YWCA), Board of Directors Minutes, 10 March 1947. They provided this dinner annually at least until 1951.

19   KW, YWCA, Board of Directors Minutes, 13 February 1950.

20   KW, YWCA, Board of Directors Minutes, 12 February 1951.

21   KW, YWCA, Board of Directors Minutes, 26 May 1969.

22   KPL, GSR, OHT 396, recorded 24 March 1987, side 2, @ 208, Gertrude (née Rake) Gill.

23   WCW, Interview, 3 August 1989, Name withheld by agreement.

24   KPL, GSR, OHT 246, recorded 15 June 1983, side 1, @ 218, Margaret (née Erb) Schreiter. She had four children, and was widowed in 1933.

25   For an excellent description of the symbolic and imaginary in Lacan and in Irigaray, see Whitford (1991, Ch. 3 and 4).

REFERENCES

Baruch, E. H. and Serrano, L., 1988, *Women Analyse Women*, London and New York: Harvester Wheatsheaf.

Bateson, G., 1972, *Steps to an Ecology of Mind*, New York, NY: Ballantine.

Benhabib, S. and Cornell, D. (eds), 1987, *Feminism as Critique*, Minneapolis, MN: University of Minnesota Press.

Braidotti, R., 1991, *Patterns of Dissonance*, Oxford: Basil Blackwell.

Burke, C., 1981, 'Irigaray Through the Looking Glass', *Feminist Studies*, Vol. 7, pp. 289–306.

Connell, W. R., 1987, *Gender and Power*, Stanford, CT: Stanford University Press.

Connolly, W. E., 1988, *Political Theory and Modernity*, Oxford: Basil Blackwell.

Grosz, E., 1989, *Sexual Subversions*, Sydney, Australia: Allen and Unwin.

Le Doeuff, M., 1989, *The Philosophical Imaginary*, London: Athlone Press.

Milroy, B. M. and Wismer, S., 1994, 'Communities, Work and Public/Private Sphere Models', *Gender, Place and Culture*, Vol. 1, pp. 71–90.

Pateman, C., 1989a, 'The Fraternal Social Contract', in Pateman, *The Disorder of Women*, Oxford: Polity Press, pp. 33–57.

Pateman, C., 1989b, *The Disorder of Women*, Oxford: Polity Press.

Rabine, L. W., 1988, 'A Feminist Politics of Non-identity', *Feminist Studies*, Vol. 14, pp. 11–31.

Whitford, M., 1991, *Luce Irigaray: Philosophy in the Feminine*, London and New York, NY: Routledge.

Young, I. M., 1987, 'Impartiality and the Civic Public', in Benhabib, S. and Cornell, D. (eds), 1987, *Feminism as Critique*, Minneapolis, MN: University of Minnesota Press, pp. 56–76.

Chapter 8

The moral mandate of the 'profession' of planning

Jerome E. Bickenbach and Sue Hendler

PROFESSIONS AND PROFESSIONALS

Increasingly, the planning literature is replete with debates about the societal purpose and ethical imperatives of planning. As a consequence, planners, wandering unguided through a maze of conflicting responsibilities, may be uncertain about their social status and duties. Inevitably, this uncertainty will raise the question of whether, and in what respects, planning is a *profession*. For a profession is more than a gainful occupation; it sets out a social good as its goal and *raison d'être*, and requires those who would call themselves professionals to strive to further that goal. A profession, in short, is characterised by a moral mandate.

That the concept of a profession embodies a normative standard is uncontroversial (Goldman 1980; Bayles 1981; Callaghan 1988). It is impossible to label someone's behaviour or demeanour 'unprofessional' without conveying the sense of untoward, inappropriate or unethical conduct. But at the same time, as critics of professionalism have argued, our understanding of professions is coloured by carefully cultivated, and universally believed, self-serving myths about the social value of being a professional (Johnson 1972; Bledstein 1976; Larson 1977). Although the boundaries of the notion are fluid, there are a few uncontroversial characteristics that occupations must possess in order to qualify as professions.

First of all, both historically and conceptually, a profession is founded upon – and would be a parody or fraud without – a corpus of specialised, esoteric, or systematic knowledge (or skills or arts) not commonly known or available to all. It is this knowledge, or set of skills, that a professional professes. The distinguishing mark of a professional expertise is not its intellectual depth, but its exclusivity: not just anyone, on their own, can become a member of a profession. So, a professional is someone who has learned (and often laboured long to learn) a required body or canon of knowledge.

The second important feature of a profession is that it is a community of like-learned individuals – people who identify themselves as professionals of a certain sort by virtue of an expertise. Thus it is that, in all professional schools, one is trained to 'think like a professional', inasmuch as this conformity is a precondition of initiation. One must be able to profess the profession to qualify; but more importantly, one must, willingly, be a part of a community defined by a common discourse and shared social meanings.

This last, almost ineffable feature of professions is essential, since it – and it alone – distinguishes a profession from an occupation, or a *métier*, vocation or, more bluntly, a job. Occupations and the rest can be learned, they can involve highly specialised knowledge or skills, and have substantial barriers to entry, preventing all but a few from entering. But occupations are not professions when the expertise does not create a community. A profession, in short, is more than a livelihood, it is a form of life (Hughes 1963).

Professions justify their special social status – the privileges and rights accorded to them – by claiming cognitive exclusiveness over their professional expertise. But, significantly, this claim would be a transparent fraud unless the services that depend on the expertise are genuinely and demonstrably beneficial to society. The social status the professional possesses is thus, in part, the result of the perception that he or she is contributing something especially beneficial to society – something society cannot do without. It is upon this perception that the normative structure of a profession rests; without this foundation in social good, the putative profession would lack the moral mandate essential for the plausibility of the claim to professional social status.

These three features of professions are central. But some commentators argue that, in addition, it is crucial that the expertise that defines a profession be controlled and sustained from within (Bayles 1981). That is, only professionals must be able to assess, validate, and contribute to their expertise. Organisationally, this means that professions are voluntary and exclusive associations that have mechanisms in place for controlling admission to the profession. These mechanisms may require the candidate to take a university programme, to article or clerk with an established member of the profession, to sit exams, face a licensing board, or to otherwise endure some ritual of initiation. The possibilities are unlimited.

What lies behind these procedures, though, is more important than the precise form they may take. For it is obviously vital to professions that they be autonomous with respect to their expertise. If outside powers dictate who can become a professional or what the expertise consists of (if, that is, there is complete, external regulation of the professional organisation), then we would be hard-pressed to call the result a true profession. A profession – if it is to remain such – must, in the face of external pressure, reserve to itself the final authority over its expertise. Professions must have that degree of autonomy. And this extends to individual professionals as well: we speak of 'professional judgements' in order to identify them as opinions to which non-professionals should defer. Thus, whenever medical professionals wish to resist further state regulation or other encroachment, their strongest argument is that shifting the decision-making power from physician to bureaucrat will inevitably undermine people's health and welfare.

In sum, then, for an occupation to qualify as a profession:

(1) it must be founded upon a corpus of specialised, esoteric, or systematic knowledge (or skills or arts) not commonly known or available to everyone;

(2) it must involve a community of like-learned individuals, professionals who share a common vision about the rationale and social value of their profession;

(3) it must offer services that are genuinely of benefit to society, in so far as they promote, or exemplify, a self-evident social good;

(4) it must be in control of, and autonomous over, the expertise that defines its special contribution to society; and

(5) it must be organised as an exclusive association, with mechanisms in place to secure its autonomy over its expertise.

The traditional professions of law, medicine and theology satisfy each of these criteria with ease. Increasingly, however, many other occupations have, to enjoy the social advantages professionalism creates, striven to join these ranks. Thus recent debates about the professional status of planning.

IS PLANNING A PROFESSION?

These days, the public manifestation and expression of the five character-istics of professions tends to take the form of a professional code. Al-though professional codes have a long history (the first probably being the Hippocratic Oath, formulated in the fourth century BC), it was not until the nineteenth century, with the rapid growth of non-medical and non-legal professions, that codes were written to govern the relationships between professionals and their peers, their employers and clients, and the public at large (Harris 1989). Given the prominent role of profes-sional codes, the status of planning as a profession might be assessed, at least initially, by consulting existing codes of conduct for planners. What do these codes say about the five characteristics of professions – special-ised knowledge, initiation, social value, autonomy and regulation? For illustrative purposes, we focus on codes from Canada, the United States and the United Kingdom.

Specialised knowledge

Historically, the roots of planning in public health, civil engineering, architecture and the natural sciences gave rise to a body of specialised knowledge grounded on technical aspects of land use. As planning ma-tured, however, it began to expand its scope to include a variety of social, economic and health issues that arise in urban and regional environ-ments.

The resulting breadth of the contemporary planning endeavour has led to the concern that there may not be a base of common knowledge for the various strands of planning thought and activity (e.g. Wildavsky 1973). Some have responded to this concern by arguing that, although planning may not possess a specific technical expertise, it does have an identifi-able ethically-centred and process-focused knowledge base. Others, though, have argued that this focus is insufficient – and perhaps inappro-priate – to distinguish planning from other fields. Planning requires a so-called 'substantive basis' to be distinct as a profession, the argument goes, but it is precisely that which it lacks.

In general, planning codes do not resolve this dispute, since they are typically silent on questions of technique and substance (see e.g. Wachs 1989). While 'professional competence' – typically understood to mean technical competence – is often stressed in the codes (RTPI 1986; CIP

165

1986), there are few references to the kinds of knowledge that planners are supposed to possess, and no identification of a discrete expertise.

The Code of the American Institute of Certified Planners (AICP) is an exception in this regard. This code speaks of the importance of ethical knowledge, and makes reference to 'planning theories, methods and standards' (AICP 1981). Yet, while one might infer from this that competence in the areas of citizen participation techniques, forecasting, environmental design and an awareness of social problems is important, nowhere are these directives made explicit, nor are they tied to academic or technical disciplines.

A 1986 article in the Canadian journal *Plan Canada* has been the principal impetus for planning schools and professional organisations in Canada to delineate the kinds of knowledge or skills that characterise the expertise for the profession of planning. Lang, Keeble and Carrothers (1986) list the following groups of skills which, in their view, define the profession: conceptual and analytical skills, evaluative, strategic, interactive and management skills, and skills of personal development. By contrast, the AICP has suggested a more substantive list of knowledge areas, including knowledge of physical structure, institutional structure, economic organisation, ethics, and planning law (PAB 1984).

These lists suggest that it is likely that planning cannot claim a unique, specialised expertise since it appears not to be a body of knowledge which – compared, for example, to that of law or medicine – is both unified and coherent. Instead, planning is an inter- and multi-disciplinary endeavour that demands a range of skills and knowledge bases.

Initiation

How does one become (or become known as) a planner? The second characteristic of a profession requires that the putative profession be a community of like-learned people, and one whose membership is restricted to those who, in one way or another, qualify. On the face of it, planning satisfies this requirement inasmuch as aspiring planners must typically have an academic accreditation, as well as gain professional experience and successfully complete professional written or oral examinations. Although the initiation ritual for planners is not as ornate or steeped in history as those of the traditional professions, that matters little if the point of it is to maintain exclusivity and so define a community of professionals.

A further move in this direction is evidenced by legislative provisions in several jurisdictions, limiting admission to the planning profession to those who have complied with specified academic and experience requirements. Although a trend, it is not one all planners agree with. In Ontario, for example, a private member's bill currently under consideration has proven controversial, with at least some planners urging that the bill 'is [a] conspiracy by some fat-cat planners to protect their own self-interest' (Sniezel 1992). The related movement toward standardisation of planning schools in Ontario has met with similar resistance.

Societal role

That planners are asked for, and make, recommendations to their clients, and that these recommendations are viewed as beneficial, is obvious. Yet when one tries to go further and specify the social good to which these recommendations, and so the planning activity as a whole, are directed, one reaches more controversial matters. None the less, the language – and, in some instances, the tone – of professional codes for planners suggest attempts to identify a suitable social goal for planners.

That goal is primarily one of promoting social justice and environmental integrity. For example, the Royal Town Planning Institute Code (RTPI 1986) explicitly directs British planners to eliminate discrimination and promote equality, while the Code of the Canadian Institute of Planners (CIP 1986) requires planners to ensure that the voices of disadvantaged groups be heard as much as possible. For its part, the American Institute of Certified Planners Code (AICP 1981) reminds planners of the necessity to plan for the needs of disadvantaged groups, as well as the natural environment, and to promote citizen involvement.

In short, if these codes are to be believed, the social goods of environmental integrity and social equity are intrinsic to what it means to be a planner, and, therefore, are part of the fabric of the profession. More significantly, these social goods are constant, irrespective of the ambient political climate. Many planners in South Africa, for example, appear to have held equity-driven, anti-apartheid views, even when the politicians employing them thought differently (Muller 1991).

Autonomy

There are two functional tests that could be used to determine whether planning is autonomous over the expertise that defines its special contribution to society. First, we could ask whether planners as a group possess a tradition of generating from within their ranks the expertise upon which practitioners rely; or, second, we could ask whether non-planners defer to the expertise of planners on issues and problems that planners purport to be able to solve.

On the first test, planning is not autonomous, since its 'specialised knowledge' is inherently multi-disciplinary, and it is debatable whether planners could be said to be in possession of a unique body of knowledge, or set of skills, that only they possess or use.

Arguably, planning might meet this criterion if we agreed to extend the notion of an expertise to include an organised endeavour at melding *multi*-disciplinary knowledge into new, *inter*-disciplinary conceptual frameworks. Consider, for example, the area of social planning, in which elements of the disciplines of sociology, ethics, geography, economics and others are brought together within an inter-disciplinary framework designed to identify and address social issues with the overall aim of improving our collective quality of life. Understood in this way, social planning might be argued to possess an integrated and systemic body of knowledge, rather than merely relying upon the expertise of various disciplines.

The question posed by the second test is easier to answer. Plainly, planners are deferred to by their clients and others. Planners are employed precisely *because* they are autonomous over their expertise, and are hired to solve planning problems because their judgement is prized. This being so, one might argue, it is not particularly relevant whether this expertise is multi-disciplinary or unique to planning.

Yet, here too we should be realistic. Research on planning practice has shown that planners are often frustrated in their work because their recommendations are not followed by their employers or clients (e.g. Krumholz & Forester 1990; Hendler 1990a). Worse yet, planners are sometimes pressured into altering their 'independent professional judgement' in order to conform more closely to their employers' values and preferred directions. So, while it may be true that planners are hired for their expertise and professional judgement, sometimes there is a reluctance to defer to that expertise and judgement.

Self-regulation

In this area, planning certainly takes on the air of a profession. Planning organisations make a point of identifying unethical behaviour, educating their members about ethical norms and, when necessary, applying sanctions and other correctives to those who fail to meet these standards. These bodies also provide resources for their members when they are faced with allegations of unethical conduct from peers, clients, employers and members of the public. Thus planning organisations, like all professional bodies, are in the business of both disciplining and defending their members. To be sure, the institutional machinery for self-regulation is not nearly as impressive for planners as it is for other professionals; but no doubt there is enough in place to satisfy this characteristic of a profession.

Conclusion

Now, taking all of this together, does planning qualify as a profession? It would appear that – setting aside the difficulty of finding a suitably unique and specialised expertise – planning possesses all of the characteristic traits of a profession, to one degree or another. Furthermore, as noted above, if we were willing to recognise as a discrete expertise the blending and restructuring of multi-disciplinary fields of learning, then we could be far more confident in that judgement.

Still, doubts remains. To return to the case of Ontario again, efforts to create before the Ontario legislature the Ontario Professional Planners Institute (OPPI) have met with resistance from within the 'profession'. Among other things, the proposed legislation would make 'professional planner' and 'OPPI' *legal* designations, misuse of which would attract a substantial fine. Legally enforceable restrictions on the use of professional designations is a perfectly natural concomitant of the social status of a profession. Therefore, it is very significant indeed that at least some members of Ontario's planning community have voiced strong opposition to this proposal.

The depth and origins of this opposition are not entirely clear, though part of it arises from the fact that the OPPI is seen by many to represent predominantly the interests of land-use planners. Social, health, strategic, economic and other sorts of planners have largely felt disenfranchised from the workings of the OPPI and its national counterpart, the Canadian

Institute of Planners. These planners seem not to hold membership in such organisations in particularly high regard, and may have found it difficult to pursue full membership. At the same time, and for at least some related reasons, relationships have been strained between academic and practising planning factions.

Now, while it may be rash to infer anything about the broader question of the status of planning as a profession from the situation in Ontario, this case does provide examples of potential areas of controversy that arise in most jurisdictions. It seems true, however paradoxical it sounds, that the major obstacle to planning being a profession is the reluctance of its members to conceive of themselves in professional terms, if that means abandoning what they perceive to be the appropriate normative focus of their work.

In the end, though, the major issue that has to be decided if planning is to qualify as a profession is one we have treated only superficially so far – namely, what, if anything, is the moral mandate of planning? That is – professional codes aside – do the distinctive roles that planners play give rise to particular responsibilities and social obligations? Obviously, every profession – indeed every occupation – is under general obligations to perform its roles competently and honestly. Those moral values are given. But the more important and more difficult question is whether planners, solely by virtue of their special skills and social roles, have obligations that are unique to them.

WHAT IS THE MORAL MANDATE OF PLANNING?

It should be clear by now that the way this question is answered depends in large part upon our perception of the proper role of planning in the municipal structure, the function of planning in the political process, and the overall place of planning in contemporary societies. In other words, answering this question will necessarily involve making a decision about the nature of the social good that planning (as a possible profession) seeks to secure and maintain, for it is this which would count as its moral mandate.

There are at least four approaches to defining the moral mandate of planning. These approaches would involve:

(1) an examination of the context in which planning functions and the role(s) it has developed;

(2)   an identification of the values planners hold and express in their work;

(3)   an analysis of professional planning codes; and

(4)   a critical or philosophical argument as to the social niche planning and planners should occupy.

Each of these approaches presents its own distinctive set of professional ethical considerations.

First, and with respect to the context and associated societal role of planning, planners often work in planning departments that represent only one part of a city or region's administration. Other departments address issues of public works, finance and social services, among others. Apart from specific concerns about such things as parkland and infrastructure, the development and conservation of the municipality's land base is left largely to planners. It thus becomes their task to integrate the directives of other departments and make concrete recommendations about what should happen 'on the ground'. The integrity of the land base and the integration of disparate aspects of a municipality's territory represent, therefore, substantive elements of the planner's role.

Another set of distinctive tasks for planners arises from the processes used in municipal decision-making. While participation in these processes by members of the public is widely valued, few municipal employees have had training in facilitation, animation and other participative methods. As a consequence, these participatory tasks are often left to planners, some of whom have learned appropriate consensus-building, mediation and related techniques in their education and other experience.

A third, process-driven, aspect of planning pertains to the short-term nature of the political structure in our societies. Politicians who employ planners are predominately elected for three or four years, and are thus especially interested in issues and activities that can be addressed during this relatively short time-span. This leaves questions requiring a longer period of thought and action to other employees of government who, of necessity, take on the tasks of identifying concerns, forecasting consequences, and selecting appropriate mitigating policies and plans. Again, this is a role reserved for, and taken up by, professional planners.

These, then, are the major, substantive and methodological responsibilities of planners. There are, however, more social aspects of planning work that might generate distinctive ethical directives. That is, the role of planning in a democratic, justice-oriented society brings with it the ob-

171

jective of representing interests that are otherwise poorly articulated. As is intuitively obvious, wealthy, educated and empowered persons can express their opinions freely and openly in municipal, decision-making processes, and their voices are heard. Less well-off and more marginalised individuals, by contrast, are far less likely to participate in such processes because of an apathy born of powerlessness, either perceived or real. Usually, then, others must be advocates for the interests of disadvantaged individuals and groups. Planners are often such advocates.

Thus, planners assume roles – and accompanying moral mandates – of the environmental ethicist (land management); the mediator (of values, discourses and expertise); the advocate (of the disadvantaged), and the futurist (protector of long-term interests). Conflicts among these roles are inevitable, and may be the source of public frustration manifested in perceptions of those on the political 'Right' that planners are socialist, anti-development tree-huggers, and those on the 'Left' that planners are paper-pushing, capitalist facilitators of development.

Whether planners' professional values conform to these roles is the second approach to an investigation of the moral mandate of planning. As a matter of fact, in many countries planners have often accepted the challenge of accommodating the kinds of interests just described. Not only do planners, as a rule, value the input of the disadvantaged, they also place importance on expressing the interests of those whose views are not represented. Moreover, planners often strive to bring perspectives into the scope of planning that might well be ignored. The perspectives of the natural environment and future generations are obvious examples.

Support for the prevalent belief in the existence of these 'professional' obligations comes from empirical studies of planners' values (e.g. Howe & Kaufman 1979, 1981; Hendler 1991a; Lang & Hendler 1990; Howe, forthcoming), analyses of planning language and decisions (e.g. Krumholz & Forester 1990, Throgmorton 1993), and examinations of planning codes (e.g. AICP 1981), as well, of course, as assertions and theoretical arguments (e.g. Davidoff 1978; McConnell 1981; Haworth 1984; Udy 1980; Blanco 1993). Whether the source of these perceived responsibilities is the people who become planners, or the planning organisation/ profession that attracts prospective professionals, probably does not matter much (see, however, Alterman & Page 1973).

We do know, from preliminary studies of students in planning schools, that students express planning values similar to those of practitioners, but apparently only as they gain practical planning experience (as in Hendler

1991a). One could hypothesise from this that the ethical obligations planners have, or feel they have, are generated through the work planners do and the expectations that others have of them. At same time, of course, these obligations could be enshrined in planning through the professional codes adopted by professional organisations (see Hendler 1991b).

Most of the studies of planners' values have been carried out in countries characterised by fairly liberal approaches to their social, political and economic endeavours. These include Canada (Hendler 1991a; Lang & Hendler 1990), the United States (Howe & Kaufman 1979, 1981; Howe, forthcoming), Israel (Kaufman 1985), and Sweden (Khakee & Dahlgren 1990). While values of social equity, democracy and justice, as well as environmental integrity, characterise the results of these studies, a question arises as to the generalisability of such findings. While the professions of law, medicine, and architecture involve sets of values largely consistent over the face of the globe, can this be said about planning?

We do not have sufficient data to answer this question. International, cross-cultural studies of planners' values are few and far between (see Kaufman 1985). Kaufman's comparison of US and Israeli planners, however, is one piece of evidence that indicates that values of the sort listed above are not immutable across political, geographic, and cultural boundaries. Further research is needed in order to test whether differences in values are simply variations in intensity or, more significantly, dramatic conflicts among values reflecting different political or philosophical orientations.

Another reflection of planners' values is the professional codes to which they adhere. Depending upon how such codes are developed and implemented (see e.g. Kaufman 1990; Hendler 1990b, 1991b), they can provide a concise and thoughtful statement as to the normative stance of a professional planning organisation.

Having said this, however, codes are not much help in ascertaining a definitive moral mandate for planning. Obligations to the natural environment, for example, vary among planning codes (Gowdy 1993). Some codes, such as that of the American Institute of Certified Planners (1981) and the draft code of the Canadian Institute of Planners (1992), are quite explicit in directing planners to protect the integrity of our biophysical surroundings; other codes, however, such as that of the Ontario Professional Planners Institute (1986), contain no explicit mention of nature, and may allude to it only implicitly as part of the 'public interest'. Such reference gives little guidance to planners, and does not address crucial questions regarding the kind of value accorded to nature (i.e. instrumental or intrinsic), the definition of nature as a moral community, and so on. Other values pertaining to the interests of disadvantaged individuals, public participation and heritage conservation follow a similar pattern. Thus, the lack of consistency in planners' values appears also to be manifest in professional planning codes.

The fourth and final way of identifying planning's moral mandate is by the development of philosophical critique and rational argument. Udy (1980) and Blanco (1993) are two prominent examples of this approach. The former presents a case for truth, goodness, beauty, and love as being the *raison d'être* for planning; the latter argues that reason, democratic process, community, and nature provide the moral glue that does – or should – hold the planning profession together. There is sufficient overlap between these two examples to postulate the beginnings of a coherent moral posture for planning. However, other writers propose a diverse array of competing normative directions; these include autonomy (Haworth 1984), Rawlsian social justice (McConnell 1981; Marlin 1989), equity (Davidoff 1978), environmental integrity (Richardson 1990), and liberalism (perhaps libertarianism) (Sorenson 1982, 1983). The list seems endless.

This diversity, corresponding to different ethical, political and other divergent contexts, further supports the notion that a single, unifying basis for planning is, at best, elusive. And, if there could be said to be one particular moral mandate supported by planners' work, their professional values, ethical codes and philosophical treatises, it could only be called the 'public interest' (see Howe 1992; Marcuse 1976). This, however, is a slippery term, in which may be lumped all of the preceding, often conflicting, values. Fleshing out anything more specific and useful will require much in the way of cross-cultural, international work, in the form of both empirical research and theoretical discourse.

CONCLUSION

Taking any, or all, of the four approaches to the issue of the moral mandate of planning outlined above seems to lead us to the prospect of diversity and incoherence. Significantly, though, the problem here is exactly parallel to the earlier worry about the existence of a single, unified and coherent planning 'expertise'. There we suggested that, while the search for a distinctive, 'specialised knowledge' may be futile, there is nothing that stands in the way of extending the notion of an expertise to include the restructuring – and reintegration – of several co-operating expertises within the structure of an inter-disciplinary framework. Perhaps the same suggestion is relevant here. Rather than searching for a single value, or even a single set of values, at the heart of the planning endeavour, one might argue that it is the resolution of a range of competing and conflicting values that gives the planner her or his moral mandate. The role of planning, as discussed above, can provide a context for this admittedly difficult and contentious activity. And this struggle may indeed result in planners coming to an agreement on their professional ethics which reflects their 'concern for long-term consequences and ... the costs and benefits to people outside the immediate circle of decision making' (Stollman 1979, p.9). Thus, dealing with the ambiguity of moral dimensions of planning can actually *be* the moral mandate of planning, and can be part of its basis for claiming professional status.

REFERENCES

Alterman, R. and Page, J., 1973, 'The Ubiquity of Values and the Planning Process', *Plan*, Vol. 13, pp. 13–26.

AICP (American Institute of Certified Planners), 1981, *Code of Ethics and Professional Conduct*, Washington, DC: AICP.

Bayles, M. D., 1981, *Professional Ethics*, Belmont, CA: Wadsworth Publishing.

Blanco, H., 1993, 'Community and the Four Jewels of Planning', in Hendler, S. (ed), *Planning Ethics: A Reader in Planning Theory, Practice and Education*, New Brunswick, NJ: Center for Urban Policy Research, Rutgers University.

Bledstein, B. J., 1976, *The Culture of Professionalism: The Middle Class and the Development of Higher Education in America*, New York, NY: Norton.

Callaghan, J. C., 1988, *Ethical Issues in Professional Life*, New York, NY: Oxford University Press.

CIP (Canadian Institute of Planners), 1986, *Code of Professional Conduct*, Ottawa, Ont.: CIP.

CIP (Canadian Institute of Planners), 1992, *Draft Statement of Ethical Principles and Code of Professional Conduct*, Ottawa, Ont.: CIP.

Davidoff, P., 1978, 'The Redistributive Function in Planning: Creating Greater Equity Among Citizens of Communities', in Burchell, R. and Sternlieb, G. (eds), *Planning Theory in the 1980s*, New Brunswick, NJ: Center for Urban Policy Research, Rutgers University, pp. 69–72.

Goldman, A. H., 1980, *The Moral Foundations of Professional Ethics*, Totowa, NJ: Rowman and Littlefield.

Gowdy, A., 1993, *The Environmental Values of Ottawa Planners and the Role of these Values in a Professional Code*, MPL thesis, Kingston, Ont.: Queen's University.

Harris, N. G. E., 1989, *Professional Codes of Conduct in the United Kingdom – A Directory*, London: Mansell Publishing.

Haworth, L., 1984, 'Orwell, the Planning Profession, and Autonomy', *Environments*, Vol. 16, pp. 10–15.

Hendler, S., 1990a, 'How Planners Choose', unpublished manuscript. Available from the author.

Hendler, S., 1990b, 'Professional Codes as Bridges between Planning and Ethics: A Case Study', *Plan Canada*, Vol. 30(2), pp. 22–9.

Hendler, S., 1991a, 'Ethics in Planning: The Views of Students and Practitioners', *Journal of Planning Education and Research*, Vol. 10, pp. 99–105.

Hendler, S., 1991b, 'Do Professional Codes Legitimate Planners' Values?', in Thomas, H. and Healey, P. (eds), *Dilemmas of Planning Practice*, Aldershot: Avebury Technical.

Howe, E., 1992, 'Professional Roles and the Public Interest in Planning', *Journal of Planning Literature*, Vol. 6, pp. 230–48.

Howe, E., forthcoming, *Acting on Ethics in City Planning*, New Brunswick, NJ: Center for Urban Policy Research, Rutgers University.

Howe, E. and Kaufman, J., 1979, 'The Ethics of Contemporary American Planners', *Journal of the American Planning Association*, Vol. 45, pp. 243–55.

Howe, E. and Kaufman, J., 1981, 'The Values of Contemporary American Planners', *Journal of the American Planning Association*, Vol. 47, pp. 266–78.

Hughes, E. C., 1963, 'Professions', *Daedalus*, Vol. 92(4), pp. 655–68.

Johnson, T., 1972, *Professions and Power*, London: Macmillan.

Kaufman, J., 1985, 'American and Israeli Planners: A Cross-cultural Comparison', *Journal of the American Planning Association*, Vol. 51, pp. 352–64.

Kaufman, J., 1990, 'American Codes of Planning Ethics: Content, Development and After-effects', *Plan Canada*, Vol. 30(5), pp. 29–34.

Khakee, A. and Dahlgren, L., 1990, 'Ethics and Values of Swedish Planners: A Replication and Comparison with an American Study', *Scandinavian Housing and Planning Research*, Vol. 7, pp. 65–81.

Krumholz, N. and Forester, J., 1990, *Making Equity Planning Work*, Philadelphia, PA: Temple University Press.

Kultgen, J., 1988, *Ethics and Professionalism*, Philadelphia, PA: University of Pennsylvania Press.

Lang, R. and Hendler, S., 1990, 'Ethics and Professional Planners', in MacNiven, D. (ed.), *Moral Expertise*, New York, NY: Routledge, pp. 52–70.

Lang, R., Keeble, R. and Carrothers, G., 1986, 'What Planners Need to Know: CIP Recognition of Planning Degrees', *Plan Canada*, Vol. 26, pp. 252–6.

Larson, M., 1977, *The Rise of Professionalism*, Berkeley, CA: University of California Press.

Marcuse, P., 1976, 'Professional Ethics and Beyond: Values in Planning', *Journal of the American Institute of Planners*, Vol. 42, pp. 264–75.

Marlin, R., 1989, 'Rawlsian Justice and Community Planning', *International Journal of Applied Philosophy*, Vol. 4, pp. 36–44.

McConnell, S., 1981, *Theories for Planning*, London: Heinemann.

Muller, R., 1991, 'Ethics: Theory and Practice in South African Planning', *Town and Regional Planning*, Vol. 31, pp. 17–25.

OPPI (Ontario Professional Planners Institute), 1986, *OPPI General Bylaw (1986 10 17)*, 'Appendix 1: Professional code of conduct', Toronto, Ont.: OPPI.

PAB (Planning Accreditation Board), 1984, *The Accreditation Document: Procedures and Standards of the Planning Degree Accreditation Program*, Washington, DC: PAB.

Richardson, N., 1990, 'Four Constituencies Revisited: Some Thoughts on Planners, Politicians and Principles', *Plan Canada*, Vol. 30(2), pp. 14–17.

RTPI (Royal Town Planning Institute), 1986, *Code of Professional Conduct*, London: RTPI.

Sniezel, J., 1992, 'Letter from the [OPPI] President', *Ontario Planning Journal*, Vol. 7(1), p.8.

Sorenson, A., 1982, 'Planning comes of Age: A Liberal Perspective', *The Planner*, Vol. 68, pp. 184–8.

Sorenson, A., 1983, 'Towards a Market Theory of Planning', *The Planner*, Vol. 69, pp. 78–84.

Stollman, I., 1979, 'The Value of the Planner', in So., F. (ed.), *The Practice of Local Government Planning*, Washington, DC: International City Management Association, pp. 503–515.

Throgmorton, J., 1993, 'Ethics, Passion, Reason, and Power: The Rhetorics of Electric Power Planning in Chicago', in Hendler, S. (ed.), *Planning Ethics: A Reader in Planning Theory, Practice and Education*, New Brunswick, NJ: Center for Urban Policy Research, Rutgers University,

Udy, J., 1980, 'Why Plan? Planning and the Eternal Values', *Plan Canada*, Vol. 20, pp. 176–83.

Wachs, M., 1989, 'When Planners lie with Numbers', *Journal of the American Planning Association*, Vol. 55, pp. 476–9.

Wildavsky, A., 1973, 'If Planning is Everything, maybe it's Nothing', *Policy Sciences*, Vol. 4, pp. 137–53.

Chapter 9

Political judgement and learning about value in transportation planning: Bridging Habermas and Aristotle

John Forester

This chapter explores the political judgement that planners need to learn about value in the always political world of their daily practice. The argument proceeds in four parts. Value judgement in planning is inescapable, complex, and quite poorly understood, Part 1 suggests. By considering a brief account of a metropolitan transportation planner's work in the USA, we confront immediately the inherently ethical, value-ambiguous character of planning practice. Assessing this planner's story further in Part 2, we explore the challenges and strategies of learning on the job that planners often face as they manage inter-agency working meetings. Part 3 suggests that issues of power are ever-present. In the face of power, planners must improvise sensitively and imaginatively, changing objectives, discovering and responding to novel problems, adjusting their priorities and efforts accordingly. Part 4 concludes by drawing more general implications: practical political judgement in planning must address ends as well as means, public deliberation as well as personal strategy, the recognition of value as well as the justification of action.

PART 1: POSING THE PROBLEM: LEARNING ABOUT VALUE IN A POLITICAL WORLD

Introduction: challenges of learning about value

Planners have to learn, in practice, not just about facts but about facts that matter. So they must learn about fact and value together, about consequences and consequentiality, about impacts and the significance – the value-laden character – of those impacts.

In professional schools, however, students and faculty alike appear to believe that disputes about facts can be rationally advanced through appeals to evidence, but disputes about value cannot. Disputes about value, apparently, appear only and essentially 'subjective' and 'irrational'.

To say that these beliefs – that we cannot rationally discuss, criticise, and assess value in the world – disserve prospective planners understates the case dramatically. For planners must interpret mandates and obligations, promises and threats, the significance of 'impacts' and consequences every day. To have them suppose that such interpretation is essentially irrational, that better and worse interpretations of value are thus beyond discussion, is a bit like asking them to swim with one foot heavily weighted down.

At work, planners must distinguish people's 'values' – as articulated in their expressions of commitments and enduring preferences – from specific matters of value, matters in the world to be honoured or dreaded, protected or prevented, cultivated or mitigated. For example, 'historic preservation' or 'environmental protection' may (or may not, in a given locale) be popular 'values'. But a newly-discovered archaeological find can have great value even while only a very few people know about its existence. When planners must anticipate future streams of project consequences, they have to pay attention not only to existing and projected popular 'values' but to what can go wrong, to what benefits can be realised, to the value to be gained or lost from project implementation in each alternative form.

To make matters worse, not only must planners learn about value, they must respond appropriately to it as well. Recognising a community's need for affordable housing, a neighbourhood's record of fatalities at a given intersection, a developer's record of building flimsy housing, a resident's history of attacking before getting the facts, a planner must respond in light of these relevant particulars. That planners owe every

179

person respect does not mean that planners should treat every person in precisely the same way: the student intern, the journalist out for a story, the mayor, the developer making false promises, and so on. Like a hairdresser who cut the same amount of hair no matter what, or a dentist who always drilled the same amount into every tooth, the planner who failed to respond to the relevant particulars of each new case could hardly be said to be planning well.

To do their work well, then, planners cannot simply follow rule books or recipes. Their work of ongoing practical judgement requires them to be moral improvisers. They must face new and unique situations in light of encompassing mandates, goals, responsibilities and promises, which provide them with general directions but not specific instructions.

This work of judgement and moral improvisation is constrained, but not determined; open if not wide open. Institutional mandates and obligations – like a city council's directives and declared purposes – will limit what a planner can take as an appropriate, legitimate action. But each new situation will also present possibilities to protect or realise value, to identify issues, to focus on particular problems, to recognise particular needs or options.

Yet we know too little about how practical judgement in planning works, even as we think we know too much. Some may argue that we know a good deal about how practical judgement works in planning: it works for the benefit of those in power – for those who own the land and housing, and not for those who rent; for those who own factories and corporations, not for those who have to work for those owners. Of course, power (suitably defined) prevails, but this reply not only misses the point, but distracts our attention from what we need to investigate practically and politically. This reply is a bit like responding to the question, 'How does applied statistics (or informal networking) work in land-use planning?' by saying, 'It works for the powerful, not the powerless.' Even when this is true, it tells us nothing about the character or substance of applied statistics (or informal networking), not even whether or not its use in a particular case may have taken power relations brilliantly into account, even though 'the powerful' prevailed for yet other reasons.[1]

If it is too simple and sweeping, then, to say that practical judgement in planning simply works to support the powerful, we need to understand more clearly how it can work for better or worse, what political and practical abilities are required, what its contingencies are. How can planners 'learn about value' in new situations? What sort of ethical work must they do, before and after decision-making, if decision-making is only one part – and perhaps not a big part – of their ongoing work (cf. Forester 1992)?

To explore these questions, we begin by listening to a metropolitan transportation planner, Mitch, speaking about the challenges of his work. We will assess particularly how this planner, and arguably many others too, must be able to learn about value as well as about fact, to make judgements of relevance and significance as well as calculations of costs and benefits. Only if we recognise clearly how questions of value may arise in planning can we examine in turn the better and worse ways that planners might address such questions.

A transportation planner's work: value judgement and inter-agency co-ordination

Listen, then, to Mitch, a planning graduate whose most recent job title was Manager of Policy Development in a large metropolitan area's transportation agency (Forester & Kreiswith 1993). That agency, Mitch tells us,

is in the process right now of asking for $11.5 billion from the state for capital development, and we were a big part of that process. Of all of my time there, I spent at least 60% on capital planning development. Airport access is a particular project that I worked on.

[Because] our two major city airports have no direct mass transit access ... we worked on an interagency committee trying to determine how best to serve the market, and what our goals were for providing airport access. By 'interagency' I mean very broad: we worked with the city, the regional transportation authority which operates all the airports, half a dozen city and state agencies, and the Transportation Agency. It was a very hot project. There were various goals: we were trying to minimize congestion, keep airports open, and enhance economic development. So we wrote a paper about that.

Then we developed an alignment – a way of keeping the airports open – and started working to find out whether that idea was really feasible. So we looked at the engineering of it. We looked at whether or not we could get the private sector to help fund it: are they going to kick in any money for this airport access notion of ours or are we going to have pay for this whole thing ourselves? We looked to see whether or not we had the legal representation to do this: whose sign

181

off do we have to get? Even though it's all government work, EPA is going to have to sign off on it; someone owns the roads or the right of way that we're going to carry; we'll have to develop community support programs, and we'll have to look at that. In short, we considered everything that was necessary to make the project feasible.

We found initially that the original alignment was not feasible, and we came up with a modification of the plan that will be tested. Then, perhaps in ten years or so, something will be built. But all of the work was very long-term; we had a long-term focus.

Working in a huge metropolitan area and among so many different constituencies is challenging – it's a real pain in the ass. My role varied somewhat. On airport access, I played the role of day-to-day coordinator of the project, at least in the early stages. Later on, that emphasis shifted toward a particular person within the Regional Authority. I was reporting directly to the Director of Planning, and he said, 'Mitch, handle this for me. Here's what we're doing', and I said, 'OK.'

I held regular meetings with staff from each of these agencies in order to develop the report that would detail what we were trying to do. The city had its agenda; the Regional Authority had its agenda; and City Planning had its agenda. The city actually had several representatives from different departments, so they had their own set of internal conflicts.

We all had our own agency's agendas to protect. For example, everybody down there was looking at the Regional Authority as the cash cow.

What I should say is that the city was looking at the Transportation Agency and the Regional Authority as potential funders for this project. The Transportation Agency was saying, 'This is a jointly funded project that everyone's going to have to kick into, including the state.'

Everybody – the Transportation Agency included – was saying, 'The Regional Authority really ought to come up with the money on this.' So everyone had different ideas there.

Everybody also had different ideas about what alignment we ought to take. 'How do you get from City Centre to the airports?', for example. You shouldn't go through houses; do you try and take a lane of roadway? Is it elevated or underground? Everybody had different ideas about that. We argued back and forth, and my role as coordinator was to try and come up with some sort of consensus.

To do that, you try to do a bunch of things. One is that you're very diplomatic: You always try and recognize that people have proper points of view, that they're good and right-thinking people, and they may just disagree. You try to precisely determine the disagreement. You try to clarify whether or not there really are points of disagreement. I would say, that in a good half of the cases, you really don't have an argument, you just think you have one.

One person is saying, 'I really think you can't affect local communities', and another person is saying, 'I think we have to get there by the shortest way.' Those two things are not mutually exclusive – but you can wind up in a heated argument, and we did. But if you precisely define the point of conflict by saying, for example, 'Maybe we can keep both of these as objectives', then both people start saying, 'Yeah, OK!'

You find that a lot of people have difficulty expressing what their precise concern is, so it takes a lot of probing, and you have to be gentle about it – and it takes enormous amounts of time: 'What exactly is your concern? I don't understand.'

Finally, someone will say, 'My concern is that we're going to get too far afield when we don't have the basic information we need to go to the mayor and say, "This is what we propose."' And then, once you precisely define it, you try and make some determination as to whether or not you agree, whether or not that's really a problem. If it's a problem, then you try and find a way around it. If it's not a problem, then you have to convince the other person that you don't think it's a problem because ... or: 'Well, I finally understand your point. Yeah, we do need some set of alternatives.'

PART 2: MANAGING TO LEARN

Practical entanglement and multiple forms of value

Mitch's account seems quite ordinary on its surface. Like many planners, he works in a situation of multiple actors, multiple goals, conflicting agendas, all involving multiple levels of government and large numbers of potentially affected people. Mitch speaks simultaneously of preserving institutional peace, working with the inter-agency committee, 'serving the market', and then, too, of determining the committee's 'various goals' – to 'minimize congestion, keep airports open, and enhance economic development'.

The substantive goals, Mitch tells us, had to be seen in their institutional contexts. Developing an alignment, a strategy of keeping the airports open, the committee explored feasibility in terms of private sector commitment, regulatory approval from the EPA, and necessary community support programs too. No wonder, then, that Mitch says, 'Working in a huge metropolitan area and among so many different constituencies is challenging – it's a real pain in the ass.'

The value of the proposed alignment, Mitch suggests, can be explored not only by anticipating its consequences but also by gauging its significance for relevant institutions and public groups. Mitch pays attention not only to consequences but to relationships; he seems as concerned with 'what will happen' as with 'who must be involved' or 'who will have to sign off', who will have to approve, to consent. So, he suggests, the more we can understand a project's entanglements, its relatedness to an existing social and institutional fabric, the better may we appreciate a project's value.

As Mitch refers to different contexts, he alludes as well to different forms of value. Perhaps the private sector can be persuaded to contribute some portion of the financial costs of the proposed alignment; this is one measure of the alignment's significance. Then, of course, measures of community impact and community sentiment are likely to take a quite different form – which might range from modest interest, to bodies laid down before bulldozers, and intractable community conflict. As if grappling with private sector investment calculations and gauging community sentiment did not differ enough, Mitch alludes as well to legal-regulatory sanctions and authorisation.[2]

The value problem is already worse than we may have thought. Not only do substantive goals conflict – how to compare gains in congestion reduction against minimising adverse community impact? – but projects must be evaluated in distinctively organised and politicised financial, legal and community contexts, too.

But Mitch tells us much more than this. He provides a fascinating glimpse at the internal value discussions of the inter-agency committee itself, each agency having brought 'its own agenda' to the discussions. 'Everyone had different ideas' about financing. 'We argued back and forth', and Mitch's role, he says, 'was to try and come up with some sort of consensus'.

Mitch's task is a daunting one. He's told us clearly of conflicting agendas, multiple jurisdictions, varied goals, and more. Although we might be tempted to wonder why, in such a politicised context, consensus-building in an inter-agency committee is not simply complete foolishness, we would do better to listen closely, to consider Mitch's portrayal of the value conflicts and the process of value conflict itself.

Listening and learning: specifying ends and generating means

To come up with some sort of consensus, he says, 'you try to do a bunch of things. One is that you're very diplomatic: You always try and recognize that people have proper points of view, that they're good and right-thinking people, and they may just disagree.'

Mitch's language here is at once tempered, political, and moral. He speaks of 'trying', and not just doing. He recognises and embraces a political role of diplomacy. But diplomacy, for Mitch it seems, has a certain tone to it. He portrays this role as being respectful, not manipulative, as demanding the work of recognising others' integrity, not of 'talking 'em into anything', as acknowledging rather than slighting others' 'proper' points of view. So Mitch suggests the discipline he needs in order to 'try and recognize' that these committee members – however much they may be in conflict with one another – are 'good and right-thinking people'.

Mitch suggests, furthermore, that the consensus-building process was not only about airport access but about managing and building working relationships too. In situations of conflict and high stakes, diplomacy apparently doesn't come easily, and here Mitch points to the complex demands of dealing with inter-agency conflict.

To 'always try and recognize that people have proper points of view', Mitch faces at the very same time a practical challenge – being critical in assessing what he hears – and an ethical challenge – respecting the person speaking and 'their place at the table'. Arising here in Mitch's story, these challenges grow out of a fundamental tension in political pluralism – between respecting another's 'right' to hold whatever viewpoint they do, and responding critically to whatever biases, exaggerations, posturing, threats, innuendos and political ploys, for example, those viewpoints may be expressing.

Mitch suggests he tries to recognise a good deal more than some abstract 'right' that participants may have to hold their points of view. He speaks of trying to recognise 'that they're good and right-thinking people', that they are to be valued in themselves, as good people, presumably committed to serving on the inter-agency committee in good faith (somehow construed), doing right by their own lights, and 'right-thinking' people, presumably serious, attentive to the diverse problems before them, thoughtful participants in the process.

But Mitch would surely not believe indiscriminately that all participants were equally serious, that everyone would act in good faith, that everyone would be equally thoughtful and attentive to the matters at hand. So that need to discriminate, to pay attention carefully, seems precisely what Mitch teaches us: that in situations of conflict and inter-agency politics, one of the challenges of managing the process, as Mitch has tried to do, will be to learn about the character of the participants (for 'they may just disagree'), even as one ought to begin, he suggests, with presumptions of respect, and attempts to recognise the value of others' presence and participation.

But Mitch says more too about the consensus-building process. Not only must he learn about each participant on the committee, he must learn about their relationships as they develop in real time. Seeing that 'they may just disagree', he goes on, 'You try to precisely determine the disagreement. You try to clarify whether or not there really are points of disagreement.'

This sounds simple enough, but it is extraordinarily complex – the challenge that every mediator of disputes faces (cf. Kolb 1994; Kressel & Pruitt 1989). Mitch reports his efforts, first, to explore the participants' unfolding relationships, and second, to explore 'whether or not there really are points of disagreement', matters of value in the world that really are, or may just appear to be, in dispute. Listening closely to the participants, Mitch must explore not just their individual intentions, not just what they are individually making of one another's words, and not just the evolving relationships being created in the heat of the moment, either, but also the actual issues, the 'substantive' matters of concern 'out there' in the case at hand. For, in half the cases he has worked on, Mitch claims, disagreements are not what they first seem.[3]

'[I]n a good half of the cases', he says,

> you really don't have an argument, you just think you have one. One person is saying, 'I really think you can't affect local communities', and another person is saying, 'I think we have to get there by the shortest way.' Those two things are not mutually exclusive – but you can wind

up in a heated argument, and we did. But if you precisely define the point of conflict by saying, for example, 'Maybe we can keep both of these as objectives', then both people start saying, 'Yeah, OK!'

Consider the judgement Mitch must bring to bear here. How can he come to see in a given case that, even though you 'wind up in a heated argument', you really may not 'have an argument, you just think you have one'? What exercise of judgement can help Mitch – or any of us – move from heated argument to both parties coming to see issues in a new way – acknowledging, 'Yeah, OK!' – coming to see, perhaps, that both of their objectives may be served rather than threatened?

'One person is saying, "I really think you can't affect local communities", and another person is saying, "I think we have to get there by the shortest way."' Mitch holds both voices and both views before us, and he seems to tell us about the importance of exploring both the participants and the world together.

Listening to each participant carefully (or presumably trying to!), recognising how easily 'you can wind up in a heated argument', Mitch sees that the content of what's being claimed, discussed, or argued must not be confused with the participants' working relationships in this particular committee.[4]

Distinguishing these issues, Mitch sees that, to do his job well, he has to learn both about these participants and about the particular claims they are making. Trying to learn about these participants, he has to try to distinguish each person from others who might have been sent to represent their group or agency – others more (or less) intransigent, competent, reasonable, obnoxious, or productive.

Trying to learn about their claims – perhaps to avoid an unnecessarily heated argument – Mitch tries 'precisely [to] define the point of conflict'. Mitch can only plausibly suggest the possibility of keeping 'both of these as objectives', if he can somehow consider those objectives, and the values at stake in them, in their own right.

He can only suggest that 'those two things are not mutually exclusive' – appearances in the committee notwithstanding! – if he can look beyond the expressed 'values' to learn quickly about the matters of value actually involved here. Like an attentive mediator, he must ask if and how the matters of value, the stakes and 'priorities', differ for the participants.[5]

He must explore the participants' 'ends' in two senses. First, he must try to understand what they articulate, express, and claim – their felt values. Second, he must assess what's involved more specifically in the 'end' at hand: what's actually involved in 'not impacting the community'? What does that mean, not only in intention, but in the world?

Exploring and considering different ways of specifying 'ends', Mitch must also explore available 'means'. He must also ask instrumental questions: can he imagine a way of technically satisfying both concerns at the same time?

Managing the committee, Mitch has to explore ends and means together. He has to explore the ambiguity of stated goals and the uncertain requirements of what must be done. To do that, he must make judgements about what the stated goals actually mean in the world: about what is actually involved in not affecting local communities, about what is actually involved in trying 'to get there by the shortest way'.

So Mitch has to learn about the values at stake in various options, just as he also must attend to the expressed 'values' – the beliefs, loyalties, commitments, biases, and prejudices of the participants – if he wishes to work with them successfully, to show them that he recognises them as full and serious participants, that he acknowledges and recognises their interests, that he understands their viewpoints. Only if Mitch can learn about value in the world, rather than in the attitudes of committee members, can he come to see – and possibly also help the committee to see – that protecting communities and finding 'the shortest way' are objectives that can in fact (really, objectively) be pursued together.

So Mitch tells us here about a learning process in which we – and he and the participants – witness a transition from 'heated argument' to a more joint exploration of alternatives, 'both people ... saying, "Yeah, OK!"' Managing the inter-agency committee, Mitch has to mediate its disputes. He has to try to work with conflicting agency agendas, and fashion working agreements about possible joint action: in this case, planning for improved airport access.

Notice that Mitch does not, apparently, assume that the committee members will be omniscient – models of perfect rationality. Quite the contrary: he suggests how easily 'you can wind up in a heated argument', but he does also tell us that the committee relationships need not end there, for both he and the participants may be able to learn together. So he teaches us about contingency rather than certainty, attentive pragmatism rather than sure-fire technique.

'You find that a lot of people have difficulty expressing what their precise concern is', he says, 'so it takes a lot of probing, and you have to be gentle about it ... "What exactly is your concern? I don't under-stand."'

Mitch has to learn both about the world of the committee – its particu-lar participants – and about the world beyond that committee, too. Telling us that 'you have to be gentle about it', Mitch warns us that riding roughshod over committee members – even to find out what it is they're really concerned about – just won't do. If the committee is to work well together, their working relationships will have to be explored and nur-tured, not presumed and taken for granted.

So being 'gentle' and taking 'enormous amounts of time' can pay off, Mitch suggests. 'Finally, someone will say, "My concern is that we're going to get too far afield when we don't have the basic information we need to go to the mayor and say, 'This is what we propose.'"'

Then,

once you precisely define it, you try and make some determination as to whether or not you agree, whether or not that's really a problem. If it's a problem, then you try and find a way around it. If it's not a problem, then you have to convince the other person that you don't think it's a problem because ... or: 'Well, I finally understand your point. Yeah, we do need some set of alternatives.'

Mitch shows us again the need for judgement in these situations – and the need for alternatives to accepting anyone's opening statements at 'face value'. Real value and 'face value' are not necessarily the same. Perhaps a way can be found to pursue both, apparently conflicting, objec-tives; perhaps, though, Mitch will himself be persuaded: 'Well, I finally understand your point. Yeah, we do need some set of alternatives.'

Perhaps, too, he will disagree with one or more of the participants, so that he will then have to try to 'convince the other person' that what they think is a problem is really not one. So Mitch teaches us here about judgements that are contingent – partially open to evidence and argu-ment, to persuasion and testimony. But what if others will not be con-vinced?

PART 3: POLITICS, SENSITIVITY, AND IMPROVISATION

Ever-present power, ever-important judgement

Mitch's story about the airport access case is instructive here, for it suggests that the play of power is never far from processes of practical judgement (Forester & Kreiswirth 1993):

> The city's point of view, for example, was always that we needed to do a full-blown alternatives analysis, which meant coming up with several different alignments, weighing the pluses and minuses of each of them, and then coming up with our prescribed choice – the one that we thought was absolutely the best – and [the reasons] why. [Our] Agency in particular did not think that was the best course of action. We kept saying, 'This thing has been studied to death.' And frankly, it has: Airport access has been on the table, so to speak, for at least 25 years.
>
> We thought that we pretty much knew all the pluses and minuses – or could make good guesses at them – and that really wasn't going to help us a whole lot. What we needed to do was forge ahead to really get something on the table, to try and begin forging this coalition that would get the job done, because we knew it was going to be very expensive. Previous alignments and suggestions [about] improving airport access had been killed for a variety of reasons. That's what we wanted to work on. We wanted to abate community pressure.
>
> Ultimately, that was not resolved. The city was cut out of the process by fiat. That happened because they kept harping on this alternatives analysis, and ultimately we could not get a precise reason as to why that was so necessary.
>
> They would say, 'What about this alignment?'
>
> We would say, 'That was shown to engender community pressure and opposition that would stop it.'
>
> They said, 'We're not sure this is the best way', and we'd say, 'Come up with a better way.'
>
> But they never did that. They never came up with a viable alternative that was well-thought-out and avoided most of the problems.
>
> Then they said, 'We're not sure that we have much to offer in this process.'
>
> And we said, 'Just give us a clear problem statement, and we'll be happy to consider it.'

But they got stymied – that stumped them.

So the Transportation Agency and the Regional Authority just went ahead without them. The city continued to be a player in this, but in a more minor role. It was about this time that the city's budget problems were becoming clear, and this was not the highest priority for the city.

Anyway, that gave us the space to go on with our own agenda. We realized that we disagreed, and we couldn't find a way to resolve the conflict except by agreeing to spend the next two years doing alternatives analysis – and we didn't want to do that. We were under pressure from our boss, the Director, who said, 'Find me a solution, and do it quickly', because he was under pressure by the governor and the mayor. So everything was, 'We have to do something. Let's do what we can do.'

We came up with a solution that was probably viable, but it wasn't completely viable because we could not generate enough public sector interest in helping to fund it, and that's why it had to go through a modification. Financing was a very big concern, frankly.

I think there's an important lesson to learn here: Sometimes you just don't resolve conflicts. Things get resolved by who has more power or by fiat. The city disagreed. After the city got stymied in coming up with a viable alternative, we kicked it upstairs from our point of view and started dealing with the Director of the Transportation Agency and the Executive Director of the Regional Authority. We planned to go to the mayor's chief assistant and say, 'Here's what we want to do. We're having difficulty getting anywhere. We are happy to pick up the ball at this point and present you with a final solution.'

That actually never happened, but we were fully ready to go that route, and the city – the staff level of the city – knew it. I think they were getting the message, and they weren't getting the creativity from their own people that they had hoped for. The point is that sometimes conflict doesn't get resolved.

So Mitch's story is as much about power politics as it is about consensus-building. He points to arguments and counter-arguments about how the airport access alternatives analysis would be carried out, but such processes of persuasion went only so far. He points, too, to budget problems, other priorities, pressures from the governor and mayor, and financing concerns: 'The city was cut out of the process by fiat', he says. But the resulting solution proposed by Mitch's agency without the city's participation also 'wasn't completely viable because we could not generate enough public sector interest in helping to fund it'.

'There's an important lesson here', Mitch tells us: 'Sometimes you just don't resolve conflicts. Things get resolved by who has more power or by fiat.'

Mitch's every move, we may now appreciate, takes place on an institutional stage structured by relations of power, expertise, access, information, and so on. Does this mean we should disregard Mitch's earlier remarks about consensus-building?

Hardly, for Mitch's story is about the contingencies of power – about both the possibilities of consensus-building and the possibilities of power plays. His story can help us to recognise, first, that power shapes processes of participation and judgement and, second, that planners' actual judgements can affect what happens within and through existing relations of power.

Precisely because relations of power are ever-present, always being strengthened or weakened, reproduced or resisted, Mitch cannot avoid the dangers of poor judgement. Put another way, in a world in which dialogue prevailed, in which the better argument gained the consent of all affected, Mitch's judgements might be less important. But the more power relations threaten to protect bureaucracies rather than communities, to line the pockets of downtown interests and displace the less affluent, to disregard public welfare in favour of the lucrative opportunities of the few, the more the practical and political judgement of public-serving planners will matter.[6]

Mitch had more to say about his difficulties of diplomacy at work:[7]

How do I learn on the job? Mostly by butting my head up against the wall. Take the 'problem agency' that I was talking about before. I was getting nowhere, going absolutely nowhere. My supervisors had taken a very antagonistic approach to begin with, and I was seen as an extension of them (I was new on the job then). So I started out being antagonistic, saying, 'We're headquarters. You should do what we're telling you to do.' That went nowhere in a hurry. It did not produce results ...

Being antagonistic was not providing any kind of results – this agency was doing what it wanted to do anyway – so I had to stop, and backtrack: 'OK. What's not working about this? We're pissing people off. That's not a good idea.'

Mitch was not blind to the history of relationships he inherited, but, initially, he was not particularly critical of them either. Not only was he perceived by others as an extension of his supervisors' prior antagonism, but he actually adopted that role – which he then came to realise, 'went nowhere in a hurry'.

He notes the power relationships here too: 'this agency was doing what it wanted to do anyway'. Going nowhere, Mitch had to stop and 'back-track', to ask practically, 'What's not working about this?'

He was able to ask that question – and answer it, too, apparently – to realise: 'We're pissing people off. That's not a good idea.'

So, in this instance, Mitch had to learn less about airport access or substantive transportation issues than about his own performance, his own strategy and style of action. Recognising and rejecting the more antagonistic strategy, Mitch had to try another approach:

So I changed my tactic and started saying, 'All right, can we start fresh?' That's difficult to do, but eventually you can get to the point where you start anew. Faces change and players change – you get the chance to do that. Yet even that did not work to my full satisfaction; it wasn't like people automatically understood where I was coming from. They said, 'Oh, strategic planning. What is that, anyway?'

You learn about them as individuals and you learn about the history of the organization and their history within the organization.

You also change your objectives. Reaching for a mountain at any point in time will pretty much get you tired and not achieve your objective. But if you start, saying, 'Well, OK, let's keep talking, let's try and find a way to communicate, easily, so that there is a lot of communication.'

Then when you get that done, you say, 'OK, now we're communicating. What is it you need me to do in order to help you develop this strategic planning process?' Very often they couldn't describe that, so you have to go back and learn more about the agency.

Mitch stresses both the need 'to communicate easily' and the extraordinary difficulties of achieving such communication. Meeting with another agency's representative, he must improvise as he tries to develop a strategic transportation planning process:

So much of it is intuitive. Essentially, you keep butting your head up against the wall and saying, 'No, that didn't work', 'No, that didn't work', 'All right, how about a different tactic, smaller objectives, closer objectives? Instead of trying to develop a strategic planning process, let's try talking to this one person, right now. Let's talk about describing the external environment of the agency. If we can get that done this year, maybe that's a good idea.' You start by doing that. Maybe that works. So you can accurately describe the problems the agency faces. And then you say, 'OK, now let's talk about the internal problems.'

Mitch is not simply considering various means to his ends here. Instead, he tells us about reconsidering and changing the very ends themselves. His attention shifts from the broader goal of developing the strategic planning process to the much more limited objective of building relationships with perhaps just 'this one person right now', to describe the external environment of the agency at hand.

As he evaluates his practice and recognises, 'No, that didn't work', 'No, that didn't work', Mitch reconsiders what he has done and what he might now try to do, what he might now try to achieve as practical 'ends'.

Reflecting on his work, Mitch says:

...some of the things that I used to suggest to them were politically insensitive. For example, I said, 'Maybe you have too many people. Maybe your headcount – the number of employees that you have – is way too many for the job you're doing. Is this a problem for you?'

Well, it might be, but the agency was never going to admit that, never going to put it on paper. Maybe this is a problem. But instead of suggesting it, you start saying, 'Just between you and me – I would never write this, of course – is this one of the problems?'

And most people will say, 'Yeah, that's really one of the problems. But no, we're not going to put it in a document' – now we're getting somewhere!

The ambiguities of power necessitate improvisation

Notice the necessarily improvised character of the learning Mitch has to do here, given the power relations that make his apparently simple question *not* simple but threatening. His changing of ends and objectives, his reconsideration of style and approach, his finding a way 'off the record' of breaking through and having the feeling, 'now we're getting somewhere!' – all this is quite ordinary, unexceptional, commonplace, but it is extraordinary too, for it exemplifies the improvised character of practical judgement in the planning process. Mitch tells a story of his own initially fruitless attempt to learn about another agency. Coming now to see his own earlier line of questioning as 'politically insensitive', blind to the vulnerabilities of other agency staff, Mitch goes on to tell us about the political contingencies of learning at work, and the improvised 'sensitivity' required to attend to those contingencies.

He strengthens the point by referring to his own boss:

In this kind of work, there are no clear rules and regulations as to how you carry out your daily job responsibilities. So I prioritize and decide what I need to do on a daily basis by the seat of my pants. Communication is absolutely essential, and that's at all levels.

I've gone through a number of bosses. Sometimes you have a good rapport with your supervisor and you understand what he or she wants to get done. But they're not always that clear either: 'Give me this, you know. Give me a study on X, Y, Z.'

He's a busy person, he doesn't want a million questions about this, and sometimes he's physically out of the office so that you can't ask him. So you have to find a shorthand way of saying, 'Do you want this or do you want that? Do you want the four-month study or do you want the six-month study? What are the boundaries?' You try and work through it slowly, but you have to establish the communication so that you get the scope of what they want done and the urgency with which they want it done.

Of course, you also have your own agenda of things that you want to accomplish, and you have to fit that in with everything else. So you begin to juggle. You say, 'OK, I've got to do a little bit on that, get an interim something to this person. But I really want to work on this.' And it was typical of me to have four, five, six, eight projects running at the same time. So you have to meet this deadline over here, and then you say, 'OK, I need to do this ...'

Again Mitch describes his work to learn about values, about what matters, about what, in fact, he should be doing, what his mandate is, what his responsibilities are. But learning about responsibility and goals, here, is intimately tied to questions of power, access, ambiguity and agenda-setting.

The presence of power within and between organisations in the planning process does not make attentiveness, judgement and improvisation on Mitch's part less necessary, it makes them more necessary.

'So you begin to juggle', Mitch says. Mitch's need to improvise, he suggests, is as political as it is interpersonal, as ethically difficult as technically uncertain. Mitch must juggle and improvise, he tells us, if he is even to figure out what his own assignments and mandates are. He must interpret the 'scope' and 'urgency' of what his supervisors really want. There are, he says, 'no clear rules and regulations as to how you carry out your daily job responsibilities'.

Mitch is far from suggesting that he can do whatever he wants, that 'anything goes' in his juggling or improvisation. He provides us with no recipes, no prescriptions, but with a more rough and ready pragmatic sense of 'good' work. He stresses the need to pay attention to several projects at once. He has told us of the need for a 'political sensitivity' in which interpersonal sensitivity, too, seems to play a clear, if subordinate, role. He notes, as well, the need for communication and rapport, and the need to juggle and improvise, because any communication and rapport seem fickle at best.

Mitch tries to learn about what matters here – what matters to his supervisors, and to others, too. But he is no blank slate himself: 'Of course, you also have your own agenda of things that you want to accomplish, and you have to fit that in with everything else.'

He points here to issues of day-to-day politics and ethics: the conflict of agendas, the possibilities of analysts' agendas pre-empting those of public officials, and the need to 'fit' a given day's work into a broader context of practice, too. We do not know enough here about the particular content and setting of Mitch's work to evaluate it with respect to any one project. But Mitch's account presents a challenge to us, nevertheless: if planners need inevitably to improvise politically and ethically – because of the ambiguities of value and power relations, to take the most obvious reasons – what attentiveness, what rationality, does such public-serving work require? We turn to this question below.

Mitch's improvising is hardly without its own stresses:

When things did get frustrating, what kept me going was a good bottle of Jack Daniels and a weekend away. It can be frustrating – you can get dumped on, it's all very much left to fate and chance. You try and do the best job you can do, and yet people will come down on you because you're not doing the job that they want you to do, or there was a misunderstanding and you are supplying a different product than what was asked for. Sometimes there's even malfeasance in that people are deliberately misdirecting you to keep you away from things that they don't want you to see or keeping you out of a process that you should and need to be in on.

Noting the role of 'fate and chance', Mitch speaks even more pointedly here about political power, deliberate misdirection, the calculated invisibility of 'things they don't want you to see', what he refers to as 'malfeasance'. Significantly, Mitch neither minimises and dismisses politics, nor does he make 'everything so political that nothing can be done'. This, surely, is one of the real messages of his own practice story: brute political power is real, inescapable, pervasive and frustrating, but not so total that no good work can be done; not so total that some significant bad work cannot be avoided.

Lacking rationality, adding analysis

But Mitch – unlike others, no doubt – seems to thrive on political challenges. He seems to believe that he has a special contribution to make – not despite, but because of the politics of his job:

The thing that I think that I've learned about myself is that the agenda that I bring, the thing that I am always trying to work on, is trying to get more decisions made on a more rational basis. Because by and large – as a lot of people have stated, and I have found to be true – decision-making is far from a rational process. Some politician wants this, he or she's got a lot of power, and that's the way it's going to be, goddammit. So they're done by fiat rather than by a good, intellectual, analytical process.

My agenda has always been, 'Let's try and interject just a little bit more analytical thought into this.' And sometimes I'm successful and sometimes I'm not. Sometimes I get dumped on for reasons that are unfair or unjust, and sometimes I'm the beneficiary of great good luck, where I haven't done anything and have gotten credit for it.

So Mitch has few illusions that actual decision-making processes are terribly rational. He is as clear about the politicians with the power to dictate 'that's the way it's going to be, goddammit' as he is about the apparent opportunity to 'interject just a little more analytical thought into this'. Again, though, Mitch points to the role of contingency: he is sometimes successful, sometimes not, sometimes 'dumped on for reasons that are unfair or unjust' and sometimes 'the beneficiary of great good luck'.

We need to ask, then, what sort of judgement is needed by planners and policy analysts who face situations like Mitch's. We can give Mitch the first, if not the last, word:

> I've learned numerous lessons on this job that I'll bring to my next position. Number one, always be tactful. Always. The old saying that a teaspoon of honey will get you further than a quart of vinegar is definitely true. I don't think I've learned it on this job, but it's been hit home more directly here.
>
> Dealing with social problems is enormously complex, and – depending on your point of view – you can come up with very rational ways of dealing with issues, depending on how you define the issue, what the problem is, or what aspect of the problem you find most compelling … There are always points of conflict and contradiction. Some of those go away with good analytical thought; some of them remain because you're concentrating on different aspects of the problem; and some can be resolved.

In Mitch's view, then, power has a role, but it has its limits too. His account could be read as contradictory, but it is far more clearly listened to as complex and practical: arbitrary power matters, and so does analytical thought. How much one or the other matters in a particular case will be contingent, structured by relations of power and language, access and discourse, but contingently shaped by fluid inter-agency politics, by multiple readings of ambiguous goals and mandates, by personality, chance, analytical skills and practical judgement, too.

So, in each particular case, Mitch has to bring judgement to bear. He has to learn about this political and technical situation, its more general institutional structure, and its quite specific peculiarities and particularities. He has to learn, in this case, about the possible play of power, the opportunities that may exist or be created, the coalitions there to be formed, the values in the world and the concerns of parties to be protected, clarified, enhanced, or counteracted.

PART 4: PUBLIC DELIBERATION AND PRACTICAL POLITICAL JUDGEMENT

Concluding lessons: learning about value and the necessities of ethical and political improvisation

What can we learn from Mitch's story, then, about the demands of practical judgement or moral improvisation in planning? What can we learn from Mitch's own struggles to assess the stakes of particular proposals, to assess his own responsibilities and mandates, to learn about other agencies?

We find insights here that do not specify 'how to do it', no matter what the situation at hand, but that suggest, rather, how planners need to approach the challenges Mitch has identified. We can frame these suggestions in the form of practical needs or requirements.

First, *the need to learn about value*: we need an account of judgement in planning that recognises its imaginative and exploratory role as much as it recognises its judicial or justificatory role. Mitch does try to come up with strategies and suggestions that will gain others' consent, that he can justify as legitimate to them but, *before* he can do any of that, he must explore and assess what's at stake in various proposals or options, what value in the world may be threatened, whether others have expressed explicit concerns about such matters or not (yet). Not only must planners attend to the details – the distinctive and relevant particulars – of new situations, but they must often re-interpret multiple ends and mandates themselves in new ways in each situation – as new 'facts that matter', for example, are discovered (interest rates have just skyrocketed; buried wastes have just been discovered at the building site, and so on).

Second, *the need to exploit ambiguity*: we need an account of judgement that will be interpretive and probing rather than solely calculative; hardly one accepting at face value what co-participants say, but rather one exploring articulated ends as well as proposed means, recognising ambiguity as an abiding source of opportunity rather than as a persistent source of confusion.[8]

Third, *the need for deliberation about ends as well as means*: planners must explore explicit ends and objectives, goals and mandates, so we need an account of practical judgement that takes seriously the practitioner's deliberative search for value, the practitioner's reflection upon the question, 'What should we want?' (individually and collectively). Mitch, for example, recounted both the inter-agency committee's goal-setting efforts and his own 'juggling' of agendas and priorities. Neither preferences nor 'interests' are 'given' once and for all in each practical situation: ends and goals, mandates and responsibilities, obligations and commitments must be interpreted, specified anew in new situations. How can and ought this to be done in different contexts?

Fourth, *the need to appreciate that practical judgement is reconstructive as well as justificatory*: our notion of practical judgement in planning cannot be reduced to one of adequate justification. If practical judgement is a three-legged stool, perception or recognition constitute one leg, justification constitutes another, and the crafting or fitting of action to the circumstances at hand constitutes the third. Amelie Rorty (1988, p.286) has put this powerfully in her discussion of 'the myth of justificatory judicialism':

[J]udicialism tends to distinguish the judicial function of rationality from (what gets relegated to) the craftsmanly imagination exercised in constructing integrative solutions. Emphasis on judicialism unfortunately tends to focus on the moment of radical, selective choice, rather than on the delicate and difficult processes that precede choice, the processes of generating and articulating the range of alternatives.[9]

A notion of judgement that depends so heavily upon procedures, tests, or methods of justification that it obscures the prior work of problem perception and recognition, and the crafting of action (Mitch's 'you have to fit that in with everything else') must be an inadequate one.

Fifth, *the need for public deliberation in the face of power*: we need a notion of judgement that will be dialogical, communicative and political – that will conceive of judgement as growing from a communicative, deliberative, *thoughtful* and *careful* process staged and shaped by existing, and fluid, contingent relations of power. Issues of inclusion and exclusion, power and agenda-setting, arise clearly and problematically in Mitch's account of his work.

Public deliberation depends less upon technique than upon conversation – inevitably a thoroughly political conversation – in which affected parties have always vulnerable, contingent abilities to participate, to voice their concerns. Practical judgement, then, comes to depend less on instrumental calculation and more on potential consent – consent given the benefits of the best available instrumental knowledge as one among many considerations. So public deliberation is always itself contingent and vulnerable, shaped by the quality of public participation as well as knowledge, by well-informed consent as well as true beliefs, by reconstructive dialogue as well as simple bargaining. Searching for an understanding of judgement that could combine moments of perception and justification, Seyla Benhabib (1988, p.39) quotes Hannah Arendt in apt ways to develop this point:

> The power of judgment rests on a potential agreement with others, and the thinking process which is active in judging something is not, like the thought process of pure reasoning, a dialogue between me and myself, but finds itself always primarily, even if I am quite alone in making up my mind, in an anticipated communication with others with whom I know I must finally come to some agreement. From this potential agreement judgment derives its specific validity.

Of this anticipated communication, Arendt continues:

> And this enlarged way of thinking, which as judgment knows how to transcend its individual limitations, cannot function in strict isolation or solitude; it needs the presence of others 'in whose place' it must think, whose perspectives it must take into consideration, and without whom it never has the opportunity to operate at all.

Sixth, *the need to bridge Habermasian and neo-Aristotelian accounts of practical rationality*: we need an account of judgement that is as attentive to Habermasian inclusiveness and participation as it is to more Aristotelian perception and recognition of value, as attentive to issues of 'right' as to issues of 'good'. Without the perception of value, participants can have little to say; without the inclusion of citizens, deliberation can have little legitimacy. Seyla Benhabib (1988, pp. 46–7) puts these demands eloquently:

> Between the basic institutions of a polity embodying principles of the morally right and the domain of moral interactions in the life world, in

which virtue often comes to the fore, lie civic practices and associations of a society in which individuals face each other neither as pure legal subjects nor as moral agents standing under ties of ethical obligations to each other, but as public agents in a political space. The gap between the demands of justice, as it articulates the morally right, and the demands of virtue, as it defines the quality of our relations to others in the everyday lifeworld, can be bridged by cultivating qualities of civic friendship and solidarity ... Whereas the traditional liberal model from Kant to Rawls sees a rupture here between the public virtue of impersonal justice and the private virtue of goodness, it is possible to envisage, not their identity, but their mediation.

The discourse model of ethics, which enjoins enlarged thought by making the perspective of all involved in a dialogue situation the *sine qua non* of the moral standpoint, allows us to think of this continuity and mediation ... The articulation of differences through civic and political association is essential for us to comprehend and to come to appreciate the perspective of others. The feelings of friendship and solidarity result precisely through the extension of our moral and political imagination, not *in vacuo* or via a Rawlsian thought experiment, but through the actual confrontation in public life with the point of view of those who are otherwise strangers to us, but who become known to us through their public presence as voices and perspectives we have to take into account.

We have, here, no recipe or technique for public deliberation and practical judgement. We have, instead, an approach to deliberation and judgement that appeals to the public recognition and engagement of difference, a discursive ethics protecting and nurturing voice, an argumentative planning that seeks not deal-making but public imagination and reconstruction. Mitch asks us for no less when he acknowledges incessant and pervasive politics, malfeasance, and wilfulness, but nevertheless reminds us that tactfulness and analysis can make a difference, that some issues can be resolved, that neither technique nor brute power are all there is. His story – if we are to understand the possibilities of practical political judgement in planning better than we do – is worth taking to heart.[10]

NOTES

1   We need always to understand the challenges of planning in the face of power. One of those challenges, certainly, is to address the ethical relativism promoted both by a scientistic view of the world and an uncritical, post-modern, pluralist view. The scientistic view reduces value to subjective preferences, making no assessable cognitive claims; the uncritical post-modern view is so concerned about privileging a 'foundational' set of ethical standards that it loses any basis for the criticism of 'other' ethical views. Scientism presumes ethics cannot get started; uncritical post-modernism presumes ethics can never arrive at non-arbitrarily imposed destinations. Both pretend to 'respect' value positions and doubt their rational evaluation or assessment; both confuse respecting a person with believing their claims are justified (cf. Putnam 1990).

2   Working in a situation of obvious institutional conflict, what forms of value does Mitch have to consider? Compare: assessing problems of deliberation, paternalism, the public interest, justice, evaluation of consequences, and the character of good agreements. Note that this chapter depends less upon the accuracy or 'truth' of the details of Mitch's account – for perhaps he has been somewhat self-serving – than it depends upon his story's enabling our characterisation of ethical challenges plausibly haunting quite ordinary planning practice. No doubt Mitch has left a great deal out of his account, but no story, and no analysis of ethics, can ever be 'complete'. The question is not whether we have the last word but, as we explore the ways practitioners learn about value in a political world, if we even have helpful first words. The proof's in the pudding.

3   It is not that participants do not know what they themselves are talking about, though their 'minds may change' as they learn new things; they are simply a good deal less clear about what precisely their counterparts are saying.

4   This point reflects a central truism in communications research (see e.g. Watzlawick 1976) and negotiation literature (see e.g. Fisher & Ury 1983). Content and context must be related, but must not be equated. This has been explored politically in appropriations of critical social theory, too (see e.g. Forester 1993).

5   Lawrence Susskind argues that an essential part of dispute resolution in planning involves 'exploiting differences' between parties: trading across differing priorities so that both parties can gain on their more highly-valued priorities in exchange for giving way on less-valued concerns (see e.g. Susskind & Cruikshank 1987).

6   This is obviously not to say or assume that planners have much influence or power in general. But our question here is: what is involved in planners using whatever influence they *do* have in the highly political settings in which they work? For an extensive account of case experiences and analyses, see Krumholz and Forester (1990).

7   His remarks hardly provide 'how to do it' instructions, but they can teach us more about his work of practical judgement and, in particular, his learning about value in practical cases.

8   For related work, see Fischer and Forester (1993), Forester (1992) and Krumholz and Forester (1990: Part 2).

9   Rorty continues: 'A sophisticated and modest form of judicialism recognizes that the justificatory model of rational action is not sufficient to explain, let alone to generate, the delicate tonalities of the *petites actions* that constitute a large part of acting well ... [R]easons individuate as well as justify actions. Judicialism ... is incomplete as a moral theory because it does not by itself provide a substantive

theory of virtue, or principles and criteria, for what is good and right. And however essential the judicial model may be to a rationally constructed practical life, it is incomplete as a psychological theory because it does not exhaust, nor can it serve as the model for, the many functions of thought in forming appropriate actions' (p.286).

10   Thanks for comments on an earlier draft of this chapter to Raphael Fischler, Susan Hendler, Jean Hillier, Beth Howe, Michael Savonis, and Huw Thomas.

REFERENCES

Benhabib, S., 1988, 'Judgement and the Moral Foundation of Politics in Arendt's Thought', *Political Theory*, Vol. 16(1), pp. 29–51.

Fischer, F. and Forester, J. (eds), 1993, 'The Argumentative Turn', in *Policy Analysis and Planning*, Durham, NC: Duke University Press.

Fisher, R. and Ury, W., 1983, *Getting to Yes*, New York, NY: Penguin.

Forester, J., 1992, *On the Ethics of Planning: Profiles of Planners and What they Teach us about Practical Judgement and Moral Improvisation*, Cornell Working Papers in Planning, Ithaca, NY: Cornell University.

Forester, J., 1993, *Critical Theory, Public Policy and Planning Practice: Towards a Critical Pragmatism*, Albany, NY: State University of New York Press.

Forester, J. and Kreiswirth, B. (eds), 1993, *Profiles of Planners in Land Use, Transportation and Environmental Planning*, Ithaca, NY: Department of City and Regional Planning, Cornell University.

Kolb, D., 1994, *When Talk Works*, San Francisco, CA: Jossey Bass.

Kressel, K. and Pruitt, D., 1989, *Mediation Research*, San Francisco, CA: Jossey Bass.

Krumholz, N. and Forester, J., 1990, *Making Equity Planning Work*, Philadelphia, PA: Temple University Press.

Putnam, H., 1990, *Realism with a Human Face*, Cambridge, MA: Harvard University Press.

Rorty, A., 1988, *Mind in Action: Essays in the Philosophy of Mind*, Boston: Beacon Press.

Susskind, L. and Cruikshank, J., 1987, *Breaking the Impasse*, New York, NY: Basic Books.

Watzlawick, P., 1976, *How Real is Real*, New York, NY: Vintage.

Chapter 10

Values and planning education

Charles Hoch

DOING GOOD AND BEING RIGHT

If a tree falls in the forest, but no one hears it crash, does the tree make a sound? Pondering this question as an adolescent, I decided that most definitely the tree made a sound when it hit the earth, no matter that no human ears registered the noise. Later, after undergraduate studies, I changed my mind. Sound, I learned, was the product of sensation, an active process of physiological response. No responder. No response. No sound.

The falling tree example illustrates a kind of understanding that separates the workings of nature from human intention and action. The question presumes two worlds: the real world and the world we experience. It's a set-up. A lumberjack busy deciding which trees to cut and how best to do it would find the question puzzling; so too would the deaf hiker. But the planning theorist on holiday in the woods would understand.

> Look [she might say], there are causes and reasons, objects and ideas, cities and plans, facts and values. Facts command assent, values evoke intention. Facts are hard, values soft. Facts are objective, values subjective. Facts the object of scientific rational inquiry, values the subject of moral reflection. We need planning theory to unite the two worlds. Good planning theory provides a rational foundation upon which to build relationships between the two worlds.

Pausing only for a short breath, she continues:

> The forces of urbanisation shape and channel the geography of every-day life in obscure and complex ways. Even though urbanites each pursue their own purposes, the collective consequences of their individual actions litter the urban landscape – troublesome trees that fall unannounced. Good planning theory will uncover the social and economic sources of urban blight, amplify the sounds of decay, and propose remedies that cure and heal. Good theory offers rational reassurance about the coherence and predictability of our efforts to reduce the undesirable uncertainties of modern urban life.

Applause among the other members of her outing party. (Well, maybe not.)

The salience of epistemology (How do you know it's true? How can you be sure?) in planning theory conversations flows from the persistent belief in this dualism. If you believe in the dualism, theory becomes important, because only theory can bridge the gap between scientific fact and moral value. However, many planning practitioners do not believe in the dualism. For them planning theory appears peripheral and irrelevant. Many practically-minded students who dutifully endure theoretical education quickly cast it aside when they get their first job. Even those who believe in theory find little to reinforce that faith in the world of practice. Given our (other planning teachers' and academics') belief in the importance of theory, how is this possible? How is it that students-turned-planners can find gainful employment as professional planners and not use theory? How do these practitioners bridge the gap between fact and value without theory?

There are three responses planning educators and analysts might make:

- *Pedagogical* The students failed to understand the theory we taught (or we failed to teach theory in a manner students found understandable) and so, as practitioners, they cannot build workable bridges. Instead of serving truth they serve political interests. Instead of using the standards of theory to guide practice, they make up arguments to justify what they do. These practitioners mistakenly clothe subjective opinion in the language of truth. We must find ways to improve how we teach theory so that planners will use it and not abuse it on the job.

- *Theoretical*   The theories we have developed so far remain tentative and incomplete. Planners find theoretical knowledge provides insufficient insight and information to bridge the gap when they try to put theoretical knowledge into practice. We must create more coherent, comprehensive and compelling theories – theories that will not only analyse causes, but identify more clearly causes for action.
- *Heretical*   Planning theories and theorists reproduce a fact–value dichotomy which only theoretical concepts can bridge. When students leave the university setting and theoretical conversation, the gap simply disappears. Theoretical knowledge, in many cases, handicaps students who seek to carry on theoretical discussions among accomplished practitioners. We need to teach theory, not as a foundation, but a rhetorical and pragmatic supplement to the learning skills students acquire as they cope with the practical problems of anticipating and alleviating the consequences and causes of collective uncertainty.

I prefer the last response, not for theoretical or epistemological reasons, but historical and pragmatic ones. In this essay I will conduct a brief historical reconnaissance, arguing that the relevance of the first two responses can be tied to the adoption of the social sciences at the core of university planning education in the United States since about 1950. Many planning academics adopted theoretical ideas drawn from the social sciences that fostered the split between theoretical understanding and practical reason. This effort not only imported epistemological problems of the social sciences into academic planning debates, but it simultaneously separated these debates from the practical moral and political concerns of students and alumni pursuing careers in a rapidly-growing profession. I am concerned that we enliven debates about the purposes and scope of democratic planning to attract and educate practitioners from outside conventional planning organisations, and to stimulate attention and respect for the importance of the complex uncertainties which planning seeks to comprehend and reduce.

A HISTORICAL RECONNAISSANCE

Theory plays an awkward role in an applied profession. Professionals can learn to act in useful and effective ways without knowing why their actions work. The founders of city planning made practical proposals and vivid plans. They did not write rational or scientific theories. The craft of planning, such as it was, was taught on the job. Planners learned their craft in the studio and the office. Most – first schooled as architects, engineers and landscape architects – learned to plan the city as an object of practical design.[1]

But, as planning became a function of government, the standards of the design craft were revised and expanded by occupational criteria and government policy. The widespread adoption of zoning regulations, planning commissions and master planning by municipalities, especially after the Second World War, placed new demands on planners as government employees. Planners now addressed the problems of metropolitan congestion, transport, infrastructure, economic growth, public services, and more. Addressing these issues required making comprehensive plans.

Preparing such a plan required foreseeing as clearly as possible the major technological, economic, social and political changes likely to affect the area, as well as some of the ways in which various kinds of change might manifest themselves. Had city planners the knowledge and prescience to undertake so formidable a task (Scott 1969, p.332)?

The problem of fitting population to place using government powers and revenues did not lend itself to conventional planning, with its heavy emphasis on physical design. The functional procedures of government bureaucracy abstracted from the particular and favoured the uniform. This shift from the physical master plan to the comprehensive policy plan represented not just a broadening of scope, but a change in the kind of knowledge needed to practise planning. The social sciences of economics, sociology, political science and public administration offered methods that analysed problems of inefficiency, disorder and inequality among parts of an entire city population. The collection and analysis of abstract measures was guided by socio-economic theories and political objectives organised to meet the demands of government agencies.

Planning education in the university

The rapid growth in employment opportunities for planners in the 1950s and 1960s stimulated the formation and expansion of graduate schools of planning, preparing students to meet the growing demand. The number of graduate planning degrees conferred increased from about one hundred per year in 1955 to almost 1 500 per year in 1975 (Krueckeberg 1984, p.79). The impact on the educational background of practising professionals was twofold. First, university graduate education virtually replaced (and discredited) professional apprenticeship as a prerequisite for professional acceptability. The old guard resisted, but the rapid growth in demand overwhelmed conventional on-the-job training methods. Second, the proportion of planning professionals from the design disciplines of architecture, landscape architecture and engineering declined as well. Surveys of professional planners document this dramatic shift in the educational background of professional planners. In the early 1950s virtually all professional planners had their training or undergraduate degrees in architecture, landscape architecture and engineering. Few had graduate education. By the late 1950s the planning graduate degree was still relatively rare. But the proportion of planners drawn from fields other than design, especially the social sciences, was evident. By 1959 only 40 per cent of professionals had undergraduate degrees in architecture and landscape architecture, while 16 per cent held degrees in the social sciences. The share of designers had declined to 33 per cent by 1967, and barely 25 per cent in 1974. Meanwhile, those with bachelor's degrees in the social sciences had increased their share to about 33 per cent by 1967, where it remained until 1974. Over the same period, the proportion of professional planners with graduate degrees in planning increased from 7 per cent in 1959 to 49.2 per cent in 1974 (AICP 1967; Vasu 1979, pp. 208–9). In the UK, the Town Planning Institute, which had trained and certified professional planners, peaked in 1949, rapidly replaced by planners educated in university and, later, polytechnic planning schools (Cherry 1974, p.227).

Newly-formed university-based planning schools emphasised the production and dissemination of knowledge at the expense of traditional design skills. Faculty and research analysts in the schools adopted forms of inquiry and expectations for professional practice shaped by theoretical and methodological concepts drawn from the practice of social scientific research. The scope of planning expanded to include a wide array of social and economic problems. Preparing students to work as government employees rather than independent consultants required knowledge about organisations. This emphasis on the study of institutional and behavioural relationships pushed questions of physical design toward the margins.

The combination of social science and institutional knowledge into a planning curriculum was laid out for schools in the United States by Harvey Perloff in his book *Education for Planning* (1957):

Perloff argued that planning's claim to professional status could not be realized without a research and theory base for the field ... He looked to social science for the research orientation of planning. At the same time developments in government and in the social sciences concerned with government called for a change in planning process. The rational planning model attempted to provide a framework for both the planner's social scientist role as a generator of knowledge and staff role as an administrator. This very inventive combination of the knowledge base and process issues made the rational planning model very appealing, and it was subsequently widely adopted. (Hemmens 1988, p.87)

Ironically, efforts to legitimise and solidify the identity of new planning faculty and schools in the university elevated theoretical and methodological activity above practical and applied activity. Faculty were drawn together from diverse disciplines, mainly the social sciences. While the schools, for the most part, had an applied and professional focus, few new faculty had professional experience as planners of sufficient depth or breadth to allow for overlapping domains of practical experience among the faculty. Lacking a shared experience with planning practice, and trained in diverse, often exclusive specialities, faculty did share a commitment to the protocol of scientific inquiry, and the methodological norms necessary to safeguard its proper use.

Perloff had optimistically summarised his planning curriculum design as a planning core with a social science specialisation. He expected faculty would use the social sciences to advance new theories of planning based on the discipline of research rather than principles of design. Planning students exposed to such knowledge could then put it to use as well-informed staff, offering rational guidance to powerful government decision-makers. But, implemented in the university setting with an interdisciplinary faculty, efforts to produce the generalist with a speciality produced unexpected results. The core was treated much as undergraduate liberal arts is treated – a general preparation for the more important and valued graduate education in a specialised field. It ended up providing generic survey and skill development courses that prepared students for participation in a number of different specialisations.

The specialisations were not tamed and directed by the professional concerns that make up the core of everyday practice, nor adapted to supplement and enhance the education of students in planning knowledge well-suited to a variety of practical institutional domains. Rather, specialisations were used to frame students' choices of professional preparation and occupation. The core was less and less made up of practical modes of inquiry and design, and increasingly centred in theories of rational scientific inquiry and methods of scientific investigation – the basic modes of inquiry that faculty from diverse social sciences shared and found important. The widespread adoption of the rational model and social science research methods made scientific knowledge the primary source of reliable and valid understanding about planning.

Social science analysts studied policy rather than master plans. The values of artistry and craft used to design physical plans lost status. Designers judged a plan for its beauty and utility as a visual image of a city's future physical form. Analysts treated planning as a process of ongoing inquiry, punctuated occasionally with written policy reports. They claimed the designers had not grasped the complexity of cities. The social scientists analysed the complexity of urbanisation, developing and testing theories they hoped would identify and classify the relationships of cause and effect that make up the modern metropolis. Such knowledge was crucial in preparing and justifying comprehensive plans for social, economic and administrative reform, supported by funding from national government and implemented by local and, preferably, regional government.

Adopting the sceptical scientific approach required its faculty proponents to suspend, or even reject, commitments to particular planning reforms. Value neutrality gained pride of place as analysts worried that moral commitments to professional planning would undermine the integrity of their research and analysis. Older planning reformers and designers – who had assumed science was on their side – now faced a growing group of university-based analysts whose critical scepticism not only separated scientific inquiry from practical efforts at reform, but elevated the status of scientific knowledge above the knowledge of professional experience.

Rational planning model and the theory–practice dualism

The rational planning model attempted to provide a framework for both the social scientist role as a generator of knowledge and the staff role as an administrator. This very inventive combination of the knowledge base and process issues made the rational model very appealing, and it was subsequently widely adopted. An important common assumption of the social science ideal and the administrative process ideal was belief in the efficacy of information. Right information in the right place was expected to be a powerful force in democratic process, and contribute to the quality of public decision-making (Hemmens 1988, p.87).

George Hemmens goes on to argue that the reaction to the earlier design tradition in planning was an over-reaction that unwisely promoted a preoccupation with the objective integrity of analysis and the pursuit of abstract procedural theories to integrate the increasingly fragmented specialisation of analysis. But this proliferation also reflected and fostered the functional specialisation of the planning occupation. Not only did governments adopt a wider variety of functional programs, generating demand for specialists, but the universities hired faculty with backgrounds in these specialities to meet this demand (Krueckeberg 1984).

During the decades of growth in the planning profession after the Second World War, the bureaucratisation and specialisation of planning occupations increased the range and complexity of everyday practice. The knowledge and protocols of the design consultant proved inadequate and inappropriate to cope with the regulatory, financial and organisational problems government planners faced. In a 1963 article, Melvin Webber argued that the reform spirit that offered moral justification for planning activity in the first half of this century had been replaced by the pursuit of professional values that accompanied the rapid growth of government planners during the 1950s.

The growing prominence and popularity of planning theory among planning academics and intellectuals in the universities, however, did not foster theoretical consensus or build support for theory among practitioners. Belief in the rational model – and renewed efforts to modify and justify its reach – did not unify the practical and theoretical. Instead, theoretical arguments multiplied, and intensified the paradoxical relationship between the two. This paradox persisted at the centre of theoretical debates about rational planning as intellectuals scrambled to revise, supplement and otherwise salvage a rationale able to bind together science and practice. Practitioners had little interest in the theoretical debates, and theorists cared little for the practical problems of the planner-bureaucrats.

This fact–value dualism still structures the organisation of the curricula of planning schools. Students take courses in methods (e.g. statistical analysis, evaluation, research design, cartography) and in specialised subject areas (e.g. housing, transportation, land use). In the United States

212

the subject areas are usually divided into a small cluster of core courses and a large group of specialised courses organised along functional lines. Methods courses draw heavily on the techniques of quantitative social science analysis. They are 'hard'. (The metaphor implies that this knowledge offers a solid foundation for arguments and judgements, but one difficult to build.) Substantive courses about policy and practice draw from history, case studies and experience. They are 'soft'. (The metaphor implies this knowledge offers a less reliable foundation for understanding, but one easy to construct.) Theoretical coursework seeks to bind the two together, and so assumes the central role in the curriculum. A hierarchy emerges (see Figure 10.1).

Direction	Subject
Top	Planning Theory
↑	Scientific Methods
↕	Specialisations
Bottom	Practical Fieldwork

Figure 10.1 The value hierarchy and the planning curriculum

Faculty who believe deeply in the importance of theory teach students to do the same. Correspondingly, the curriculum structure elevates the learning of theoretical concepts, methods and specialities above practical experience. Students learn to think critically and analyse causes and patterns. Students learn to test hypotheses, interpret findings and write explanations.

A recent study of faculty and students of thirty graduate schools offering PhDs in the United States and Canada found students complaining bitterly about the ambiguous and overwhelming expectations they face. The schools offer inter-disciplinary faculty, and rely on ideological commitment to applied research to bind their diverse interests together. However, the programs reward research products based in a specialised discipline (e.g. economics) rather than an applied product that draws on a variety of disciplines. Vague references to problem-solving or action research accommodates, but does not integrate, the teaching and use of different disciplinary theories and methods (Innes et al. 1992).

Practical difficulties emerge when schools attempt to teach how to improve the practice of planning. Field study, studio and internship (on-the-job) learning usually require detailed study of particular settings and problems. The people experiencing and coping with these problems want advice that will offer relief that fits the situation – that works. But giving good advice – advice that clients comprehend, trust, appreciate and can use – does not depend on mastery of the scientific method, urban theory or a comprehensive knowledge of facts. As Martin Krieger, and more recently John Forester, have written so insightfully, it requires a relationship of trust among persons (Krieger 1981; Forester 1989, 1990, 1991, 1992).

Rejection of positivism and epistemological worry

As social scientists, planning faculty criticised designers for relying on superficial ideas about the causes of urbanisation (e.g. physical determinism). Designers based their advice on what the social scientists claimed were narrow, professional design conventions (e.g. avant-garde aesthetic ideas). But, like the designers they criticised, the social scientist planners still hoped to teach students to apply knowledge to guide and improve cities. The scientific method, however, does not offer insight about desirable purposes or how to pursue them. The lack of practical conventions for teaching applied social science for planners leaves a gap between social science method and practice.

Placing the social sciences at the centre of professional education posed a serious legitimisation problem. Scientists analyse and pursue generalisations, planners compose and propose particular schemes. Designers do. Scientists study. Furthermore, design professionals and educators rely on the values implicit in their techniques – techniques supported by the traditional conventions of a parent discipline with social and cultural standing (e.g. architecture). Social scientists, however, are members of relatively new traditions, whose members are anxious to protect the integrity of their analytic enterprise by jealously guarding their methodological scepticism. This scrupulous attachment to methodological conventions drawn from the well-established physical sciences fostered respect for detached testing and analysis, and suspicion of precisely the sorts of moral and artistic judgements designers make.

Planning educators now worry about values and planning precisely because we have, for a generation or more, laboured under the conventions of social science, which favour objectivity and punish moral sentiment. Instead of arguing about the merits of different purposes and policies using the languages of morality, politics, history and design, we have done so using the languages of the social sciences. The social sciences offered institutional legitimacy and the promise of greater degrees of certainty than the applied arts. But institutional status and theoretical certainty came at a price.

Widespread concern about epistemological ('being right') and value ('doing good') questions among planning analysts and intellectuals is, I believe, a result of this successful capture of planning education by the values of social science theory and analysis. Planning analysts are raising questions about their epistemological presuppositions, in large part, because many social scientists are doing so. Many social scientists now critique and reject the value-free pursuit of scientific certainty as an unnecessary positivist tradition. These analysts have introduced forms of moral inquiry into their studies that violate earlier conventions. Many planning analysts have followed their lead (e.g. Marris 1982; Schon 1983; Forester 1989; Throgmorten 1992).

CONCLUSION

Professional planners offer an important – if not exclusive – service. They spend their time and energy focusing on the problems posed by the general conditions of modern urbanisation. Take traffic congestion, for example. Individual commuters seek dependable and speedy routes to work. Together their individual trips produce congestion. Each commuter wants his or her own trip to be quick and easy, without concern for the trips of others. Planners, however, worry about the relationships between the different kinds of trips, and how these change in relation to different modes of travel, routes, etc.

Professional planners develop schemes to reduce congestion, and offer advice to various government agencies, executives and legislatures about the relative merits of these schemes. Where these professional planners differ from others (e.g. neighbourhood advocacy groups, development firms, banks) who may offer more politically attractive advice is in the effort and care taken to respect the relevant inter-dependencies in offering the advice. The painful irony professional planners face is that their activity remains on the margin of social importance, while the problems they seek to address increasingly touch the lives of almost everyone. It seems understandable that planning educators and professionals would seek to enhance the legitimacy of their advice by claiming it has special validity – a quality of scientific truth that transcends the limited moral purposes of the people involved and their limited powers to shape the environment. But this belief will not offer relief. It raises unrealistic expectations and makes impossible demands, as critiques of the rational planning model make evident. It fosters public contempt for planners among the practically-minded. Worst of all, it prevents those who believe they know the truth recognising and acknowledging the usefulness and value of non-professional allies and colleagues.

My own pragmatic vision of planning places this activity at the core rather than the periphery of public life. The ultimate hope – echoing the ideas of many anarchist, socialist and populist professionals involved in the early years of the planning movement (e.g. Geddes, Marsh, Mumford, Goodman) – would have the special profession of planning disappear altogether – at least in so far as this means a group of experts who know the proper and right ways to solve the problems of urban inter-dependency. The profession would be replaced by a diverse variety of institutional practices incorporated within modified occupational and cultural relationships which reflectively and purposefully take inter-dependencies into account. Presently, in liberal societies, we routinely take self-interest into account in the formulation of plans, but seldom does this address the inter-dependencies.

As planners, we can each provide evidence of the impacts of existing inter-dependencies on individual choice – from the health risks of ozone depletion to the public burdens imposed by a brokered development deal. Although we hardly need fear the cultural absorption of professional planning in the near future, the inter-dependencies keep growing, with little evidence that the panacea of *laissez-faire* initiatives or state-sponsored bureaucracy will address them adequately. Professional planners should not advocate a single position or plan (whether out of scientific conviction or self-interested gain), but should offer promising and workable alternatives that take the plans of others into account. In this (pragmatic) sense they inform, and so improve, democratic deliberations about urban improvements.[2]

I would like to believe that countering the forces of fragmentation and totalisation that sceptical (some argue, cynical) critics like Foucault (1979, 1991) write about in such chilling detail is an inevitably developing practice of popular democratisation. But my sceptical knowledge of history makes my own desire for a reassuring sense of inevitability appear silly. Our freedom is contingent, fragile and subject to constant attack. So I take Foucault – and other post-modern criticisms of the sort of liberal reforms planners initiate – as a warning against the all too pervasive belief that our efforts serve a greater good – progress or the public, for instance – that excuses our use of expertise, rhetoric and other kinds of power. For Foucault – and for a pragmatist like me – when we do good we use power. When we help some we exclude others.

Lessons for planning educators

If we do not separate values from planning practice, then we don't need to worry about putting values back into planning school curricula and pedagogy. 'Value' simply refers to the purposes planning educators and professionals rely on to identify other planners, and to judge the quality of these planners' actions. But *which* values? The lack of unanimity here has meant disagreement and conflict between academics and practitioners. In the United States, competition for limited employment opportunities over the past two decades has fuelled calls for restrictive licensing and more vigilant control over professional credentials. The expansive and specialised curricula of university planning schools have been criticised for so expanding what counts as planning that almost anyone with a social science degree could legitimately apply for a planning job (Levin 1979, 1992).

I treat planning in our time as an activity that both presumes and fosters a liberal democratic culture. I believe that we cannot be indifferent to the responsibilities of democratic citizenship and still be good planners. Values are an important topic in liberal societies, since each member, upon reaching adolescence, is expected to construct his or her own moral identity as an individual citizen. We may inherit moral beliefs and customs based on our social standing, but we are still expected to craft our own moral identity from an assortment of moral traditions and beliefs. Coping with this multiplicity poses a serious obstacle to establishing a shared notion of either the good life for an individual or the common good for a group of individuals. When individual planners offer advice they seek to order this multiplicity. How do we prepare professionals to do this well, especially when we no longer expect theory to certify their beliefs?

Instead of treating theory as an intellectual foundation for worthy planning activity, we might better treat theory as a kind of reflective

217

inquiry about puzzling and troublesome problems. Instead of serving as judge, theory could act as ally when routine inquiry goes awry. Instead of a vertical orientation, a developmental curriculum would have a horizontal orientation. Students would start their education with (simulated or bounded) practical experiences requiring the use of planning methods and knowledge. Students would be challenged to address questions of efficacy, craft, and value, drawing on this limited experience. For instance, students might be asked to prepare a plan for a suburban settlement in a relatively short time. Only the most rudimentary and conventional methods, knowledge and purposes would be offered by the teacher. The experience should be complex and difficult enough to provoke questions from the students about what to do, how to do it and why. The importance of one or another question shifts with the particular details of practice, but no type of question should be treated as privileged inquiry, able to trump its competitors. The major kinds of inquiry that make up the curriculum would be introduced in the context of practice from the outset. Students would be pressed to make value judgements, and to follow up, evaluating the consequences.

This initial experience of practical inquiry and problem assessment would be followed by conventional course work in theory, specialised subjects and planning methods. However, in each course there would be expectations of consistent reference to the varieties of practice and practical problems. Those committed to teaching pure science or theory unsullied by the corruptions of practical inquiry would appear iconoclastic and eccentric, although not receive censure. Questions of value would not appear as another specialised field of knowledge offered in a single course, but as questions which define the ongoing network of pathways (customary and innovative, radical and conservative) linking understanding and action in the planning field. Many teachers already teach in this fashion, but others teach specialised courses, relying on the values of the discipline rather than its use for planning.

Emphasising practical reasoning rather than scientific analysis as the primary mode of understanding would dramatically affect what gets taught and how. For instance, specialised courses on such topics as housing, land use, transportation and the environment would include history, case studies and scientific analysis (with a small 's'). Interpretation and understanding would displace the primacy of (but not exclude) explanation and prediction. In methods courses, emphasis on technique would take a back seat to craft. Instead of always learning the most recent, sophisticated and powerful methods of analysis, students would learn how to apply methods which are useful, well-known, but rarely used in practice properly.

In their final term, students would conduct planning in a practical context, as at the outset. Only now the students would be expected to design their own inquiry and select their own actions. Judgement of their efforts and performance would include not only themselves and their teachers, but others with whom they might work, or for whom the plan had important consequences. Students would learn how to compose arguments and judgements that offer diverse alternatives, rather than unilateral prescriptions. Such learning occurs already in many settings, but rarely inspires an entire curriculum.

These curriculum ideas illustrate how to break from Perloff's notion of the generalist with a speciality – a model that continues to shape the accreditation standards for planning schools in the United States. Perloff believed in the efficacy of specialised knowledge because of his allegiance to the rational model. But, as I have argued throughout this essay, once you break away from practice in the pursuit of rational certainty, it is hard to get back. Dropping the complex baggage of context to race ahead in the pursuit of scientific, methodological or theoretical knowledge appears less attractive when we can no longer convince ourselves that such inquiry will offer practical pay-offs later. Better not to leave, but to broaden and deepen the understanding of planning in practice.

There are serious criticisms and impediments to adopting this pragmatic approach. First, having established institutional standing in research universities, planning schools will find little support from their university hosts to return to a role associated with professional schools. In response, I would not argue that faculty should give up their research pursuits, but consider broadening and changing its purpose and audience; adopt comparative and interpretive methods of inquiry that explore theoretical questions through the study of specific institutions and practices; carry out research designed to speak to several audiences, rather than just the community of analysts.

Second, the move from science to craft represents a loss of rigour and scope. Yes, but such a shift offers relevance and utility in return. The scientists among us can, and should, continue their inquiries, but we need not expect they will offer us much that is practical and useful. Nor should we expect that we can find and use a scientific method to serve as the correct and proper guide for analysing and evaluating the values of others. Values do not make sense in the abstract. We grasp the meaning of values through particular actions in a specific time and place.

Third, treating the pursuit and study of planning as an inherently contingent activity introduces relativism into planning. Rational methods and argument must possess a truthfulness that justifies our judgements, independent of particular biases and commitments, otherwise these judgements lose legitimacy and authority. Such relativism appears threatening only so long as we expect to find rational theories of social behaviour and moral practice that shield us from the ambiguity, diversity and contingency of practical life. For instance, we value tolerance and detachment in our research community, not because we possess superior rational arguments in their defence, but because we have come to share their value for our efforts to conduct useful research.

NOTES

1   As I write this I am glossing over important details. My speculations here draw heavily from my knowledge of US history. I am using the historical sketch to suggest that what appear as epistemological and theoretical problems among planning analysts may be 'rationalisations' for difficult, practical, institutional problems.
2   Interesting theoretical debates among political theorists offer competing accounts of the proper form for such deliberation. These include variations of the conventional pluralist approach, as well as challenging notions of republicanism and communitarianism.

REFERENCES

AICP (American Institute of Certified Planners), 1967, 'Analysis of the AIP Membership Survey', *AIP Newsletter*, No. 218, August.

Cherry, G. E., 1974, *The Evolution of British Town Planning*, New York, NY: John Wiley and Sons.

Forester, J., 1989, *Planning in the Face of Power*, Berkeley, CA: University of California Press.

Forester, J., 1990, 'The Politics of Storytelling in Planning Practice', paper presented at the American Collegiate Schools of Planning Annual Meeting, Austin, Texas, October.

Forester, J., 1991, 'Practice Stories and the Priority of Practical Judgment', paper presented at the joint American Collegiate Schools of Planning/Association of European Schools of Planning Conference, Oxford, July.

Forester, J., 1992, 'On the Ethics of Planning: Profiles of Planners and What They Teach us About Practical Judgment and Moral Improvisation', paper presented at the Conference of the American Planning Association, Washington DC, June.

Foucault, M., 1979, *Discipline and Punish*, Harmondsworth: Penguin.

Foucault, M., 1991, 'Questions of Method' and 'Governmentality', in Burchell, G., Gordon, C. and Miller, P. (eds), *The Foucault Effect*, Chicago, IL: University of Chicago Press, pp. 97–164.

Hall, P., 1988, *Cities of Tomorrow*, Cambridge, MA: Blackwell.

Hemmens, G., 1988, 'Thirty Years of Planning Education', *Journal of Planning Education and Research*, Vol. 7, pp. 85–92.

Innes, J. et al., 1992, *Report of the Commission on the Doctorate in Planning, to the Association of Collegiate Schools of Planning*, 19 October.

Krieger, M., 1981, *Advice and Planning*, Philadelphia, PA: Temple University Press.

Krueckeberg, D., 1984, 'Planning and the New Depression in the Social Sciences', *Journal of Planning Education and Research*, Vol. 3: pp. 78–86.

Levin, M., 1979, 'Bumpy Roads Ahead', *Planning*, Vol. 45(7), pp. 28–35.

Levin, M., 1992, 'We Have Met the Enemy and it Ain't us', *Planning*, Vol. 58(5), pp. 26–7.

Marris, P., 1982, *Community Planning and Conceptions of Change*, London: Routledge and Kegan Paul.

Perloff, H., 1957, *Education for Planning: City, State and Regional*, Baltimore, MD: Johns Hopkins Press.

Schon, D., 1983, *The Reflective Practitioner*, New York, NY: Basic Books.

Scott, M., 1969, *American City Planning Since 1890*, Berkeley, CA: University of California Press.

Throgmorten, J., 1992, 'Planning as Persuasive Storytelling About the Future: Negotiating an Electric Power Rate Settlement in Illinois', *Journal of Planning Education and Research*, Vol. 12, pp. 17–31.

Vasu, M., 1979, *Politics and Planning: A National Study of American Planners*, Chapel Hill, NC: University of North Carolina Press.

Webber, M., 1963, 'Comprehensive Planning and Social Responsibility: Toward an AIP Consensus on the Profession's Roles and Purposes', *Journal of the American Institute of Planners*, Vol. 29, pp. 232–6.

Index